JOHN BARTON

➤➤ ◄◄

Playing Shakespeare

John Barton has directed many productions for the Royal Shakespeare Company and conducts Shakespeare workshops in the U.K., the U.S., and Europe. He has been an associate director of the RSC for more than thirty-five years and is now an advisory director. As a playwright he spent twenty years developing *Tantalus,* a ten-play cycle based on the Greek tragedies, which was recently produced by the Denver Center for the Performing Arts and by the RSC in England. He lives in London.

Playing Shakespeare

An Actor's Guide

Playing Shakespeare

An Actor's Guide

JOHN BARTON

Foreword by Trevor Nunn

ANCHOR BOOKS

A Division of Random House, Inc.

New York

FIRST ANCHOR BOOKS EDITION, AUGUST 2001

Library of Congress Cataloging-in-Publication Data
Barton, John.
Playing Shakespeare / John Barton ; with a foreword by Trevor Nunn.
p. cm.—(A Methuen paperback)
Originally published: London : Methuen Drama, 1984.
ISBN 0-385-72085-8
1. Shakespeare, William, 1564–1616—Dramatic production.
I. Title. II. Series.
PR3091 .B37 2001
792.9'5—dc21   00-052597

Author photograph © Simon Chapman

Book design by Rebecca Aidlin

www.anchorbooks.com

Printed in the United States of America
10 9 8 7 6 5 4 3 2 1

Contents

Actors

who took part in Playing Shakespeare

PEGGY ASHCROFT

TONY CHURCH

SINEAD CUSACK

JUDI DENCH

SUSAN FLEETWOOD

MIKE GWILYM

SHEILA HANCOCK

LISA HARROW

ALAN HOWARD

BEN KINGSLEY

JANE LAPOTAIRE

BARBARA LEIGH-HUNT

IAN McKELLEN

RICHARD PASCO

MICHAEL PENNINGTON

ROGER REES

NORMAN RODWAY

DONALD SINDEN

PATRICK STEWART

DAVID SUCHET

MICHAEL WILLIAMS

Foreword

The young man with the Renaissance face was John Barton. I had heard of him, of course, but there on the stage of the Arts Theatre Cambridge, directing a battle scene for a Marlowe Society production, was the man himself, with tapered trousers and bulky cardigan, giving him a seventeenth-century silhouette confirmed by a noble beard, high forehead, an expression in the eyes both haught and hawk and rich brown crinkled hair. He was Essex or Raleigh—dashing, formidable and in bursts of energy, like a whirlwind. My mental picture of my first sighting of John Barton betrays something of the impressionable eighteen-year-old student I was, and something of the need eighteen-year-old students have for legends, and larger-than-life heroes and enemies. In 1959 John was a Cambridge legend; he had directed countless university productions to professionally high standards, he had become a young and romantic don as the Lay Dean of Kings, with the Elizabethan Theatre Company he had pioneered small-cast touring Shakespeare productions, and he had been invited to become a founder-director of the Royal Shakespeare Company in Stratford-upon-Avon. None of that of course contributed much to the legend—no, it was the fact that he chewed razor blades for fun, that he knew every line of the First Folio by heart, that he spoke Chaucer's English, that he was a brilliant and extremely dangerous sword fighter, that he was hilariously absent-minded, obsessed with cricket, a chain-smoker, an expert on Napoleon and somebody who enjoyed working sixteen hours a day without a break.

A lot of water has flowed under the bridges of the Cam since then; my need for heroes has diminished, while my regard for John Barton has increased. For much of the intervening time, since 1964 in fact, we have worked for the same company; we have shared similar ideals about the training and development of actors; we have collaborated on productions; we have asked for each other's aid when things have gone wrong and we have become fast friends as much through adversity as through the sweet smell of success. And to the best of my knowledge John has given up chewing razor blades.

In 1965 I had a formative experience. I had been working for the RSC for a year. I had altogether lost my way and was suffering a crisis of confidence. John Barton proposed to me that he and I should collaborate on a reworking of *Henry V,* which had been part of the famous Stratford history cycle the previous year. For the six weeks of the rehearsal period I became the world expert on John's absent-mindedness, I came to love the sixteen-hour day (I was already O.K. on cricket and Napoleon) and I learned more about unlocking a Shakespeare text than any scholarship could have taught me. I had always thought of Henry V as a role full of splendid and necessary rhetoric. Under John's direction, the mighty "set speech" we know as Crispin's Day, for example, became the spontaneous, almost desperately improvised attempt by a young leader to hold the morale of his men together as they stared at inevitable defeat; and instead of there being any sense that the actor was delivering a previously written text, Ian Holm, as Henry, thought and discovered those words out of the situation and of his character. Every clue of where to breathe, what to stress, when to run on, what to throw away was there in the text, if only like John you knew what to look for. But the poetry was not an end in itself. The words became necessary. It wasn't verse speaking. It was acting.

In 1979 John and I collaborated in a way that was new to both of us; we accepted Melvyn Bragg's invitation on behalf of London Weekend Television to make a program about the difficulties and techniques of speaking verse, and together with Terry Hands and a small group of RSC actors, we conducted a session in front of an audience similar to the demonstration lectures all of us had done years previously as part of our company's work in education. The material we shot was sufficiently interesting to make Melvyn decide that it should become not one, but two programs and *Word of Mouth,* Parts 1 and 2, was duly transmitted to considerable acclaim in 1980.

The actors were articulate, Terry and I did what was required of us, but the star of the programs was John Barton, partly because he appeared not to know that the cameras were there, and partly because he did know so much more about the subject than all the rest of us put together. A series was proposed. John and I attended many hours of meetings delineating a structure and content for thirteen programs, but shortage of money and studio time postponed the whole project. I was relieved and delighted when the idea was taken up again and although I was unavailable to contribute, John agreed to make it his main RSC task for the second half of 1983. It was a very happy accident.

What the programs, and now the published texts of the series, reveal, is the method and principle of an approach to acting Shakespeare which has been fundamental to the Royal Shakespeare Company since it was formed. This approach is not didactic or political or scholastic or literary. It relies a good deal on analysis, but just as much on common sense and pragmatism, and a sense of theater and of character; it attempts to serve the complexities and contradictions of the text, but it is also trying to make the language *work,* and to be alive and exciting in the theater.

Generations of actors joining the RSC have benefited from John Barton's teaching, and so too of directors. The Company is founded on continuity. It is surely unique that a television series can field a cast of internationally and nationally famous performers who are present precisely because they continue to feel themselves to be members of a theater company, and who have shared the experience of trying to communicate the ambiguities and complexities of the greatest of all dramatists. I have been privileged to lead the fortunes of this Company for many years, and I confess to ferocious pride in its achievements; there is something in the texts of these programs that underpins all RSC achievements, and something which makes the series *Playing Shakespeare* an RSC achievement in its own right.

TREVOR NUNN

Preface

This book springs out of special circumstances and has one very particular aim. On the surface it is the record of nine workshop programs made in 1982 by the Royal Shakespeare Company for London Weekend Television and shown on Channel Four in 1984. At first I rather doubted whether this material should be published. I felt that the series depended quite as much on the live contributions of the actors who took part in it, whether in discussion or demonstration, as on the various expositions and explanations made by myself. And I much regret that a book cannot properly recapture their contribution and the way in which they brought many characters alive on the screen at a moment's notice. Yet my reason for wanting to publish the material is entirely to do with actors.

But first I should define what this book consists of. It sticks pretty closely to the television programs on which it is based, although I have tried to clean it up and clarify it throughout. The workshops were partly scripted and partly unscripted and were devised for a wide and not a specialist audience. Everywhere points had to be made as succinctly as possible because of the viewing time available, which explains why there are often savage cuts in the Shakespearean passages we worked on. Two chapters on Heightened Language and on Character have had to be presented as one. We recorded much more material than we were able to screen, and chapters 4, 6 and 11 therefore appear here for the first time. Much of the material had to be shot out of order, depending on which actors were able to take part on different shooting days, and the extent of each actor's involvement depended on their availability from other work.

This explains why, sadly, some of them only made a brief appearance.

Because much of our work was rough-and-ready I have here edited, cut and expanded the original material and reworded it where any of us who took part were unclear or imprecise. I have not however tried to conceal the fact that the material was begotten for television rather than for libraries. The book is set out as a dialogue because that is what *Playing Shakespeare* was: a series of conversations, rather than something conceived in literary form. I hope that this is the best way to present its subject matter clearly. I believe that acting is a subject for discussion rather than just exposition.

2

Now for this book's why and wherefore. For many years I have heard actors who were new to Shakespeare lament that they could find nothing written which would assist them directly in handling his text and particularly his verse. Although there is no lack of material about all aspects of his plays and stagecraft, most actors feel that this does not really help them as actors. One of them once showed me a Shakespearean Grammar he had got hold of in the hope of getting his bearings. It was a daunting document, full of technical terms which alarmed rather than enlightened. But what of Granville Barker? It is now over fifty years since he wrote his *Prefaces to Shakespeare*. It used to be thought that he had made a major breakthrough by looking at Shakespeare in essentially theatrical terms, but these days actors do not respond to him. They feel, and I think justly, that though his heart is in the right place and he is rich in perception, he is of little practical use to them because he is rarely specific about the details of how Shakespeare's verse *works* or how an actor should come to terms with it. They are put off by his assumption of his reader's sensibility to and knowledge of Shakespeare and by the generalized tone of a passage such as this:

> The actor, in fine, must think of the dialogue in terms of music; of the tune and rhythm of it as at one with the sense—sometimes outbidding the sense—in telling him what to do and how to do it, in telling him, indeed, what to *be*.   Preface to *Love's Labour's Lost*

This is in fact a shrewd and just comment on the passage to which it refers. Yet the one thing it does *not* achieve is to tell an actor what to do or how to do it. Granville Barker delivers an aesthetic injunction but does not go into practical or line-by-line detail. That is surprising as he was an actor and a director, and a very fine one. Though he is basically right in what he urges, the way he puts it is more likely to affright an actor than to stimulate him:

> Let him rather acquire an articulate tongue, an unfailing ear for the pervasive melody and cadence of the verse, let him yield to its impetus, and—provided, of course, that he knows more or less what it is all about, and this sympathetic self-surrender will aid him there—Shakespeare can be counted on to carry him through.   Preface to *Othello*

To an actor such advice is deadly. Acting is built upon specifics but Granville Barker is tantalizingly literary and vague. I think that today he also sounds condescending. He anatomizes the text but not the habit of mind of the actor who has to play that text. He does not, for instance, seem to understand the natural fear that many actors have of poetry. I hope that *Playing Shakespeare* may explain that fear a little and maybe help to ease it.

But what of the many scholars, especially in recent years, who have made "Shakespeare in the Theater" their theme and who have stressed over and over that his plays must be studied in relation to the stage for which they were written? Are they no help to actors either? The answer is, I think, not yet, or at least not deeply. This is not primarily due to any insensitivity in either the scholars or the actors. There is rather a problem of communication and a lack of information. The kinds of things that concern an actor in the rehearsal room are not normally written down. Consequently I believe that a book which reflects the way that actors think about Shakespeare now is needed. So I hope not only that some actors may find this book useful but also that it may serve, not as an authoritative statement, but as a useful theater document and casebook for those who study and write about Shakespeare.

One thing we would all like to know, of course, is how Shakespeare's actors rehearsed a part and what way their minds worked. I have suggested in this book some of the things they must have instinctively gleaned from the text and how an actor today can easily do the same. Much that is said here is obvious, yet I know from experience that it needs saying over and over. Much is crude or over-simplified. Much is either too narrow or too general. And some is probably plain wrong. But I must confess that I have never worried overmuch about the precise accuracy of what I may say in the rehearsal room. The test there is not whether a given statement is objectively true but whether it helps, stimulates and releases an actor at a particular rehearsal. If it does so, then the advice is useful. If it does not, however true it may be, it has no practical use in that par-ticular context. Dangerous words, but I believe that, theatrically speaking, they are realistic. It is not enough for a director to speak true. He must reach and help the actors with whom he is working, and if he does not do so then he fails them. So the kind of points I have tried to make below do not derive solely from my own inner view of Shakespeare but from a verbal tradition I have learned and shared over many years in the hurly-burly of the rehearsal room. I much regret that the need to compress things for television has led to my too often laying down the law. When the questions covered in *Playing Shakespeare* come up in rehearsal they of course emerge in a more freewheeling way.

The twelve chapters that follow cover what seem to me the most important areas in which an actor needs to find his bearings. I have tried to concentrate throughout on the pragmatic question, "How does Shakespeare's text actually *work*?" I realize of course that what I have to say must often represent my own subjective response to the text rather than a completely objective account of what goes on. Even so, I think it will be found that most of the first six chapters do present a reasonably objective analysis. The second half of the book is certainly more subjective, but I believe that most of the ground covered is to do with common sense rather than with anything mys-terious. I have also tried to keep away from the question of directing the plays as irrelevant to the main purpose, though I have of course handled it by implication. If these chapters help a few actors to find their way with Shakespeare I shall be content. If they stimulate scholars and critics to take a similar approach but to do it better, I shall be delighted. In spite of the important work which has been done on Shakespeare's text in the theater and in the study over the last forty or fifty years, I believe that the way actors handle that text still has a long way to go. In the meantime I should like to dedicate *Playing Shakespeare* to the actors, not only all those who took part in these workshops, but all the actors I have ever worked with. It is from them that I hope I have learned something of what a Shakespearean actor needs to know.

◄◄　◄◄　◄◄　◄◄　◄◄　◄◄　◄◄　◄◄　◄◄　◄◄　◄◄　◄◄　◄◄　◄◄　◄◄　◄◄　◄◄

Note: all the Shakespearean quotations have been standardized as follows:
The *Plays* follow the text of the New Penguin Shakespeare with the exception of *Cymbeline, Titus Andronicus* and *Troilus and Cressida,* which were not yet published when this book was prepared; for these the Cambridge University Press New Shakespeare was used.
The *Sonnets* follow the edition of W. G. Ingram and Theodore Redpath (Hodder & Stoughton, 3rd Impression, 1978).
Omissions within quoted texts are designated by . . .

PART ONE

✦➤ ◄✦

Objective Things

CHAPTER ONE

The Two Traditions

Elizabethan and Modern Acting

[The following actors took part in the program that
forms the basis of this chapter: MIKE GWILYM, SHEILA HANCOCK,
LISA HARROW, ALAN HOWARD, BEN KINGSLEY,
IAN MCKELLEN, DAVID SUCHET.]

*P*laying Shakespeare. Not reading him or writing about him but
playing him. Over a thousand books or articles are written about
him every year. In 1980 there were 195 books and 877 articles, many
in Japanese. And yet very little is put on paper about how to act him.
I think I can guess why. I have been urged to write about this but I
have always felt I couldn't do it. I thought that the sort of points that
need to be made could only arise truly in the living context of working with actors. On this subject each actor and his experience of acting is worth many books. So what I shall be saying in *Playing
Shakespeare* is by itself worth nothing. It only has value if it comes
alive in the performances of living and breathing actors.

The best guide to an actor who wants to play in Shakespeare
comes, I think, from Shakespeare himself, who was an actor. Listen
to Hamlet's advice to the players. It can't be quoted too often.

> Speak the speech, I pray you, as I pronounced it to you, trippingly on
> the tongue. But if you mouth it as many of our players do, I had as lief
> the town crier spoke my lines. Nor do not saw the air too much with
> your hand, thus. But use all gently. For in the very torrent, tempest,
> and, as I may say, whirlwind of your passion, you must acquire and
> beget a temperance that may give it smoothness . . . Be not too tame
> neither. But let your own discretion be your tutor. Suit the action to the

word, the word to the action, with this special observance, that you o'erstep not the modesty of nature . . . For anything so o'erdone is from the purpose of playing, whose end, both at the first and now, was and is to hold, as t'were, the mirror up to nature.   *Hamlet: III:2*

I believe that speech goes to the very heart of it. It's one of those utterances which seems a bit simple and limited at first, but if you live with it you will find that it begins to resonate and to open doors. I also believe that in the Elizabethan theater the actors knew how to use and interpret the *hidden direction* Shakespeare himself provided in his verse and his prose. I believe that the kind of points we shall be making in these workshops work best in the theater, not by a director telling an actor about them but by an actor learning them, largely by experience, and applying them for himself.

There are few absolute rules about playing Shakespeare but many possibilities. We don't offer ourselves as high priests but as explorers or detectives. We want to test and to question. Particularly we want to show how Shakespeare's own text can help to solve the seeming problems in that text. Of course, much of it is instinct and guesswork. We will try to distinguish between what is clearly and objectively so and what is highly subjective. I hope that if I'm too dogmatic the actors will challenge me. I should also make it clear what I'm *not* talking about. I shall hardly talk at all about directing, and at first I shall try to keep clear of interpretation. We won't talk much about individual characters, and we shall say even less about plays as a whole. We shall simply concentrate on finding out how Shakespeare's text *works.*

Of course what we say is bound to be personal. We don't believe that there's only one way of tackling Shakespeare. That way madness lies. But out of the infinite number of questions which come up when we work on him we have picked the ones that seem to us the most important at this time. Another actor or another director would rightly stress things differently or violently disagree with us or stress points which we shall leave out. What we say will of course be colored and limited by the fact that we are the products of a particular time. One bit of me is uneasy at holding forth about Shakespeare. I am not a pundit but a man who works in the theater at this moment and I can only talk about what seem to me the main needs and problems at this moment. I am deeply aware that these sessions will probably seem outdated and odd before many years are past. That is the nature of the theater. We can only speak about what we think and feel at this time.

We shall look at many short individual passages, often cut down, from many different plays. I believe they can all make sense out of context and that those who don't know the play in question will still be able to follow quite easily the points we are making. As ever, the audience is quite as important in all this as the actors. If we don't reach our audience we fail. We must make them listen and share and follow the story. But above all, *listen*. It's so easy for an audience *not* to listen, particularly with a knotty and difficult text. I may be cynical but I don't believe most people really listen to Shakespeare in the theater unless the actors make them do so. I certainly don't. I know that it's too easy for me to get the general gist and feeling of a speech, but just because I get the gist I often don't listen to the lines in detail. Not unless the actors make me. What I want to explore are the ways in which they can achieve that.

But you may say, "All that's very fine, but what's so difficult about acting Shakespeare? What's the problem?" Or indeed "Is there a problem?" Well, yes, I believe that there is. Two things need to come together and they won't do so without a lot of hard work and much trial and error. First, there's Shakespeare's text written at a particular time and for particular actors:

> Cut me to pieces, Volsces. Men and lads,
> Stain all your edges on me. "Boy"! False hound!
> If you have writ your annals true, 'tis there
> That, like an eagle in a dove-cote, I
> Fluttered your Volscians in Corioles.
> Alone I did it. "Boy"! *Coriolanus: V.6.*

Secondly there are the actors today with their modern habit of mind and their different acting tradition, based on the kind of text that they're more used to:

LEN: (*Mike Gwilym*): 'S great 'ere.

PAM: (*Lisa Harrow*): What?

LEN: Why did you pick me up like that?

PAM: Why?

LEN: Yeh.

PAM: Sorry, then?

LEN: Tell us.

PAM: 'Ow many girls you 'ad?

LEN: No, I tol' yer my life.

PAM: 'Old on.

LEN: What?

PAM: Yer got a spot.

LEN: Where?

PAM: 'Old still.

LEN: Is it big?

PAM: 'Old still.

LEN: Go easy.

   (*She bursts the spot on his neck.*)

PAM: Got it!

LEN: Ow!   *Saved* by Edward Bond

Well, there we are. The two chief ingredients with which we start rehearsals are Shakespeare's text and a group of modern actors who work mostly on modern plays. How do the two come together? Let's start with the second as the more accessible. Our tradition is based more than we are usually conscious of on various modern influences like Freud and television and the cinema and, above all, the teachings of the director and actor, Stanislavsky. I suspect he works on us all the time, often without us knowing it. So let's ask ourselves what are the most important things in an actor's mind as he begins work on a modern text. No, any text. What are the most important things to go for?

David Suchet: *We might do worse than start with something Stanislavsky wrote: "If you speak any lines or do anything mechanically without fully realizing who you are, where you come from, why, what you want, where you are going, and what you will do when you get there, you will be acting without imagination."*

Ben Kingsley: *Or, to put it in our own words, what is our motivation, our objective or our aim or our* intention? *We use lots of words for the same thing.*

Sheila Hancock: *Here is Stanislavsky again: "On the stage there cannot be, under any circumstances, action which is directed immediately at the arousing of a feeling for its own sake."*

Lisa Harrow: *Or, in other words, we must beware of playing only the* quality *or general emotional tone of a speech. For instance, if we have a sad speech, we mustn't just sound sad. What we play must be specific and fresh.*

Alan Howard: *So we must dig into a character socially and psychologically.*

Ian McKellen: *Yes, socially, which means being concerned with other people, our audience and other characters on the stage, impersonated by the other actors. It's not enough to be aware of our own thoughts, our own feelings, our own words. We must listen to the words and understand the feelings and the thoughts of the other characters.*

I think the most basic thing in all that is the importance of asking the question "What is my intention?" If we had to reduce our modern tradition to one single point I think it would be this. It is practical advice which always works and always helps the actor. Yet it is often confusing to people who approach a text from a literary or non-theatrical viewpoint. It seems to them to imply that we are saying a playwright always has a character's conscious intention in mind when he writes a given line, but of course that isn't necessarily so. A playwright can write a play without asking that question constantly or even most of the time. All that we in the theater are saying is that to ask that question is the way to act without falseness. It always works, though of course many other elements are involved which we shall be looking at.

Mike Gwilym: *On the other hand we all know the sort of actor who won't speak at all until he feels absolutely the inner need to do so.*

Huge, long pauses. By the time he's ready he's brilliant, but the audience is fast asleep. So perhaps it's good also to remember the story told of John Gielgud. When he was asked, "Now, Sir John, what exactly is your intention at this point?" he answered, "To get onto the stage."

Yes, here and elsewhere, we will find that we can hardly ever make any generalization about acting without adding some sort of qualification. Here is an overserious theatrical practitioner who in his way is also talking about intentions:

> *David Suchet:* "I should like to cite examples of game beats in the opening scene of *King Lear.* The game Lear wishes to play with his daughters, which might be called 'benevolent father and loving children' leads us to a model of the transactions needed to play it successfully. Now the child in Lear's child is cathected (which may be a symptom of old age, what we call second childishness) . . . Hence Lear's opening kick comes in the form of benevolent Parent and his social action is 'to divide his kingdom.' However, his object is ulterior and comes from his Cathected Child . . ."
>
> From an article by Arthur Wagner
> in *Tulane Drama Review,* Summer 1967

Beware of jargon. It can lead to *talking* about acting taking the place of actually *doing* it. Though we're exploring something complex and we must not overlook those complexities, we must all of us try all the time to be clearheaded and simple.

Well, I hope we're reasonably clear about what our modern tradition is. Actually it's a great deal more modern than we know. The key technical terms we use were not known to Elizabethan actors. They have only come into existence during the last hundred years or so. "Characterization" in our theatrical sense is a mid–nineteenth century word, though "character" in the sense of a part assumed by an actor comes in a hundred years earlier. "Motivation" seems to be a twentieth-century term and in its theatrical sense it hasn't yet got into the Oxford Dictionary. It's the same with one of our favorite words in the theater, "naturalistic." This is salutary. I'm not decrying our modern tradition, merely trying to put it into perspective. It perhaps suggests how surprising our acting style would have seemed to the Elizabethans.

> Ian McKellen: *I don't know that I agree with that. I suspect that actors through the generations have tried in their own terms to be real. After all, Hamlet's advice to the players seems to be good advice that a modern director might give to modern actors: don't be too theatrical, don't saw the air too much, but think about the reality of the situation. What is modern about our approach however is the jargon that we use. As you've just pointed out, "motivation" is not a term that Shakespeare's actors would have understood. But the feeling behind what "motivation" means, I suspect, Shakespeare and his actors would have understood very well.*

Yes, they didn't have the word "motivation" but Hamlet does talk about having "the motive and the cue for passion."

> Alan Howard: *I think that Elizabethan actors had an instinctive apprehension of all this. They didn't have some of the distractions that we have in our day. They depended more than we do on the spoken word. It was like food, and they probably used words much more sensually, almost* eating *words.*

Yes, one of Shakespeare's characters says as much. He says of another character, "He hath never fed of the dainties that are bred in a book. He hath not eat paper, as it were: he hath not drunk ink." "Eating words" is a useful phrase.

> Mike Gwilym: *What exactly do you mean when you say "naturalistic"? That word can mean different things to different people, can't it?*

Yes, you're right, we must define it. By "naturalistic" I mean the acting style and the kind of text which is the norm in the theater and film and television today. The deliberate attempt to make everything as natural and lifelike as possible. But there are two other words we ought to explain. We've touched on playing the *quality* of a speech as opposed to the *intentions* behind it. Let's try to clarify that by look-ing at an example. Give us the opening line of *The Merchant of Venice*.

> Ian McKellen: *"In sooth I know not why I am so sad."*

Now that simple line can be said in an infinite number of ways. On the one hand you could go for the mood and the quality of it. Try it, for instance, sadly.

> Ian McKellen: *Do you mean by the mood or the quality, just paint-ing it over with a color called sadness?*

Yes, the feeling only.

> Ian McKellen (sadly): *"In sooth I know not why I am so sad."*

Now try it humorously.

> Ian McKellen (humorously): *"In sooth I know not why I am so sad."*

But now try and ask what is Antonio's *intention*. Perhaps it's to try to explain himself.

> Ian McKellen: *So rather than painting the line, I should think about it and let the voice just do what it will?*

Yes, search your thoughts.

> Ian McKellen: *Make a connection between the mouth and the brain and then with the heart: "In sooth I know not why I am so sad."*

Now try changing the intention to avoid explaining yourself.

> Ian McKellen (does so): *"In sooth I know not why I am so sad."*

Or try to make light of your sadness.

Ian McKellen (does so): *"In sooth I know not why I am so sad."*

And one more: try to put an end to the conversation.

Ian McKellen (finally): *"In sooth I know not why I am so sad."*

I don't think there's much doubt about it, is there? Playing the *quality* leads to bad acting, and going for the *intention* is more interesting and alive and human. The first is general and the second specific. We learn more about the speaker and his situation.

> Ian McKellen: *Well, of course it's impossible to decide exactly how to say any line without considering many other things which are not directly related to what noise the tongue is making on the roof of the mouth. Like, Who am I saying the line to? How long have I known him? Where have we just been? What were the other words spoken before the first line of the play? Were there any words before the play began? What are likely to be the words spoken in later scenes? There's a whole complex of questions of which the sound is just the outward expression.*

So in other words, rehearsal of a scene is going to be about character and relationships and situations and certainly about social background. Today the director helps to sift those possibilities and at some point in rehearsals agreement is reached. In this case, it will probably be reached quite late on, because the possibilities are so many. Shakespeare never actually tells us for certain why Antonio is so sad. This simple example takes us, I think, to the heart of our modern acting tradition: relationships, character, intentions. So don't let us lose touch with that because we'll keep coming back to it.

But what about the Elizabethan theater? We don't know all that much about how they rehearsed, but we do know that direction in the sense of detailed analysis of the scene or play probably didn't exist.

> David Suchet: *They had no director in our sense, though the author often instructed the actors.*

Mike Gwilym: *Just as Hamlet was doing in his advice to the players. Because he actually wrote the speech that the players were going to insert into their performance it was assumed he had the right to direct it as well.*

Lisa Harrow: *Elizabethan actors had very little rehearsal, virtually none in our terms.*

Yes, the diary of an Elizabethan theater manager shows that they might have had as many as forty plays in their repertory in a year. And that they had to put on a play in a few days.

Ben Kingsley: *The outdoor theater with its particular demands and its distractions perhaps forced a cruder style on the actors than we aim for now. The traditional style of acting was formal and bombastic and Shakespeare tried to get away from it.*

Mike Gwilym: *And they didn't have the luxury of time that we have. We now approach a character rather as a psychiatrist would approach a patient. We sort of sniff around him. Very often we don't even stand up with the text till three weeks into rehearsal. We sometimes take ten weeks to rehearse a Shakespeare play.*

Alan Howard: *But Elizabethan actors didn't even have the whole text to study. Even leading actors had their parts written out separately with none of the rest of the text except their cues. I can remember when I first started in rep. that we used to get things called "cue scripts" which were only your own part with the cue immediately before it, just the last sentence. So you could tell whether you had a big part or a small part that fortnight because it would either be this thick or that thick. But you had no sense of the whole play.*

Yet Shakespeare wrote for the Elizabethan theater, and he wrote these infinitely rich and complex plays with great psychological depth. I don't think he would have done it unless his actors could have done him justice. And I hope we can show later how Shakespeare's text is full of hidden hints to the actors. When an actor becomes aware of them he will find that Shakespeare himself starts to direct him. I believe that is what happened among his Elizabethan actors, and that they did instinctively what we do consciously and intellectually. I also believe that Shakespeare both accepted his own theatrical tradition and yet transformed it. In a sense I think that he is the unconscious inventor both of characterization in depth and of naturalistic speech. There's not much of it in the theater before him. Let's look at the fashion that he inherited. First, let's hear a conqueror boasting.

> TAMBURLAINE (*Alan Howard*): I will, with engines never exercis'd
> Conquer, sack, and utterly consume
> Your cities and your golden palaces,
> And with the flames that beat against the clouds
> Incense the Heavens and make the stars to melt, . . .
> And, till by vision or by speech I hear
> Immortal Jove say 'Cease my Tamburlaine,'
> I will persist a terror to the world
> Making the meteors (that like armèd men
> Are seen to match upon the towers of Heaven,)
> Run tilting round about the firmament
> And break their burning lances in the air,
> For honour of my wond'rous victories.
>
> *Tamburlaine* by Christopher Marlowe

Very Marlovian. Here is high language, but there isn't much character or complexity. Now let's listen to a father finding his son murdered.

> HERONIMO (*Ben Kingsley*): What outcries pluck me from my naked bed,
> And chills my throbbing heart with trembling fear, . . .
> Who calls Heronimo? Speak, here I am:
> I did not slumber, therefore 'twas no dream, . . .
> But stay, what murderous spectacle is this?
> A man hanged up and all the murderers gone,
> And in my bower to lay the guilt on me:

This place was made for pleasure not for death.
Those garments that he wears I oft have seen,
Alas, it is Horatio my sweet son,
O no, but he that whilom was my son.
O was it thou that call'dst me from my bed?
O speak if any spark of life remain.
I am thy father, who hath slain my son?

The Spanish Tragedy by Thomas Kyd

There's an emotional situation there but very flat language. Yet Ben filled it out and so brought life to the spare crude text by living through the story. Now let's look at a third example of literary, Elizabethan prose, not from a play but typical of its author, John Lyly, who was also a dramatist.

Sheila Hancock: "The Rose, although a little it be eaten with the canker, yet being distilled yieldeth sweet water, the iron, though fretted with the rust, yet being burnt in the fire shineth brighter, and wit although it hath been eaten with the canker of his own conceit, and fretted with the rust of vain love, yet being purified in the still of wisdom, and tried in the fire of zeal, will shine bright and smell sweet in the nostrils of all young novices." *Euphues* by John Lyly

As you can see, character here is two-dimensional and rich language can get monotonous. And these are examples of famous texts. Yet in Shakespeare our traditions, both the modern and the Elizabethan, come together. I believe our tradition actually derives from him. In a sense Shakespeare himself invented it, with his teeming gift for characterization and his frequent use of naturalistic language, though he didn't of course know that he was doing so at the time. That's why I believe we'll find that the problem of how to marry the two traditions in fact doesn't exist once you get to know how Shakespeare's text *works*. If the actor gets in tune with it, he'll find many naturalistic clues and hints about character so that it does in fact combine the two traditions most of the time. But it may not always seem so to an actor who's new to Shakespeare. Sheila, you've only plunged into Shakespeare quite recently. Tell us your feelings about coming to terms with it.

Sheila Hancock: *Well, coming to it at my great old age, I must say I wondered whether I was going to have to alter my whole approach to my work. And indeed during the rehearsal process and in a situation like this I feel tremendously inhibited. But I found miraculously, when I got on the stage and in front of an audience and had to communicate, something quite extraordinary happened. I found that if I let it flow, just happen, it seemed the most natural thing in the world. And what's more the language was so potent that I felt I had to make less effort than I'd ever had to make before.*

Shakespeare did it for you?

Sheila Hancock: *Yes, I find sometimes that it seems better just to stand and say it. Possibly I'd absorbed a lot in the rehearsal. I don't know.*

Mike Gwilym: *I think the main thing is to trust the language. Every actor comes to this point when he approaches a Shakespeare text. Especially in emotional scenes where he thinks, "I know exactly how this character feels, I know the depth of his passion, and I know about what his brain is doing, but why have I got these flipping words in the way?" We have to come to terms with the fact that a character is not just what he says but how he says it.*

You've got to find out why the character needs those particular words.

Lisa Harrow: *I remember early on when I was just starting and you, John, were talking about the need to find the language, you said a very interesting thing. You said that the emotion in Shakespeare has to be bigger in order actually to create those words. That was a terrific note, because the moment I actually felt something more intense and bigger and then had to say those particular words I found that they did fit in with what I was feeling. And it was real.*

Ian McKellen: *We can take comfort from the fact that people who come to a theater are called an audience . . . audio . . . "hear." People who watch television are* viewers, *and look rather than listen. And we're often helped today by working in smaller theaters without the distractions of big spectacle or scenery. The audience are close enough to pick up every detail of the voice's inflections. It wasn't easy for nineteenth-century actors who were working in large theaters, or in America today where Shakespearean acting is different from ours, mainly, I think, because their theaters are much larger. This leads to a grander, more generalized, open style of acting than perhaps we favor at the moment in England.*

I think there may be a greater difference than we realize between the senses of the Elizabethans and ourselves. For instance, they probably had a much sharper sense of smell than us because of the foulness of the stench in the streets. I'm sure they also had a much sharper ear than we have and that they picked up words in a way that we don't. We're more trained to go by the eye, as Ian says, from television and from films. I'm sure Elizabethan audiences' ears were sharper than ours.

Lisa Harrow: *The language was growing too, wasn't it? It was much more of a living thing than our language is.*

That may well be true. But we should look now in more detail into this question of marrying the Two Traditions. Let's go back to the opening of *The Merchant of Venice* where Antonio the merchant is talking to his friends Salerio and Solanio.

ANTONIO (*Ian McKellen*): In sooth I know not why I am so sad.
It wearies me, you say it wearies you;
But how I caught it, found it or came by it,
What stuff 'tis made of, whereof it is born,
I am to learn;
And such a want-wit sadness makes of me
That I have much ado to know myself.

SALERIO (*David Suchet*): Your mind is tossing on the ocean,
There where your argosies with portly sail,
Like signors and rich burghers on the flood,
Or as it were the pageants of the sea,

Do overpeer the petty traffickers
That curtsy to them, do them reverence,
As they fly by them with their woven wings.

The Merchant of Venice: I.1.

Good. Now let's compare the two speeches. Antonio's is relatively naturalistic, isn't it? Or perhaps it's not?

Ian McKellen: *Yes, it's quite easy for a modern actor to get into because there aren't many old-fashioned words in it. Though I do note that it's written in verse and not prose. But it's occurred to me that I probably did it absolutely wrong and far too slow and ruminatively because Salerio says, "Your mind is tossing on the ocean."*

That's probably true. But let's press on with our comparison of the two speeches. When I say yours is naturalistic it is not strictly true. It has poetic undertones which I want to look at later. I only mean it's naturalistic in comparison with Salerio, whose text is actually much trickier for an actor because it's full of images and metaphors and similes. "Tossing on the ocean," "portly sail," "burghers on the flood," "pageants of the sea," "curtsy to them," and so on. Note specially the metaphor "As they fly by them with their woven wings." Clearly Salerio's text is not naturalistic but is what we usually call "heightened." He is coining phrases and finding unusual ways of expressing himself. So first let's ask ourselves our basic question, what's his intention?

David Suchet: *I think his intention is to cheer Antonio up. Probably by sending him up.*

Good. So having first established his intention what do you do with the language to further that intention?

Ian McKellen: *Language which you would call "heightened": can you define that? What is heightened language?*

Yes, I'm taking a favorite phrase too much for granted. I suppose the simplest way of defining it would be to say that it refers to any language which is not naturalistic. Any bit of text where there are images and metaphors and similes or rich, surprising language. If we compare the two speeches the difference is pretty obvious. Let's see what happens, for a moment, if we try to take Salerio's text naturalistically.

> David Suchet: *What, completely flat and straight? As I might speak in an ordinary conversation?*

Just try and see what happens.

> David Suchet (with many grunts and pauses):
> *"Your mind is . . . er . . . tossing on . . . er . . . on the ocean . . . Er . . . there where your argosies with . . . er . . . portly sail, Like . . . er . . . signors and . . . er . . . we . . . rich burghers on the flood . . ."*

Thank you, point made. It doesn't work, does it? We've just been listening to what is sometimes called the "naturalistic fallacy." It's unclear and it's woolly and it's deadly slow. It's just not the way it's written. Heightened speech must be something that the actor, or rather the character he's playing, *finds for himself* because he *needs* those words and images to express his intention. So you, David, need those words to cheer up and send up Antonio. We can put this idea in various ways: we can say you've got to *find* them or *coin* them or *fresh-mint* them. We can use any word we want to describe the idea of inventing a phrase at the very moment it is uttered. The vital thing is that the speaker must *need* the phrase. He must not think of such phrases as simply words that preexist in the text. They have got to be words that he finds as he utters them.

> Mike Gwilym: *A director often asks an actor to deal with a particularly heightened piece of language by putting it into inverted commas. The danger with that is that it sounds as if the actor is being very self-conscious about what he is saying. The trick is, I think, for the character rather than the actor to put the words into inverted commas. In this way he acknowledges to the audience that the language he is using is not common parlance or everyday speech. We can see him taking pleasure in choosing his words.*

Sheila Hancock: *Or we could put it another way and say, first clarify your intention about why you're making the speech. And then decide why you use those particular words in order to pursue that intention.*

That's right, every actor needs to do that. So let's take the speech again, choosing and coining the words with the intention of cheering him up and sending him up, as we've agreed.

David Suchet does so: "Your mind is tossing on the ocean,
There where your argosies with portly sail,
Like signors and rich burghers on the flood,
Or as it were the pageants of the sea,
Do overpeer the petty traffickers
That curtsy to them, do them reverence,
As they fly by them with their woven wings."

Good. You kept a fine balance there between the heightened and the naturalistic elements. *Balance* between these ingredients is something which we're always looking for and we shall keep coming back to that word. The great thing was that the speech was much clearer to follow. And it sounded as natural, I would say, as anything that we like to call naturalistic in the theater.

Ben Kingsley: *There's always a debate that rages in me whenever I find myself with a new text in a rehearsal room. It's the old debate between naturalism and realism. It's a vital distinction. I find more and more when I am onstage that naturalistic acting, that is totally reported nature, is inappropriate. Because onstage one is in an environment that is by its very nature highly organized and concentrated. So naturalistic acting is a false exercise. On the other hand we mustn't forget that to the Elizabethan mind to be "'gainst nature" or not natural was something profoundly disturbing. "To hold the mirror up to nature" or "to o'erstep not the modesty of nature" were maxims which told the actor to root himself in nature. But once he is so rooted, he must remember that his landscape as an actor, the play itself, is a compressed, organized, condensed version of the truth.*

Lear's whole destiny for instance unfolds in the space of an evening.
That is not naturalistic. But an actor must be rooted in nature for the
emotions to be contagious and real.

Yes, the word "naturalistic" is a jargon word for a particular style.
We mean by it a style which deliberately gives an impression of ordinary everyday speech and behavior. We don't mean it in the more
general sense of "being true to nature."

Ben Kingsley: *Yes, it's a dangerous word and can be confusing. But I*
think if we're clear about what we mean by it then we're on much
safer ground.

Let's go back to the point we were making about balance. There has
to be a balance between being seemingly natural on the one hand and
coming to terms with the heightened language on the other. We've
seen what happens if we do the Salerio speech totally naturalistically,
and we've seen David do it with the kind of balance I am urging.
Now let's be very unfair and see what happens if we go to the other
extreme. Let's lose the naturalness and overplay the heightened language, because that's the other trap that we have to avoid.

David Suchet: *Ham it up a bit?*

Ham it up a bit.

David Suchet does so:
"Your mind is tossing on the ocean,
There where your argosies with portly sail,
Like signors and rich burghers on the flood,
Or as it were the pageants of the sea,
Do overpeer the petty traffickers
That curtsy to them, do them reverence,
As they fly by them with their woven wings."

Well, you see why we talk about balance. To go solely for the heightened language is as dangerous as to plump totally for naturalism.

Mike Gwilym: But there's a danger in all this, isn't there? It's so easy to laugh at overdoing the language. We're all so keen to avoid it that we often get into lunacies. We try to take the curse off heightened language by trying to prove that the text is really quite modern. We sometimes pepper a bit of heightened language with little, almost subliminal, modern tags. For instance, a line like "The barge she sat in, like a burnished throne/Burned on the water" can all too easily become . . . "Well, the barge she sat in like, like a . . . sort of . . . burnished throne . . . you know . . . burned on the water . . ." If we're not careful we can do that without even being aware that we're doing it.

I have some sympathy with an actor's instinct to do that. The trouble is that it distorts as much as ham does. That's why I stress, and will do so again and again, that we have to find a balance between those two extremes. In other words an actor in Shakespeare simply has to marry the two traditions of heightened language and naturalistic acting.

Ian McKellen: I must confess I find it very difficult to draw a clear division between what you've called the Two Traditions. I'm sure you're fighting to define the difference between good acting and bad acting. As Ben has suggested, any play is going to be concerned with the playwright's organized view of the world and of the inner world of the characters we are playing. Every speech we utter, whether it's in a soap opera or by Shakespeare, is not going to be like speech in real life. So we always have the problem of coming to terms with the style of the writing. But I think the style of acting against which modern actors, of whatever generation they come from, rebel, is not so much the style of the writing as the style of the actors of the previous generation. And I suspect that actors from Richard Burbage, the man who first acted Shakespeare's heroes, right through to us today, have all been concerned with truth, reality and nature. It's just that we've all had different perceptions of it.

Our naturalism today is a reaction against the supposed naturalism of, let us say, the nineteenth century, where indeed the playing style was large, partly because the theaters were large. Partly too because in nineteenth-century England everything about the world seemed to be certain. The British Empire was going to last for a thousand years, and therefore Henry Irving could stand firmly on a stage in front of three thousand people and make declarations. We have a different perception of the world. Life is difficult, ambiguous and complicated. The British Empire doesn't exist anymore. We ask ourselves, what is our role as a nation in the world and what is our role as people, as parents, as children? This tends to direct our attention into details and away from the big gestures.

Well, of course I've been oversimplifying. What always happens when we talk about acting is that we start to use labels to help us articulate something which is very hard to define. But as soon as I put a label forward, like the Two Traditions, and offer a definition, I know I have to qualify it because I am oversimplifying. Of course there's naturalistic text in lots of Elizabethan plays and there is heightened language in modern plays, but I still think that my general point is true. Actors are normally much more at home with a naturalistic text, because that's what they work on the most today. I simply want to stress that if they can act in such a way as to *marry* the two traditions and if they can get the balance right, then there's no question of the result being either too naturalistic or too this or too that. It will work, it will be real and it will be accepted.

Ben Kingsley: *We've been talking about finding a balance and bringing the two elements of naturalism and heightened speech together. But often Shakespeare achieves a dramatic effect by deliberately switching from the one element to the other.*

Absolutely. He does so in our example from *The Merchant of Venice*. Let's look at an extreme example and switch to another play for a moment. In *Othello* there are some violent switches between naturalistic and heightened language. Here is Othello when Iago has just convinced him that his wife is unfaithful.

OTHELLO (*Alan Howard*): I had been happy if the general camp,
Pioners and all, had tasted her sweet body,
So I had nothing known. O, now, for ever
Farewell the tranquil mind! Farewell content!

Farewell the plumèd troops, and the big wars
That make ambition virtue! O, farewell!
Farewell the neighing steed, and the shrill trump,
The spirit stirring drum, th'ear-piercing fife,
The royal banner and all quality,
Pride, pomp and circumstance of glorious war!
And, O you mortal engines, whose rude throats
Th'immortal Jove's dread clamours counterfeit,
Farewell! Othello's occupation's gone!
IAGO (*Mike Gwilym*): Is't possible, my lord?   *Othello: III.3.*

Pretty telling, isn't it? That single short verse-line, "Is't possible, my lord?" after all the color and the richness that has gone before. Contrast, ringing the changes: Shakespeare does it over and over. It's true that a heightened speech may lift the emotional pressure of a scene, but it's also true that it may pave the way for something quite down-to-earth and simple which is even more telling. The one style enriches and sets off the other. Let's go back to *The Merchant* and take the scene a little bit further. Another character joins in the conversation, Solanio. This time, let's treat the scene as if it's the middle of a conversation which has been going on before the play begins.

ANTONIO (*Ian McKellen*): In sooth I know not why I am so sad.
It wearies me, you say it wearies you;
But how I caught it, found it, or came by it,
What stuff 'tis made of, whereof it is born,
I am to learn;
And such a want-wit sadness makes of me
That I have much ado to know myself.
SALERIO (*David Suchet*): Your mind is tossing on the ocean,
There where your argosies with portly sail,
Like signors and rich burghers on the flood,
Or as it were the pageants of the sea,
Do overpeer the petty traffickers
That curtsy to them, do them reverence,
As they fly by them with their woven wings.
SOLANIO (*Ben Kingsley*): Believe me, sir, had I such venture forth,

The better part of my affections would
Be with my hopes abroad. I should be still
Plucking the grass to know where sits the wind,
Peering in maps for ports and piers and roads,
And every object that might make me fear
Misfortune to my ventures, out of doubt
Would make me sad . . .

SALERIO: I know Antonio
Is said to think upon his merchandise.

ANTONIO: Believe me, no: I thank my fortune for it
My ventures are not in one bottom trusted,
Nor to one place; nor is my whole estate
Upon the fortune of this present year.
Therefore my merchandise makes me not sad.

SOLANIO: Why then you are in love.

ANTONIO: Fie, fie!

SOLANIO: Not in love neither? Then let us say you are sad
Because you are not merry; and 'twere as easy
For you to laugh and leap, and say you are merry
Because you are not sad.   *Merchant of Venice: I.1.*

That was good. A lively, balanced mixture, heightened yet very real.

Sheila Hancock: *I notice you've been basically using one word to describe Salerio's richer language; that's "heightened." You haven't used the dread word "poetic."*

"Poetic." Dread word indeed. I think it a dangerous word to use in the theater because it's so general and imprecise. If you say to an actor, "Do it poetically," I reckon alarm bells will ring in his head.

Sheila Hancock: *Well, it certainly frightens me.*

Lisa Harrow: *Don't you think poetry takes care of itself? I mean, if we use all the things we've been talking about, then the language itself and our own spirit will express the poetry.*

Well, maybe sometimes. But I rather want to dodge the question of poetry here and to come to it much later on. Not because I think it's unimportant—with Shakespeare it is of course often all-important—but because I don't believe it is helpful to *begin* work on his text by thinking about it. An actor has first to tackle the problems we're talking about tonight. He has to get on top of the thoughts before he thinks about the tune. I am using the phrase "heightened language" partly to put off the question of the poetry which I think in the end is the biggest challenge of all to an actor in Shakespeare; and partly because the coining of a simile or a metaphor or the choosing of a colored adjective is not necessarily a poetic activity. I believe that the vague idea of "the poetic" can lead an actor into troubled waters. It can lead to what I've called playing the quality or the mood and to putting a great big wash of lyricism or sentimentality over a speech. And above all it can lead to what we call "generalizing," playing a mood rather than specific thoughts or intentions.

I've deliberately started with a simple humdrum example, because I want to look at what goes on as the *norm* in Shakespeare. In our later sessions we will look at richer and more resonant bits of text. For now I just want to establish our main point. Playing Shakespeare is to do with marrying the two traditions. And in saying that I'm not suggesting that one's more important than the other. They are both vital.

> Sheila Hancock: *But it makes sense to start with our own tradition, because that's what's inside us and it's what we know best.*

Yes, that's the heart of it. We have to start with the way we are and the way we think. But look. I think we've all been falling into a trap in this discussion and I have been the worst offender. We have been *generalizing* about acting and using a lot of abstract terms. "Intentions," "tradition," "naturalistic," "real." Such words can be helpful if we use them as tools but they will undo us if we elevate them into a philosophy. We shall start to go round in circles. Abstractions don't solve acting problems. Used in moderation they can help to clear the head but we can't finally use them to pin acting down. Sooner or later we have to look at specific bits of text and seek particular solutions. I must confess that I personally find it hard and uncongenial to talk about acting in conceptual terms. But when an actor stands on his feet and begins to bring a particular passage to life then I begin to respond and sense what to say. We must hold on to that in these workshops. Our gods must not be concepts but the words that are in the text. We must keep looking at individual passages as we've begun to do this session, and we must ask what goes on in them. And in doing so we must trust our instincts and our experience. That's why I have put the Elizabethan tradition second, though most of the sessions that follow will be taken up with trying to get in touch with that tradition. So, I repeat, marrying the two traditions: it's an idea that we will keep coming back to.

CHAPTER TWO

➤➤ ◄┼

Using the Verse

Heightened and Naturalistic Verse

[The following actors took part in the program that
forms the basis of this chapter: SINEAD CUSACK, SHEILA HANCOCK,
LISA HARROW, ALAN HOWARD, JANE LAPOTAIRE, IAN MCKELLEN,
PATRICK STEWART, DAVID SUCHET, MICHAEL WILLIAMS.]

*I*n the first session I suggested that the main problem in playing
Shakespeare is how to marry the Elizabethan text and acting tradition with our modern acting tradition. There were two other important points. First, that the heightened language in a text has to be
found by the actor and not just taken for granted. And secondly, that
a right balance has to be found between the naturalistic and heightened elements in that text.

But most of Shakespeare's plays are also in verse, or else very often
in heightened rhetorical prose. Blank verse is probably the very center of the Elizabethan tradition and perhaps the most important
thing in Shakespeare that an actor has to come to terms with. Or
rather I should say that an actor *needs to get help from.* I stress that
because many actors, particularly if they're not familiar with Shakespeare, very understandably look at the verse as some kind of threat.
They know they will somehow come to grief if they ignore it or be
chastised if they do it wrong. It becomes a mountain to be climbed
or else an obstacle to be avoided. But no, it's there to help the actor.
It's full of little hints from Shakespeare about how to act a given
speech or scene. It's stage direction in shorthand. So let's try to find
out how his verse *works.* Don't let's ask what it *is,* for it's nothing
static, but let's ask what goes on in it. Shakespeare was an actor, and I
believe that his verse is above all a device to help the actor. It doesn't

necessarily or inevitably have something to do with poetry, though of course it often does. But at the beginning we can forget that. How do you all think that it helps you as actors?

> Alan Howard: *It helps us to learn the lines. Verse is usually easier to learn than prose.*

> Jane Lapotaire: *It makes a pattern on the page which is easier for the mind to retain than prose.*

> Lisa Harrow: *Yes, it helps to give us our phrasing.*

> David Suchet: *It's also full of acting hints if you know how to look for them.*

> Ian McKellen: *And because the verse is a more economical way than prose of saying something, it's likely to be more concise and more particular and exact. At the same time, because verse has a rhythm and a flow, it's perhaps more attractive to listen to and helps the actor to keep the audience's attention.*

> Patrick Stewart: *We're all talking about "verse." But what we mean is not verse in the usual sense of rhymes or couplets or other verse forms which Shakespeare only uses relatively rarely, but* blank verse.

Quite right, blank verse. Shakespeare's verse-line is sometimes called an iambic pentameter, which is a horrible phrase and I try not to use it. But what it means, and what blank verse consists of, is basically the alternation of light and strong stresses. The basic rhythm of blank verse goes like this: "de dum de dum de dum de dum de dum." Ten syllables, with light and strong stresses alternating, five light ones and five strong ones. That is the norm of blank verse. It's been pointed out that this rhythm approximates more closely than any other our natural everyday speech. In fact it's actually quite easy to pick up blank verse lines in everyday conversations, or in a book, a paper or the telly.

> David Suchet: *You've just said one: "or in a book, a paper or the telly."*

Not a very immortal line. Let's look now at two examples of unconscious blank verse in the context of speech and literature. First here is Mrs. Siddons, the eighteenth-century actress, commenting on the drink she has ordered:

Sheila Hancock: "I asked for porter and you gave me beer."

And now a bit of Dickens from the very end of *David Copperfield:*

Michael Williams: "O Agnes, o my soul, so may thy face
Be by me when I close my life indeed."

Perhaps the best way to show why blank verse is such a good verse-form for dramatic speech is to look at one or two of the verse-forms used in English drama before Shakespeare. Here is a bit from a Miracle cycle.

Michael Williams: "All hail! All hail! Both blithe and glad!
For here come I, a merry lad!
Pray cease your din my master bade
Or else the devil will you speed." *The Killing of Abel: Wakefield Cycle*

Doggerel, not speech. Those lines have eight syllables with four strong stresses, which is a bit short to accommodate our normal speech rhythms. So now let's hear another rhythm.

Ian MacKellen: "O doleful day, unhappy hour that loving child should see
His father dear before his face thus put to death should be!
Yet father, give me blessing thine, and let me once embrace
Thy comely corpse in folded arms, and kiss thy ancient face!"

King Cambises

Again, not speech but a rollicking jingle. There are fourteen syllables there and seven strong stresses. The lines are too long and clodhopping for our normal speech rhythms. Blank verse, with its ten syllables, is much closer to the way that we actually talk. In fact Shakespeare often uses it as a vehicle for *naturalistic speech,* as in

Antonio's "In sooth I know not why I am so sad" speech. Let me stress that blank verse doesn't necessarily lead to anything to do with poetry, though it often does. Its natural bias is, I believe, towards the naturalistic. Here's a good example from *Henry IV, Part Two*. Prince John of Lancaster is a very unpoetical young man:

> PRINCE JOHN (*Patrick Stewart*): Send Colevile with his confederates
> To York, to present execution.
> Blunt, lead him hence, and see you guard him sure.
> And now dispatch we toward the court, my lords.
> I hear the King my father is sore sick.
> Our news shall go before us to his majesty,
> Which, cousin, you shall bear to comfort him;
> And we with sober speed will follow you . . .
> Fare you well, Falstaff. I, in my condition,
> Shall better speak of you than you deserve.   *Henry IV, Part Two: IV.3.*

There's nothing poetic about that, is there? So how does blank verse actually work? I said that its normal rhythm goes "dĕ dūm dĕ dūm dĕ dūm dĕ dūm dĕ dūm," but actually that often isn't true. It sometimes does, but perhaps more often it doesn't. Here is a line that doesn't:

> HENRY V (*Michael Williams*): Once more unto the breach, dear friends, once more   *Henry V: III.1.*

If you try to scan it as an iambic pentameter—

> Ŏnce mōre ŭnto thĕ breach, dĕar friends, ŏnce mōre

it becomes totally unnatural. Obviously it's not written that way. So how do the stresses come naturally?

> Ōnce mōre ŭnto thĕ breach, dēar friends, ōnce mōre

Seven strong stresses. So what is Shakespeare doing there? Well, we can ask ourselves what Henry V is doing. What's his intention? To persuade his soldiers to go back into the breach. A tired, out-of-breath leader desperately trying to reach and rally his men. Now this strongly overstressed verse line reinforces this. It's a good example of a piece of hidden direction by Shakespeare.

> Once more unto the breach, dear friends, once more,
> Or close the wall up with our English dead!

The point I want to make here is that blank verse as such is neutral. Shakespeare gets his dramatic effects by the way he rings the changes on it. A basic norm is set up (de dum de dum de dum de dum de dum) and *added* stress is provided when that norm is broken. "Once more unto the breach, dear friends, once more" is a very strong line because there are extra strong stresses. There are seven "dums" here, not five. The extra stresses reinforce the sense of Henry pleading to and urging on his men. Let's take the speech a few lines further:

> Once more unto the breach, dear friends, once more,
> Or close the wall up with our English dead ...

(Note the double stress of "wall up" in the second line.)

> In peace there's nothing so becomes a man ...

(A regular blank verse line.)

> As modest stillness and humility ...

(Also pretty regular, except that there are only four strong stresses rather than the usual five.)

> But when the blast of war blows in our ears ...

(A regular line, except that "blows" is specially stressed by being put in the offbeat position.)

> Then imitate the action of the tiger ...

(Pretty regular, with a feminine ending, which we'll talk about in a minute.)

Stiffen the sinews, conjure up the blood . . .

("Stiffen" and "conjure" are strongly stressed by being put in the off-beat position. This stressing adds to the urgency of Henry's pleading.)

Disguise fair nature with hard-favoured rage . . .

(The antithesis between "fair" and "hard-favoured" is brought out and stressed because the two words are put in the offbeat position.)

Lisa Harrow: *Oughtn't you to explain what you mean by "antithesis"?*

Yes, it's a key word and we're going to make use of it a great deal. By "antithesis" I mean the setting of one word against another. For instance, "To be or not to be," or as we have here, "Disguise fair nature with hard-favoured rage." Actually two pairs of words in that line are set antithetically against each other: "Disguise fair nature with hard-favoured rage." "Fair" is set against "hard," and "nature" against "rage." To shape and clarify the thought an actor needs to stress or inflect these paired words and the verse rhythm helps him to do so.

Do you begin to see how blank verse works? The so-called iambic pentameter is the norm which Shakespeare keeps more or less going back to, but extra stresses are continually provided by putting an important word in the offbeat rather than the normal position. So we get the rhythm "dum de" rather than "de dum." Counterpoint, as in contrapuntal music. So we can say that Shakespeare uses blank verse by first setting up a norm and then significantly breaking it.

David Suchet: *So to go with the verse in the right way we need to know what are, or are not, the strong stresses in a line. But how can we be sure of that?*

I think in two ways. First, common sense will tell you the answer nine times out of ten. Ask yourself how you would naturally stress the line in everyday speech because of the meaning of what you are saying and try saying it without thinking about scansion. Look again at "Disguise fair nature with hard-favoured rage": there's not much doubt there about what the natural stresses are. Secondly, if you are in doubt there is a pretty infallible test: look for the long vowels. Look for the diphthongs. If you say such a sound slowly you can just hear that it is two sounds rather than one: "fair," "hard," "rage." All long vowel sounds usually count as strong stresses. There are very occasional exceptions which don't fit this approach, and times when common sense will tell you that a long vowel shouldn't be stressed, but for all practical purposes you'll find that it works.

> Sheila Hancock: *There's a very heavily stressed line in* The Winter's Tale. *When Leontes is questioning the goodness of Hermione and he says of her mockingly, "Good queen," Paulina answers: "Good queen, my lord, good queen, I say good queen."*

Yes, that's a wonderful example of extra stresses. It's a very special line. I believe that it has ten strong stresses out of ten: "Good queen, my lord, good queen, I say good queen." The repetition of the word "good" is given extra weight because it is put in what I've just called the contrapuntal position. "Good queen": "dum dum." That is one extreme. But there are of course some places where there are fewer stresses than usual in a line. We've just heard one: "As modest stillness and humility." The stressed words come into stronger focus because there are fewer strong words there. Another example:

There is a tide in the affairs of men.

Only four strong stresses again, not five. "There is a tide in the affairs of men." Let's have another example:

> HAMLET (*Alan Howard*): To be or not to be, that is the question;
> Whether 'tis nobler in the mind to suffer

The slings and arrows of outrageous fortune
Or to take arms against a sea of troubles
And by opposing end them.   *Hamlet: III.1.*

In the second, third and fourth lines there are only four stresses, not five. Notice how at the end of each of the first four lines there's an extra eleventh syllable. This is called a feminine ending. This extra syllable is always a light stress and not a strong one, and is simply a piece of license given to anyone writing in blank verse. An actor doesn't have to worry about it or doing anything about it, except to avoid treating it as a strong stress. If he gives a feminine ending a strong stress the line will mis-scan and will almost always sound wrong. Here's an example:

HENRY IV (*Ian McKellen*): How might a prince of my great hopes forget
So great indignities you laid upon me?   *Henry IV, Part II: V.2.*

See how it sounds if you stress the feminine ending here:

So great indignities you laid upon me.

It sounds uneasy, doesn't it? Now let's look at some other Shakespearean usages which are even more important and telling. One is a short verse line. Sometimes a line has fewer than ten syllables, maybe six or seven or even less. What do we do about that? Well, here again I believe Shakespeare is giving hidden stage directions to the actor. When there is a short line, we can be pretty sure that he is indicating a pause of some sort. Let's look at a few lines from the trial scene in *The Merchant of Venice.*

SHYLOCK (*David Suchet*): O wise and upright judge!
How much more elder art thou than thy looks!
PORTIA (*Lisa Harrow*): Therefore lay bare your bosom.
SHYLOCK: Ay his breast,
So says the bond, doth it not, noble judge?
"Nearest his heart," those are the very words.
PORTIA: It is so.

Are there balance here to weigh the flesh?
SHYLOCK: I have them ready.
PORTIA: Have by some surgeon, Shylock, on your charge,
To stop his wounds lest he do bleed to death.

The Merchant of Venice: IV.1.

Let's look carefully at that passage. You see how Portia and Shylock have two short verse lines: "It is so" and "I have them ready." Three and five syllables respectively. I've said that a short line in Shakespeare usually suggests a pause and is some sort of hint to an actor about how to play the scene. So let's ask ourselves what Shakespeare may be hinting at here.

> David Suchet: *Well, there's always a choice to be made. You can either take the pause before the line or after it. Here, I think the situation suggests that the pauses must come after the lines.*

> Lisa Harrow: *Yes, the choice you have to make arises out of your emotional and mental state in the scene. Portia is desperately trying to get through to Shylock.*

So after her short line "It is so," she pauses so that he and the court shall take in the gravity of the situation?

> David Suchet: *That's right. And Shylock, because of his emotional state and his confidence, is in no doubt about what he's doing here and comes in bang on cue with each speech.*

So, it's Portia who has the pauses because she is weighing Shylock up and deciding how to handle him. When she pauses after he has said he has the scales ready, the pause marks her disgust at his eagerness, and she weighs her words before she goes on. So we can see how Shakespeare's short lines can always tell us something, usually about the characters' intentions.

> David Suchet: *It is part of your thing about Shakespeare himself directing the actor.*

Lisa Harrow: *There's another kind of direction by Shakespeare here. What about the shared verse lines? "Therefore lay bare your bosom/Ay his breast." Portia begins the verse-line but Shylock finishes it. Shakespeare often splits a blank verse line like that.*

That's a terrifically important point. He does it over and over, and almost always we'll find that it means one thing. The second speaker is meant to pick up the cue at once, as surely as if Shakespeare had written in the stage direction, "don't pause here." So here are two of the most important ways in which he uses the verse to help the actor. A short verse line suggests a pause, and a shared verse line says, "pick up the cue."

Lisa Harrow: *Shakespeare's text is full of acting clues.*

"Clue" is a good word, because we cannot always be a hundred percent certain that we are analyzing the verse rightly. One can't be a hundred percent clear about what is or isn't a strong stress. I admit I am judging this subjectively. But that doesn't in the end matter. The important thing is our habit of mind. We must always look for the clues and play the detective, and usually we can find the answer in the text.

Jane Lapotaire: *Earlier, you said, "Pick up the cue at once." What I think you meant is "Think faster." I know a lot of people, myself included, when we first come to Shakespeare tend to put in a lot of pauses while we think the thought and before we speak it.*

Absolutely. What you've just said is perhaps the most important point that's come up so far in this session. It's no good if the richness and complexity of the verse leads one to think slowly and laboriously. Our naturalistic bias makes us use a larger number of pauses, both at the end of the line and within it.

But let's go on looking at this device of the shared verse-line. Let's take the famous example from *King John* where the king, speaking to his accomplice Hubert, proposes the murder of the boy Arthur. Imagine the lines played tightly and quickly.

KING (*Patrick Stewart*): Death.
HUBERT (*David Suchet*): My lord?
KING: A grave.
HUBERT: He shall not live.
KING   Enough.
King John: III.3.

So how do you think Shakespeare is using the verse there?

Patrick Stewart: *Well, what we've got are two verse lines. Though the first one's only got one word in it: "Death." And the second verse line is very much shared: "My lord?/A grave./He shall not live./Enough."*

Right. So what do we think about taking it lightly and quickly as you did, and which I liked, and the other possibility of doing it with pregnant pauses?

David Suchet: *I remember rehearsing it once with Emrys James. He played the king and I was playing Hubert. He said "Death," and then moved right away from me. I stood there and thought about it very carefully before saying . . . (pause) . . . "My lord?" Then he came round my other side very slowly and said . . . (pause) . . . "A grave." in my other ear. I stood there . . . (long pause) . . . "He shall not live." . . . (long pause) . . . "Enough." I remember your comments afterwards. You made us do it quickly.*

Patrick Stewart: *There is another choice, isn't there? Because we've got two verse lines, you could reasonably take a pause after "Death," i.e., at the end of the first short verse line instead of running the whole thing together. Can we try that and see what happens if we take a pause there?*

KING: Death
     (*Pause*)
HUBERT: My lord?
KING: A grave.

HUBERT:	He shall not live.
KING:	Enough.

Yes, that's possible. It's what I call an earned pause. If we have lots and lots of pauses we will probably overload things. But if we have one in the right place, particularly at the end of a verse-line, it can be very telling.

> Patrick Stewart: *And the briefness here is terrific, because they're talking about something which can't be talked about openly, which is the murder of a young child. That's why it's so terse.*

> David Suchet: *Probably you earn a pause after the exchange rather than by lengthy indulgences in the middle of the line.*

> Patrick Stewart: *It's what Jane said about thinking on the line instead of between the lines.*

Absolutely. Now let's look at something else that Shakespeare's verse does. What about the ends of the lines? The norm here is for Shakespeare to put a grammatical pause or the end of a clause, or of a sentence, at the end of a verse-line. When that happens, the verse is described as "end-stopped." So let's go back now to the opening speech of *The Merchant of Venice*.

> ANTONIO (*Ian McKellen*): In sooth I know not why I am so sad.
> It wearies me, you say it wearies you;
> But how I caught it, found it, or came by it,
> What stuff 'tis made of, whereof it is born,
> I am to learn.   *The Merchant of Venice: I.1.*

Four end-stopped lines where the grammatical pause comes at the end of the verse-line. Then there is a short half-line, "I am to learn." What does that half-line suggest to you?

> Ian McKellen: *I think when the rhythm of the blank verse as it were enters an actor's soul, and when that rhythm is interrupted because*

there are not words to complete the line, it indicates that the mind is going on ticking. Even if the words are not coming out to explain what the thoughts are. Then of course you have to come in with the next line with a bit more of a push because of that.

Yes, short lines do that nine times out of ten. But this is also a good example of end-stopped verse. The thoughts and the lines go together and that's very helpful to an actor when he's learning at speed and mapping it all out in his mind.

Ian McKellen: *Yes, and if the speech is a long one, and the punctuation indicates that the thoughts are flowing and it is all in fact one sentence, the ends of the verse-line may indicate points where an actor can breathe, if not actually stop speaking. You have to stop speaking when you breathe but only fractionally.*

Sometimes there are sentences which take up fourteen or fifteen lines of verse. They would be impossible to say if the verse didn't phrase it all for us. Let's look now at a sonnet which is all one sentence.

Sheila Hancock: "When, in disgrace with Fortune and men's eyes,
I all alone beweep my outcast state,
And trouble deaf heaven with my bootless cries,
And look upon myself and curse my fate—
Wishing me like to one more rich in hope,
Featur'd like him, like him with friends possess'd,
Desiring this man's art and that man's scope,
With what I most enjoy contented least;
Yet in these thoughts myself almost despising
Haply I think on thee, and then my state,
Like to the lark at break of day arising
From sullen earth, sings hymns at heaven's gate:
    For thy sweet love remember'd such wealth brings
    That then I scorn to change my state with kings."   *Sonnet 29*

It would be virtually impossible to say that if it wasn't shaped by the verse. The speaker wouldn't know how to phrase so long a sentence.

But what Sheila did with it, and the verse helped her, was to carry us with her and make us listen. The flow of it helped us to follow the argument. And even though it was a very, very long sentence indeed, it didn't seem so.

> Sheila Hancock: *It felt it to me. There is one place where I don't quite know how I should phrase it: the bit about the "Lark at break of day arising." The sentence overruns the verse-line there.*

"Like to the lark at break of day arising": end of line. And then the new line begins with "From sullen earth, sings hymns at heaven's gate."

> Sheila Hancock: *So what do you do there?*

Should you run on the line or should you not? Ask yourself that question and simply decide which feels better. Shakespeare gives you a choice. If it's better for you to run the line on, run it on. But if the verse actually helps you to phrase the line then that's the right answer. Personally I think that if you lift the word "arising" at the end of the first line, it is quite easy to take a small pause after it, perhaps a naturalistic pause for breath. Let's look at an extreme example of this kind of question. It comes from a late Shakespeare play, *The Winter's Tale*. In his later plays Shakespeare's verse is much less end-stopped and the lines continually overrun. That is to say the grammatical stops and the ends of verse-lines don't go together. Here is Leontes with his little son. He is mad with jealousy of his wife and his best friend.

> LEONTES (*Patrick Stewart*):   Gone already!
> Inch-thick, knee deep, o'er head and ears a forked one!
> Go play, boy, play: thy mother plays, and I
> Play too—but so disgraced a part, whose issue
> Will hiss me to my grave . . .   *The Winter's Tale: I.2.*

> Patrick Stewart: *Now, John, there's one line there which runs on: "Thy mother plays and I/Play too . . ." What about that? Surely it's natural to run on there.*

Well, is it? You have to ask that question and then decide.

Patrick Stewart: *It's possible to pause at the end of the verse-line and for it to sound natural and like spontaneous everyday speech. But if you pause here, it begins to sound slightly unnatural: "Thy mother plays and I . . . (pause) . . . Play too." And yet to stress it in that way might tell us something about Leontes.*

Well, of course you could stress it that way if you emphasized the word "play" and said, "And I/*Play* too." In other words, it would work if you picked out that deliberate theater metaphor and put the words in inverted commas.

Go play, boy, play, thy mother plays, and I . . . (pause)
Play too . . .

That's possible, isn't it? We're talking about possibilities, not laws. Particularly with Shakespeare's late verse. All I'm saying is that you need to judge the question each time and then decide. This passage also contains another very common Shakespearean usage: a break at what's called the caesura, which means a grammatical pause halfway through the verse-line.

Patrick Stewart: *"Go play, boy, play: . . . (colon) . . . Thy mother plays and I . . ."*

Yes, "Go play, boy, play:" . . . (colon). Now what do you do about that? Do you pause in the middle of the line or do you run on to the end of it?

Patrick Stewart: *The answer is common sense. It's to do with charac-ter. If the general tenor of the speech suggests rapid, teeming thought then the actor should run it on, after all we often do when we speak.*

Yes, you have just done so. I agree with you. Whenever you ask questions about the verse, there is usually a good acting reason for the answer.

Patrick Stewart: *Yes, invariably.*

Well, let's see what happens if we take the whole speech and have to decide what to do with both the caesura and the ends of the lines. Should you run on or should you not? See what happens if on the whole you phrase it so that you run on at the caesura, or half-line, but tend to have a slight break at the ends of the lines. In other words, phrase it *with* rather than *against* the verse-lines. See whether it sounds natural to you or whether it's a forced exercise.

Patrick Stewart: *When do I breathe?*

You breathe at the end of the verse-lines. I myself believe that in Shakespeare's later verse it is still right more often than not to phrase with the verse-line. Some people would not agree with that, but I think such verse is in part a form of naturalistic writing by Shakespeare. That is to say, he catches our trick of often pausing in ungrammatical places and running on at full-stops. If you look at it that way you will be surprised how often it works. I am also inclined to believe that Shakespeare wrote in blank verse partly to help actors phrase out-of-doors, where they perhaps needed to control their breathing more carefully than in indoor theaters. It's been said that's one reason why blank verse was so popular in the Elizabethan theaters—that it made life easier for the actors. Have a go.

LEONTES: Gone already!
Inch-thick, knee deep, o'er head and ears a forked one!
Go play, boy, play: thy mother plays, and I
Play too—but so disgraced a part, whose issue
Will hiss me to my grave. Contempt and clamour
Will be my knell. Go play, boy, play, there have been,
Or I am much deceived, cuckolds ere now;
And many a man there is even at this present,
Now, while I speak this, holds his wife by th'arm,
That little thinks she has been sluiced in's absence,
And his pond fished by his next neighbour, by
Sir Smile, his neighbour. Nay there's comfort in't

Whiles other men have gates, and those gates opened,
As mine, against their will. Should all despair
That have revolted wives, the tenth of mankind
Would hang themselves. Physic for't there's none:
It is a bawdy planet, that will strike
Where 'tis predominant; and 'tis powerful, think it,
From east, west, north and south. Be it concluded,
No barricado for a belly.   *The Winter's Tale: I.2.*

I thought you used the verse wonderfully there. You had control and yet a driving rhythm. The verse carried you and yet you weren't tied to it totally. If an actor follows the verse slavishly it can be a bad thing, and if he ignores it totally, that's a bad thing also. How did it feel to you?

> Patrick Stewart: *It gave me the sensation of somebody who was beginning to spiral out of control. And in fact it's characteristic of the play that as Leontes disintegrates, his verse also fragments and disintegrates and becomes less and less regular. But I wonder how much an audience would have followed me. It seemed to me I was very fast and it's a complex speech to follow.*

In all honesty I think that an audience wouldn't have totally followed what you did. But I thought it was a very healthy stage of work. You were grappling with a really difficult bit of verse. I thought that the balance between going with it and having a freedom from it, which you have to have in a late play, was pretty good. Of course, we've taken an extreme example here. It's from one of Shakespeare's very late plays, where the verse is not only difficult but at first sight looks chaotic. His earlier plays are much easier as far as the verse is concerned. The verse-lines tally with the grammatical pauses and phrasing is therefore easy. Here's a bit from a very early play, a soliloquy by the king in *Henry VI, Part Three*.

> HENRY (*Alan Howard*): This battle fares like to the morning's war,
> When dying clouds contend with growing light,
> What time the shepherd, blowing of his nails,

Can neither call it perfect day nor night.
Now sways it this way, like a mighty sea
Forced by the tide to combat with the wind;
Now sways it that way, like the self-same sea
Forced to retire by fury of the wind.
Sometime the flood prevails, and then the wind;
Now one the better, then another best;
Both tugging to be victors, breast to breast,
Yet neither conqueror, nor conquered:
So is the equal poise of this fell war.   *Henry VI, Part Three: II.5.*

The problem here is quite different. The easy regularity of the verse can lead to monotony, but there are enough contrapuntal stresses to give the rhythm variety. Listen to the last line again: "So is the equal poise of this fell war."

Now I think I've listed all the main points that an actor needs to know about Shakespeare's verse. It's been a crash course, so I'll come back to many of them later on in other examples. But there are some other minor points as well which we may as well clear up.

David Suchet: *Can you start by saying something about* elision?

Yes, elision. Very often a line seems to mis-scan because it has more than ten syllables. But where two vowels come together in a sentence or in a word, they are elided together so that the line still scans as ten sylla-bles. It isn't really something an actor need worry about. All it means is that a writer is building into his verse the natural elisions and slurrings of vowels and little syllables that occur in our normal everyday speech. It's probably good for an actor to be aware when there are elisions because it means he is awake to the way the verse works. But here at any rate he doesn't have to do anything about it. Here are some lines of Imogen's from *Cymbeline,* another late play. She's waking out of a drugged sleep and she finds a headless body lying beside her.

IMOGEN (*Lisa Harrow*): Yes, sir, to Milford Haven, which is the way?—
I thank you. By yond bush? Pray, how far thither?
'Ods pittikins, can it be six mile yet?

> I have gone all night. Faith, I'll lie down, and sleep.
> But soft, no bedfellow! O gods and goddesses!
> These flowers are like the pleasures of the world,
> This bloody man, the care on't. I hope I dream,
> For so I thought I was a cave-keeper,
> And cook to honest creatures. But 'tis not so.   *Cymbeline: IV.2.*

Look at the number of elisions there. First of all, "Yes, sir, to Milford Haven, which is the way?" "Haven," as we in fact naturally say it, becomes one syllable in the scansion of the line, not "Haven" but "Hav'n." The second one also tallies with the way we actually speak: "I have gone all night" scans as "I've gone all night." So does the next one, "I'll lie down and sleep" instead of "I will lie down and sleep." Elision sounds a learned word but basically it's to do with our actual habits of speech. It's not something grammatical or abstract. Let's look at the next example: "But soft, no bedfellow. O gods and goddesses." This is slightly trickier. The "-esses" of "goddesses" is scanned as two light stresses. It's a relatively rare example of a double feminine ending. It takes into account the fact that when we say the word "goddesses" we are apt to slur the middle syllable. You actually did that when you did the speech. The next example is "This bloody man the care on't": "on't" instead of "on it," a usage which was common in Shakespeare's day but is not one of our speech habits today. And the last very simple one is of course "But 'tis not so," for "But it is not so."

Now the interesting thing is that virtually all those examples are things you would yourself naturally elide when speaking, especially if you were saying them in a naturalistic play. One other point. One line actually doesn't scan properly in spite of the elision in it. "This bloody man the care on't. I hope I dream" has eleven syllables not ten. This does occasionally happen in Shakespeare's text, especially in the late plays. That's because he was a swift and intuitive writer and obviously didn't worry about occasional lapses of meter. So we needn't be too reverent about the seeming intricacies of his verse. Once you get the knack of it, you'll find it pretty commonsensical and simple.

David Suchet: *But what about the pronunciation of particular words? Some words keep cropping up in Shakespeare which were*

pronounced differently in his day. What should we do about them?
They do affect the scansion of the verse.

Ian McKellen: *I think this often gives Shakespearean actors a bad*
name with the public, who don't quite understand why we do use
what are now archaic pronunciations. For instance, there's a line in
Richard II *where he's divesting himself of his majesty and he says*
"My manors, rents, rĕvḗnūes I forgo." We're familiar enough with
the word "rĕvénue," as in "Inland Revenue," but if you are playing
Richard *you can't say "My manors, rents, rĕvḗnues I forgo,"*
because, although it has its own sort of rhythm, it's contrary to the
rather stately rhythm of the rest of this particular speech. So if you
hear a Shakespearean mispronouncing a word, he's actually mispro-
nouncing it because it's what Shakespeare wants.

Of course it's argued that the old stresses are hard for the audience
to follow. But are they? I personally believe we should use the
old pronunciation, partly because the rhythm of the line sounds better, but partly too because in context the old pronunciation is often
actually easier to say. There is a good example in *Antony and*
Cleopatra. Antony is dead and Cleopatra is saying that she will kill
herself.

CLEOPATRA *(Jane Lapotaire)*:   Rather a ditch in Egypt
Be gentle grave unto me! Rather on Nilus' mud
Lay me stark nak'd and let the waterflies
Blow me into abhorring! Rather make
My country's high pyrămīdes my gibbet
And hang me up in chains!   *Antony and Cleopatra: V.2.*

Good. Now we may be used to saying "pyrămīds," but
"pyrămīdes" is clear enough, and the alternative would be a tongue-
twister. Try saying it as "pyrămīds" and see what happens.

CLEOPATRA: Rather make
My country's high pyrămīds my gibbet
And hang me up in chains!

Not so easy, is it?

> Jane Lapotaire: *I find it hard to think of the word in the wrong way, the modern way. I suppose that's because the blank verse sets up such a rhythm that to go against it consciously is an effort.*

Once you accept the verse it's actually much easier to go with it than against it. Let's take another example from another play. In *Troilus and Cressida*, Cressida is desperate because she's been taken from Troilus, whom she loves. Pick it up at "Be moderate, be moderate." At first scan the tricky word in it in what would be the modern way.

> CRESSIDA (*Jane Lapotaire*): Why tell you me of moderation?
> The grief is fine, full, perfect that I taste,
> And vīolĕnteth in a sense as strong
> As that which causeth it.   *Troilus and Cressida: IV.4.*

The crux is "vīolĕnteth," which you found difficult to say.

> Jane Lapotaire: *Yes, I really have to stop and think when I get to that word, to do it that way. It's quite an effort.*

Let's listen to it again: "And vīolĕnteth in a sense as strong." It sounds wrong, doesn't it? But if we scan it as Shakespeare scanned it, and say vīolĕnteth, it falls into place.

> Jane Lapotaire: *When one does it the wrong way it sounds hurried, as if one is snatching at the word.*

Yes, "vīolĕnteth in a sense as strong" sounds like a tongue-twister. Let's see what happens when you say it Shakespeare's way.

> CRESSIDA: Why tell you me of moderation?
> The grief is fine, full, perfect that I taste,
> And vīolĕnteth in a sense as strong
> As that which causeth it.   *Troilus and Cressida: IV.4.*

It's much easier, isn't it?

Jane Lapotaire: *Yes, it seems to flow much more.*

I think that's a very good example. Sometimes there are single bits of pronunciation which don't actually affect the verse like that but which also sound better.

Jane Lapotaire: *I remember you saying that in* Troilus and Cressida *there's a character who today we call "Hecter" but the Elizabethans would have called "Hector." It's a much richer, much more powerful sound than "Hecter."*

Yes. They also pronounced what we call "Troilus" as "Troilus," which sounds more romantic as befits his character. But Shakespeare sometimes scans the word as two syllables and sometimes as three. It depends on how he uses the word in the verse-line at a given moment. Here's an example.

CRESSIDA (*Jane Lapotaire*): And is it true that I must go from Troy?
TROILUS (*Ian McKellen*): A hateful truth.
CRESSIDA: What, and from Troilus too?
TROILUS: From Troy and Troilus.
CRESSIDA: Is't possible?

Troilus and Cressida: IV.4.

You see, it scans differently in the two verse lines. In "A hateful truth. What, and from Troilus too?" it is treated as two syllables. And then in the next verse-line, "From Troy and Troilus. Is't possible?" it is scanned as three. Shakespeare often does that with his names and simply scans them according to the needs of the verse.

Ian McKellen: *Do you think the Elizabethans didn't pronounce their names constantly but had different pronunciations?*

No, it's really to do with the laws of meter. Most poets take this license and sometimes scan a word one way and sometimes another.

Let's look at a more important example and see how the scansion of the verse makes a big difference to the pronunciation and the effect of a word in the different context. First, from the opening soliloquy of *Richard III*.

> RICHARD III (*Alan Howard*): Now is the winter of our discontent
> Made glorious summer by this sun of York,
> And all the clouds that loured upon our house
> In the deep bosom of the ocean buried. *Richard III: I.i.*

Look at the last line and how it scans: "In the deep bosom of the ocean buried." There are eleven syllables here, not ten, and "Buried" is another feminine ending. "Ocean" scans simply enough as two syllables: "Ōceăn." But now let's look at some lines from another king, Henry V. It's from his "Once more unto the breach" speech.

> HENRY V (*Alan Howard*): Then lend the eye a terrible aspect;
> Let it pry through the portage of the head
> Like the brass cannon; let the brow o'erwhelm it
> As fearfully as doth a galled rock
> O'erhang and jutty his confounded base,
> Swilled with the wild and wasteful ōceăn. *Henry V: III.i.*

Now something funny happens there. "Swilled with the wild and wasteful ōceăn" is rousing stuff but it seems to peter off at the end. So if we think about the last line, how does it really scan?

Alan Howard: *Ōcĕān.*

That's right. At first sight, "Swilled with the wild and wasteful ocean" looks like a nine-syllable line, which would be unusual. So if we're to have ten syllables we have to make "ocean" three syllables. And surely we're glad to do so in this context because it sounds much better. The whole line is obviously onomatopoeic. The swish and swirl of the word sounds like the sea-swell:

Swilled with the wild and wasteful *ōcĕān.*

Lisa Harrow: *John, I know we've talked about elision but what about the vexed question of whether we should pronounce "-ed" or not? Is it always clear?*

Well, you have to do a little mathematical sum with each particular verse-line, don't you? You have to see how it scans as ten syllables and then you have the answer. Let's take two lines from the speech we've just looked at.

Disguise fair nature with hard-favoured rage.

There, "favoured" is two syllables. The "-ed" isn't pronounced. Now listen to another line.

As fearfully as doth a galled rock.

One has to say "galled," if the line is going to scan properly. Once again, if you mis-scan the line it's going to sound odd, like this:

As fearfully as doth a gall'd rock.

A bit of a hiccup, isn't it?

As we've heard lots of little examples, let's try a longer, swift-flowing passage: a piece of ding-dong dialogue where two actors will get lost if they don't go with the rhythm and pick up the cues as Shakespeare wrote them. Often in this passage a character comes in halfway through the verse-line. Richard III is wooing the Lady Anne over the dead body of King Henry VI.

ANNE (*Sinead Cusack*): Didst thou not kill this King?
RICHARD (*Alan Howard*):   I grant ye—yea.
ANNE: Dost grant me, hedgehog? Then God grant me too
Thou mayst be damnèd for that wicked deed!
O, he was gentle, mild and virtuous!
RICHARD: The better for the King of Heaven that hath him.
ANNE: He is in heaven, where thou shalt never come.
RICHARD: Let him thank me that holp to send him thither;

For he was fitter for that place than earth.

ANNE: And thou unfit for any place but hell.

RICHARD: Yes, one place else, if you will hear me name it.

ANNE: Some dungeon.

RICHARD: Your bedchamber.

ANNE: Ill rest betide the chamber where thou liest.

RICHARD: So will it, madam, till I lie with you.

ANNE: I hope so.

RICHARD: I know so. But gentle Lady Anne . . .

Is not the causer of the[se] timeless deaths . . .

As blameful as the executioner?

ANNE: Thou wast the cause and most accursed effect.

RICHARD: Your beauty was the cause of that effect . . .

ANNE: If I thought that, I tell thee, homicide,

These nails should rent that beauty from my cheeks.

RICHARD: These eyes could not endure that beauty's wrack; . . .

As all the world is cheerèd by the sun,

So I by that. It is my day, my life.

ANNE: Black night o'ershade thy day, and death thy life!

RICHARD: Curse not thyself, fair creature—thou art both.

ANNE: I would I were, to be revenged on thee.

RICHARD: It is a quarrel most unnatural

To be revenged on him that loveth thee.

ANNE: It is a quarrel just and reasonable

To be revenged on him that killed my husband.

RICHARD: He that bereft thee, lady, of thy husband

Did it to help thee to a better husband.

ANNE: His better doth not breathe upon the earth.

RICHARD: He lives, that loves thee better than he could.

ANNE: Name him.

RICHARD: Plantagenet.

ANNE: Why that was he.

RICHARD: The selfsame name, but one of better nature.

ANNE: Where is he?

RICHARD: Here. (*She spits at him.*) Why dost thou spit at me?

ANNE: Would it were mortal poison for thy sake!

RICHARD: Never came poison from so sweet a place.

ANNE: Never hung poison on a fouler toad.
Out of my sight! Thou dost infect mine eyes.
RICHARD: Thine eyes, sweet lady, have infected mine.

Richard III: I.2.

The verse works there like a rally at tennis. You both served the text up to each other, which is clearly the way it's written.

> Sheila Hancock: *All these things we've been talking about could be a bit daunting to an actor. How conscious should we be of the verse in performance?*

I think we should be very conscious of the verse in rehearsal but we shouldn't think about it in performance. If you've got it into your system it should then work on your subconscious. I've had to cram a lot of points into this session, but I wouldn't try to make them all at once if we were rehearsing. In practice I don't think it's that complicated. There's no mystique about the kind of points we've been making. A number look after themselves most of the time, such as stress, feminine endings and elision. Two simple qualities will see an actor safely through the supposed minefield of Shakespeare's verse: common sense and a feeling for what sounds right. If you decide in rehearsal that you want to go against the verse at a given point, of course you must be free to do so, but if you choose to ignore it, I think you should try to make it a rule to do so *knowingly*. Don't just overlook the verse. Ask first if following it actually isn't better and more helpful. That's the most important point I'm trying to make. But what do you all think?

> Sheila Hancock: *Well, that sounds a bit as if there's a danger of eliminating spontaneity in performance. I mean, you're saying that one has to get the pattern of the verse into one's head.*

Yes, just as you have to learn the lines. All acting is a balance between what is worked out and what is spontaneous, isn't it? Once again I'm back to my favorite word, "balance." Of course if one becomes too verse-conscious that is as bad as to ignore it. It always works best when an actor is able to go with it intuitively. And some actors are lucky and can do that without having to analyze it first. I'm sure that is the best way. But if you don't happen to have that luck, it is necessary to analyze what goes on in the verse. If you find you are getting bogged down in the process then of course you have to stop. On the other hand, we mustn't dodge our obligations. People who criticize us in the theater for not doing justice to the verse do have a point. If we are sloppy or insensitive about it we are not doing our job properly. Because Shakespeare is a great poet, an audience has as much right to expect us to be faithful to his text as they would to hear an orchestra play the right notes in the right time. That's obvious. But the truth is that the verse and its problems sometimes do annoy us because it seems to detract from exploring character. And then we overreact and go against it.

I also think the problem varies from play to play and sometimes from scene to scene and from speech to speech. I find that I need to stress what goes on in the verse much more in some plays than others. Sometimes in rehearsal I talk about it very little because it comes easily off the tongue without much thought. The norm of the verse in *Othello* and *King Lear* is like that. There are difficult, highly charged passages in those plays but on the whole the verse is easy. The late plays are harder. But I also found when working on one relatively early play, *Richard II*, that it was necessary to bring out points about the verse all the time. Mainly because the characters in the play are consciously using rhetoric as characters, not just because Shakespeare felt like writing it that way.

Ian McKellen: *I think what you're saying is pretty revolutionary. Most people when they go and see Shakespeare expect somehow to be able to hear that the actors are "speaking verse." It is related to what they know of poetry from poems they've learned at school. But of course you can sit through a whole Shakespeare play without being aware of it being written in verse at all. You keep stressing that the verse—and I absolutely agree—the verse is there to help the actors, and not for the audience to wallow in something vaguely poetic. We don't want them, as they're sitting through a play, to be aware of all this work that we've done. We must have absorbed it so that what we are saying is easy to listen to and more understandable and more beautiful and precise.*

Yes. But you have brought up the word "poetry," which I have been steering clear of. I think I ought to explain why. It's because I've been talking only about the grammar rather than the soul of the verse. Yet verse in itself is not necessarily poetic. It can of course accommodate poetry but as we have seen, it is very often the vehicle for naturalistic speech. Conversely, we shall also find out later on that poetry does not necessarily have anything to do with verse. That may sound confusing at this point, so all I will stress here is simply that the verse is the norm which Shakespeare uses for dramatic speech. An actor needs to find his feet with that before he can tap the text's poetic juices. He has to become easy with it so that it is second nature to him.

Patrick Stewart: *How often we've seen when an actor forgets his lines, whether it's one word or a whole speech, that the* ad lib *he makes to cover it comes out as blank verse. That's because the verse has become so ingrained that, although he may use different words, the rhythm will remain the same.*

Sheila Hancock: *If you forget your lines and substitute a one-syllable word where there should be a two-syllable word, it's like an electric shock. It jars and feels awful.*

David Suchet: *I think you've left out something very important. With the verse, there is always a very difficult stage in rehearsal where you begin to be highly aware of the verse subtleties. This can be very inhibiting until you break through that awareness, so that it doesn't impede your building of a character and your relationships with other people. Sometimes this verse-consciousness can dominate too long. And sooner or later you've got to get rid of it to release other areas of the play: relationships and all the rest of it. You've got to get through that stage.*

That's right. I must confess that I feel very self-conscious expounding verse in the way I've just been doing. I'd feel much happier mak-

ing specific points about it in the cut-and-thrust of rehearsal. Good
verse-speaking is not really about general principles but comes from
experience and practice. So although it's up to us to analyze the verse
as well as we can, in the end we must treat it intuitively. We must
trust it and let it be organic rather than conscious.

It is perhaps worth ending with two contemporary references to
Shakespeare's fluency as a writer. One is by Heminge and Condell,
the two actors in his company who edited the First Folio:

> His mind and hand went together: and what he thought he uttered with
> that easiness that we have scarce received from him a blot on his papers.

"He uttered with that easiness": there's a moral for us there. And
Ben Jonson, his friend and rival playwright, wrote:

> He flowed with that facility that sometimes it was necessary that it
> should be stopped.

Another good moral. So it is with the analysis of his verse: sometimes it is necessary that it should be stopped.

CHAPTER THREE

✦ ✦

Language and Character

Making the Words One's Own

[The following actors took part in the program that forms the basis of this chapter: SINEAD CUSACK, LISA HARROW, BEN KINGSLEY, MICHAEL PENNINGTON, ROGER REES, PATRICK STEWART, DAVID SUCHET, MICHAEL WILLIAMS.]

POLONIUS: What do you read, my lord?
HAMLET: Words, words, words . . .   *Hamlet: II.2.*

"Words, words, words." The Elizabethans loved them: they relished them and they played with them. Probably they used many more words in a day than we do and were eager to pick up new ones. Here, for instance, is the Clown, Costard, in *Love's Labour's Lost.* Another character gives him a letter and tips him.

ARMADO (*Ben Kingsley*): Bear this significant (*Giving Costard a letter*) to the country maid Jacquenetta. There is remuneration . . . (*Gives money and goes out.*)

COSTARD (*Roger Rees*): Now will I look to his remuneration. 'Remuneration'! O, that's the Latin word for three farthings . . . Three farthings—remuneration. 'Remuneration'! Why, it is a fairer name than French crown. I will never buy and sell out of this word.

(*Berowne enters.*)

BEROWNE (*Michael Pennington*): My good knave Costard, exceedingly well met.

COSTARD: Pray you, sir, how much carnation ribbon may a man buy for a remuneration?

BEROWNE: What is a remuneration?

COSTARD: Marry, sir, halfpenny farthing.

BEROWNE: Why then, three-farthing worth of silk.

COSTARD: I thank your worship. God be wi' you.

BEROWNE: Stay, slave. I must employ thee.
As thou wilt win my favour, good my knave,
Do one thing for me that I shall entreat.
The Princess comes to hunt here in the park,
And in her train there is a gentle lady;
When tongues speak sweetly, then they name her name,
And Rosaline they call her. Ask for her,
And to her white hand see thou do commend
This sealed up counsel. There's thy guerdon—go.

(*Costard looks at the coin Berowne has given him.*)

COSTARD: Guerdon, O sweet guerdon. Better than remuneration—elevenpence farthing better. Most sweet guerdon. I will do it, sir, in print. Guerdon! Remuneration!   *Love's Labour's Lost: III.1.*

Verbal relish . . . today we're a bit apt to fight shy of it. But until we love individual words we cannot love language, and if we don't we won't be able to use it properly. As most actors' instincts push them towards the naturalistic, they often don't go far enough. I believe that in rehearsal, at any rate, we should tend to go too far, because we can always pull back later. Let's start exploring Shakespeare's language by looking at one or two individual words. What would you say, if any, is the most important word in Shakespeare?

Lisa Harrow: *What about "Time"?*

"Time," yes indeed, "Time." It's dangerous territory, that word. There was a wonderful skit on television not long ago about a director telling an actor how to use the word.

DIRECTOR: All right, let's start right at the beginning, shall we?

ACTOR: Right, yeh.

DIRECTOR: What's the word, what's the word, I wonder, that Shakespeare decides to begin his sentence with here?

ACTOR: Er, "Time" is the first word.

DIRECTOR: Time, Time.

ACTOR: Yep.

DIRECTOR: And how does Shakespeare decide to spell it, Hugh?

ACTOR: T-I-M-E.

DIRECTOR: T-I?

ACTOR: M.

DIRECTOR: M-E.

ACTOR: Yep.

DIRECTOR: And what sort of spelling of the word is that?

ACTOR: Well, it's the ordinary spelling.

DIRECTOR: It's the *ordinary* spelling, isn't it? It's the *conventional* spelling. So why, out of all the spellings he could have chosen, did Shakespeare choose that one, do you think?

ACTOR: Well, um, because it gives us time in an ordinary sense.

DIRECTOR: Exactly, well done, good boy. Because it gives us time in an ordinary, conventional sense.

ACTOR: Oh, right.

DIRECTOR: So, Shakespeare has given us time in a conventional sense. But he's given us something else, Hugh. Have a look at the typography. What do you spy?

ACTOR: Oh, it's got a capital T.

DIRECTOR: Shakespeare's T is very much upper case, there, Hugh, isn't it? Why?

ACTOR: Cos it's the first word in the sentence.

DIRECTOR: Well, I think that's *partly* it. But I think there's another reason too. Shakespeare has given us time in a *conventional* sense—and time in an *abstract* sense.

ACTOR: Right, yes.

DIRECTOR: All right? Think your voice can convey that, Hugh?

ACTOR: I hope so.

DIRECTOR: I hope so too. All right. Give it a go.

ACTOR: Just the one word?

DIRECTOR: Just the one word for the moment.

ACTOR: Yep.

 (*He howls the word*)

DIRECTOR: Hugh, Hugh, Hugh. Where do we gather from?

ACTOR: Oh, the buttocks.

DIRECTOR: Always the buttocks. Gather from the buttocks. Thank You.

ACTOR: Time!

DIRECTOR: What went wrong there, Hugh?

ACTOR: Um, I don't know. I got a bit lost in the middle actually.

Cambridge Footlights 1981

An awful warning. So we mustn't be too solemn about our work. But we mustn't dodge things either. Words in Shakespeare do have to be searched and savored. Particularly dipthongs: long vowels like "Time." Shakespeare himself was obviously haunted by the word, and did indeed often give it a capital letter. So in spite of this dreadful warning, I intend to dig into it a bit later on. For now I simply want to make the point that the correct pronunciation, played as it were at three-quarter speed, is "Time": virtually two vowel sounds. And the word does have two meanings. First, something factual as in "What's the time?" and secondly a poetic resonance, a heightened meaning, i.e., that which is inexorable and wears down human endeavor. Shakespeare often uses it as a synonym for Death: something relentless and not to be avoided. Here are some examples:

"Time doth transfix the flourish set on youth."

"Despite of cormorant devouring Time."

"And that old common arbitrator Time."

Now I don't want to get you all gathering from the buttocks but you do have to do something about the word in those contexts, don't you? You all did in fact put it into inverted commas. You knew you had to make the word *do work*. So let's look at a passage now where the speaker is entirely concerned with working on his audience with words and where nothing else matters. It's a chorus speech from *Henry V.* Let's work on it in the way we talked of at the outset. First, let's ask what the speaker's intentions are, and secondly how we should use the language.

David Suchet: *But what about the character of the Chorus?*

I'm not going to talk about the character, because you yourself, David, *are* the character if you're playing the Chorus. It's not a character in the normal sense of the word: it is *you* painting a verbal picture. So feel your way with the words. You have said in the beginning of the play, "On your imaginary forces work": so, on our imaginary forces work. Your intention is to make us feel, smell and see what it's like on the battlefield. So you've got to find the language at the moment that you speak it. Let me repeat something I stressed in our first session. The words must be *found* or *coined* or *fresh-minted* at the moment you utter them. They are not to be thought of as something which preexists in a printed text. In the theater they must seem to find their life for the first time at the moment the actor speaks them. Because he needs them. So here you use the words which you, David, need. Have a go.

> CHORUS (*David Suchet*): Now entertain conjecture of a time
> When creeping murmur and the poring dark
> Fills the wide vessel of the universe.
> From camp to camp, through the foul womb of night,
> The hum of either army stilly sounds.   *Henry V: IV*

I think that sounded a little bit too prepared. It's got to come out of you spontaneously. You don't know what you're going to say till you find the words to express what you feel.

David Suchet: *More excited?*

Inside you, yes.

> CHORUS: Now entertain conjecture of a time
> When creeping murmur and the poring dark
> Fills the wide vessel of the universe.
> From camp to camp through the foul womb of night,
> The hum of either army stilly sounds,
> That the fixed sentinels almost receive
> The secret whispers of each other's watch.
> Fire answers fire, and through their paly flames
> Each battle sees the other's umbered face.

> Steed threatens steed, in high and boastful neighs,
> Piercing the night's dull ear; and from the tents
> The armourers, accomplishing the knights,
> With busy hammers closing rivets up,
> Give dreadful note of preparation.

I thought the first half of that was great . . .

> David Suchet: *But then I went wrong?*

You fell into a trap.

> David Suchet: *I split it up too much?*

No, you set up the general atmosphere of the battlefield splendidly. But though the text starts that way, it soon becomes much more tactile and concrete. For instance, after you've reached "Each battle sees the other's umbered face" the text goes "Steed threatens steed" and the verse rhythm goes "dum dum de dum." So the neigh of the steed breaks into the stillness of the night. In the same way, the word "piercing" in the phrase "Piercing the night's dull ear" does pierce the atmosphere which the verse has previously set up. And then comes the clang of the armorers "accomplishing" the knights and the word "accomplishing" sounds busy and practical. So individual words and images break into the initial atmosphere which you have set up and which has been still and drowsy. Take it again from "Each battle sees" and make the images more concrete.

> CHORUS: Fire answers fire, and through their paly flames
> Each battle sees the other's umbered face.
> Steed threatens steed, in high and boastful neighs,
> Piercing the night's dull ear; and from the tents
> The armourers, accomplishing the knights,
> With busy hammers closing rivets up,
> Give dreadful note of preparation.

You took us with you much more then. Like a camera the speech moved in from a long shot of the army to a close-up of what is happening within the scene. This raises a point we're going to find important when we talk about set speeches. It's a great trap with Shakespeare's text if you get on to one note, one tone and one tempo. This is true of all dramatic texts but it is especially so with Shakespeare. You have always to look within the verse for variety.

> David Suchet: *That's often the difficulty, isn't it? When you are trying to coin phrases and words and images at the same time as trying to get the flow of the blank verse.*

Yes, you can mesmerize yourself with the words. But here, if you go for the contrapuntal stresses in the verse, you will find the gear changes quite easily.

We've talked about intentions and of how the verse works and we're beginning to marry the two traditions, Shakespeare's and ours. We're beginning to get a balance by finding the language and by making it our own. Notice that once again I have not been using the word "Poetry." But don't think because I don't use it that I believe the poetry in Shakespeare is unimportant. In the end, it may well be the most important thing of all, but I don't believe in rubbing an actor's nose in it at the outset. To do that blocks and inhibits him, which is why I am hardly going to touch poetry till our last session. But in the meantime, if we come to terms with what I call the "heightened language," we shall be equipping ourselves towards unlocking the poetry. So let's look now in detail at some of the major ingredients of language. First of all, what about *resonance* and *onomatopoeia?* Let's have some examples, and let's relish them:

> Roger Rees: *"Swilled with the wild and wasteful ocean . . ."*

> David Suchet: *"But when the blast of war blows in our ears . . ."*

> Ben Kingsley: *"That the fixed sentinels almost receive*
> *The secret whispers of each other's watch . . ."*

I liked that because it was probably closer than usual to how Elizabethan actors would have taken it. We rather fight shy of such relish in performance. I want to try to push us too far in that direction for a while to see whether we don't normally fight shy of the language. If the language is as rich and vivid as that which you've just quoted, you do have to take it that far. The need for verbal relish is obvious: not too little, but of course not too much. You must still sound and be real. Again it's a question of balance. It's perhaps worth pointing to some words whose richness is not so apparent today. Shakespeare's pronunciation was different from ours; it was rougher and perhaps more onomatopoeic. "War" for instance was pronounced "Wahrre"; and "eye" was pronounced "Ay-ee" and "Time" was pronounced "Tay-eme."

> Roger Rees: *I'm fascinated to know what it could have sounded like. I know you can do it a bit so why don't you show us? What was the noise in 1590 like on the South Bank?*

Well, I'm not an expert and I'm bound to get it wrong, but I'll try to give you the general feel. I'll do a bit of the speech we've just listened to. In the 1590s it went a bit like this:

Now[1] entertain conjecture[4] of a time[3]
When[5] creeping murmur[4] and the poring dark[7]
Fills the wide[3] vessel of the universe.[4]
From camp to camp through the foul womb of night[1]
The hum[6] of either[3] army[7] stilly sounds.[1]

⤙ ⤙ ⤙ ⤙ ⤙ ⤙ ⤙ ⤙ ⤙ ⤙ ⤙ ⤙ ⤙ ⤙ ⤙ ⤙ ⤙

Note: Very approximate renderings of the above:
1. Pronounced "n-eow" as in our genteel "now."
2. "r" is burred throughout (even before consonants) as in "law-r-and order."
3. Pronounced "tay-eme," a longer version of our genteel pronunciation of the word.
4. Pronounced as in the last sound in "china."
5. Pronouuced "hw" as in Scots.
6. Pronounced "oo" as in Yorkshire and Lancashire.
7. Pronounced with a short "a" as in "cat."

Roger Rees: *That's marvelous.*

David Suchet: *That would actually have helped me a lot the first time I did it.*

Roger Rees: *It's almost like the West Coast of Ireland or the West Country.*

Yes, a funny mixture of West Country, Ireland, a bit of American.

David Suchet: *How do they know what it sounded like?*

Well, they work it out, partly from spellings and rhymes, but mainly from the way a language changes. They ask, How did English get from Anglo-Saxon to Middle English and so to us today? If it started as one thing and has ended up as another, it must have gone through certain changes.

David Suchet: *How does it all relate to the American use of English?*

I think that American is actually closer to Elizabethan English than our current English speech. That's ironic, because American actors are often worried about not speaking what they call Standard English, yet they're actually doing it closer to Shakespeare's way than we are.

Lisa Harrow: *Yes, we sound much more genteel now, don't we?*

Genteel, yes, that's a good word. Elizabethan English is rougher—isn't it?—and tougher. There is still a glimmering sense of this old richer sound in many actors today. I suppose it's a sort of thespian folk memory. Rather more at the beginning of the century than now. Let's listen to a recording of Sir Frank Benson, playing Mark Antony fifty years ago. He made two syllables out of the word "ears," for instance, and about four out of the word "bones."

Friends, Romans, Countrymen, lend me your ears,
I come to bury Caesar, not to praise him.

That evil that men do lives after them,
The good is oft interrèd with their bones . . . *Julius Caesar; III.2.*

Well, somewhat overdone, but not entirely un-Elizabethan. I think the big difference between that and what we are used to is that he's much more sentimental than we'd be today. And a healthy verbal relish has become in him a mannerism. Even so, diphthongs *are* in fact two vowel sounds, not one, and that's a point the Elizabethan pronunciation brings up. Vowel sounds are important. I don't want to labor the point because anybody who knows poetry knows it and it doesn't just apply to Shakespeare. I just want to stress that there's a tendency in our acting tradition to run away from verbal relish, especially of vowels.

Lisa Harrow: *We do run away from consonants too, don't we? Surely they're just as important?*

Yes, if there's a danger of us wallowing in vowels, it's useful to think of consonants as a goodly contrast and a stern corrective. Often they're more important than the vowels. Just listen to those two lines about the sentries again from *Henry V.*

David Suchet: That the fixed sentinels almost receive
The secret whispers of each other's watch.

The whispering is there in the sounds, isn't it? The effect of the alliteration is obvious. The text embodies the whispering. Alliteration is important and I don't think we always relish and point it up enough. Those two lines of the Chorus show why I have the instinct to push our verbal relish as far as we dare. It's partly because Shakespeare wrote with those old sounds in mind, but it's partly because we do these days tend to give short measure. Once more it's a question of balance. But we can't go far wrong if we just keep remembering Shakespeare's own view of the matter. So, let's remind ourselves of Hamlet's advice to the players.

HAMLET (*Ben Kingsley*): Speak the speech, I pray you, as I pronounced it to you, trippingly on the tongue . . . Be not too tame . . . [Oh, that's a wonderful word, isn't it? because we do get so *tame*] . . . Be not too tame, neither. But let your own discretion be your tutor. Suit the action to the word, the word to the action.   *Hamlet: III.2.*

It's all there, isn't it? Not too little, not too much. I'm always struck by the sentence "Suit the action to the word, the word to the action." I'm not sure, but I think Shakespeare is here partly expressing in Elizabethan terms what we've been expressing by the word "intention." "Intention" equals "What are you doing?" and "Action" equals "That which you are doing." So suit the action to the word, the word to the action.

That sentence of Hamlet's reminds me of a vital point about Shakespeare's language which we have not yet made. If I were to offer one single bit of advice to an actor new to Shakespeare's text, I suspect that the most useful thing I could say would be, "Look for the *antitheses* and play them." "Suit the action to the word, the word to the action" is a good example of a double antithesis. We can easily overlook it because we don't use antithesis very much today, particularly in our everyday speech. Yet Shakespeare was deeply imbued with the sense of it. He *thought* antithetically. It was the way his sentences over and over found their shape and their meaning. Sometimes he laughs at this and sends the habit up. Listen to Falstaff.

FALSTAFF (*David Suchet*): Harry, I do not only marvel where thou spendest thy time, but also how thou art accompanied. For though the camomile, the more it is trodden on the faster it grows, yet youth, the more it is wasted the sooner it wears.   *Henry IV, Part One: II.4.*

There's a triple antithesis there, and they're not at all uncommon. The trouble is that antithetical words are not always so apparent and it is easy to overlook them. For instance in "To be or not to be" we have about as simple an antithetical thought as one can get. But Hamlet's next sentence has key words which are not quite so obvious.

HAMLET (*Michael Pennington*): To be, or not to be—that is the question;

Whether 'tis nobler in the mind to suffer
The slings and arrows of outrageous fortune
Or to take arms against a sea of troubles
And by opposing end them.   *Hamlet: III.1.*

"Antithesis" is in a way a bad word for something very practical. It sounds obscure and learned. Perhaps it would be better to use a phrase of Shakespeare's and talk of *"setting the word against the word."* In the sentence we've just heard, "in the mind to suffer" is set against "to take arms," and "by opposing" is set against "end them." So that is what you have to do: set one word or phrase against another. If an actor doesn't point up antitheses, he will be hard and sometimes quite impossible to follow. Here's the beginning of Richard II's long soliloquy in Pomfret Castle.

> RICHARD II (*Michael Pennington*): I have been studying how I may
> compare
> This prison where I live unto the world;
> And for because the world is populous,
> And here is not a creature but myself,
> I cannot do it. Yet I'll hammer it out.
> My brain I'll prove the female to my soul,
> My soul the father, and these two beget
> A generation of still-breeding thoughts,
> And these same thoughts people this little world,
> In humours like the people of this world.
> For no thought is contented; the better sort,
> As thoughts of things divine, are intermixed
> With scruples, and do set the word itself
> Against the word. . . .   *Richard II: V.5.*

"Set the word itself/Against the word." That really is a useful piece of direction by Shakespeare, isn't it? It tells us how each new word in a sentence qualifies what has gone before or changes the direction of that sentence. If we don't set up one word, we won't prepare for another to qualify it. And if the next word doesn't build on the first and move the sentence on, both the audience and the actor may lose their way. That's what I mean by urging actors to think antithetically.

Michael Pennington: *Yes. And as far as this particular speech is concerned, which I don't know very well, there seem to be two separate techniques being used. Richard's opening proposition is based on a kind of antithesis, "I have been studying how I may compare/This prison where I live unto the world;/And for because the world is populous,/And here is not a creature but myself,/I cannot do it." The first strong intention of the speech comes with "Yet I'll hammer it out" and then something different happens. There seems to be an accumulation of ideas which involves picking out one word from the end of a line and setting it against a word at the beginning of the next, "My brain I'll prove the female to my soul,/My soul the father, and these two beget/A generation of still-breeding thoughts," and so on. So for the actor scanning the text for clues, the verse and the antitheses suggest an accumulating energy and a forward movement.*

That's right. Always look for the story line in a long speech. A speech must move the story on.

Lisa Harrow: *Pushing the thought through is really to do with the problem of inflection. You haven't talked about that yet. Like antithesis, it's not something we as modern actors use every day. Yet we need it to carry the impetus of the thought forward, don't we?*

Yes. I wish I had a nice helpful definition of what an inflection really *is.* It of course involves stressing something important. But partly, as Mike's just been saying, it's an invitation to the audience or the person you're addressing to *go with you.* It introduces a new thought or it changes the direction of a sentence. It's like cutting from shot to shot on the television screen: the new shot, i.e. the inflection, is a new piece of information. And so the story moves on.

Lisa Harrow: *But what do we mean by inflection? We often talk of upward and downward inflection but . . .*

Michael Pennington: *It's the shortest possible route between the speaker and the audience, isn't it? It's a way of communicating. The actor has the privilege of and the good fortune of having lived with*

the language for a long time at rehearsals, but he has only one oppor-
tunity to convey it to an audience whose attention may be difficult to
hold. The inflection is the clearest and most economical way of doing
that. For instance you could say "To be, or not to be—that is the
question" without inflection and you'd probably be understood. But
it would be more helpful if you inflected it and said, "To bé, or nót to
bé—thát is the quéstion." Or you could overpoint it and say exagger-
atedly: "To BE, or not to BE—THAT is the QUESTION" and insult the
audience's intelligence. It's just a matter of hitting the mean, isn't it?

Yes, balance again. But you're right, it's really an invitation to the
audience to go with you. That's a good definition.

Lisa Harrow: *It carries the thoughts on from the end of one verse-*
line into the next. By inflecting, you, as it were, keep the ball in the
air from line to line.

The reason it's difficult to talk about is that we're moving here from
something which is objectively present in the text to something
much more impalpable and subjective. As we've looked so far at a lot
of short examples, let's stand back now and have a look at the verbal
impact of a whole speech. We'll take Henry V's speech rallying his
soldiers at Harfleur which we've heard bits of already. An awful lot
could be said about this speech and there's no end to the ways in
which it could be taken, but I want to concentrate here on Henry's
use of his language. His intention is to rally his troops and so his language is heightened because of his intention, not because it is a set
speech. He wants to fire them, so he works on them with words.

Michael Williams: *I think this particular speech relies very much on*
the army and their reactions to what he says. It would be a help if we
could get the audience to heckle me a bit. And perhaps the other
actors can come and do some work too.

Yes, come and join Henry's army. All of you try to make it as difficult for Mike as possible and then you'll make it easier for him than
if there's a reverent silence. So resist him and heckle him.

HENRY V (*Michael Williams*): Once more unto the breach, dear friends,
once more,

Or close the wall up with our English dead!
In peace there's nothing so becomes a man
As modest stillness and humility:
But when the blast of war blows in our ear
Then imitate the action of the tiger;
Stiffen the sinews, conjure up the blood,
Disguise fair nature with hard-favoured rage;
Then lend the eye a terrible aspect;
Let it pry through the portage of the head
Like the brass cannon; let the brow o'erwhelm it
As fearfully as doth a gallèd rock
O'erhang and jutty his confounded base,
Swilled with the wild and wasteful ocean.
Now set the teeth and stretch the nostril wide,
Hold hard the breath, and bend up every spirit
To his full height! On, on, you noblest English,
Whose blood is fet from fathers of war-proof!
Fathers that, like so many Alexanders,
Have in these parts from morn till even fought,
And sheathed their swords for lack of argument.
Dishonour not your mothers; now attest
That those whom you called fathers did beget you!
Be copy now to men of grosser blood,
And teach them how to war . . .
I see you stand like greyhounds in the slips,
Straining upon the start. The game's afoot!
Follow your spirit, and upon this charge
Cry, "God for Harry, England, and Saint George!"   *Henry V: III.1.*

Of course I'm not suggesting the reactions should be as crude as
that. They would have to be rehearsed and orchestrated for a proper
performance. But this exercise serves to remind us that language
doesn't exist in a vacuum but is a response to a situation and an
attempt to work on that situation. An oration like that needs that
amount of comeback for Henry to work on and to help whoever's
acting him to be real in the theater.

Do you see why I'm taking this particular speech? The heightened language so obviously has a dramatic purpose here. It's not just poetic because it's Shakespeare: the character *needs* that language to handle the situation and to kindle his soldiers. This is an obvious and extreme example, but I believe that the same principle will be found to apply to almost all, no, perhaps all, heightened speeches which we come to look at.

> Roger Rees: *Everything you've said so far has been about language. But we haven't talked at all about character. Isn't it dangerous to split the two?*

Yes, it is, because the nature of the language tells us about the nature of the character, or maybe we should say the language *is* the character. I've separated the two rather artificially because I'm concentrating in this session on heightened language. So you're quite right to remind us that character is all-important to an actor, and it is dangerous to split it off as I seem to have been doing. I should however explain that I've been taking the importance of character for granted, simply because any actor who is worth his salt knows that to find the character is vital. More importantly, any actor knows how to do it because he is used to it. There is no basic difference between approaching a character when he plays Shakespeare and when he plays any other author, ancient or modern. So though character is one of the chief elements in playing Shakespeare, it doesn't need exposition from me, except perhaps to bring out character points in individual bits of text as we come to them. But I do believe—though you may well challenge me—that there are times in Shakespeare when the language is more important than character and, as it were, takes the driving seat. What about speeches that are obviously choric? I mean text which is primarily to do with whatever it describes and not with the character who's speaking it.

Very often Shakespeare gives a wonderfully colored speech to somebody who isn't important in the play as a character. He means us to be interested in the words that are spoken, not in the person who speaks them. As an extreme example, let's take the opening speech of *Antony and Cleopatra*. Philo is an unknown soldier who says this one speech and never speaks or appears again in the play. Really relish the words.

> Ben Kingsley: *Yes, this is the first utterance in the whole play . . .*

> Roger Rees: *. . . So it's like the introduction. It tells us the whole story, so it's not about character.*

That's right, so its function is choric. We want to know about Antony and we want to know about Cleopatra, but we're not particularly interested in poor old Philo.

> Ben Kingsley: *So when I've finished I go round and count the house, take the tickets, do the teas and sweep the car park?*

That's right, have a go.

> PHILO (*Ben Kingsley*): Nay, but this dotage of our general's
> O'erflows the measure. Those his goodly eyes,
> That o'er the files and musters of the war
> Have glowed like plated Mars, now bend, now turn
> The office and devotion of their view
> Upon a tawny front; his captain's heart,
> Which in the scuffles of great fights hath burst
> The buckles on his breast, reneges all temper,
> And is become the bellows and the fan
> To cool a gypsy's lust.   *Antony and Cleopatra: I.1.*

> Lisa Harrow: *But there is a character point here, isn't there? The character himself is angry about what he's describing. It's not just a choric speech. Although it's giving the audience a situation and information, the actor has got to get into the character's feelings.*

You're absolutely right. I'm cheating if I just say it's choric. What I am really saying is "Make the language your first concern." And that's what Ben did. Now I'd say to him, "Having focused on the language and started to make it work on your audience, show us more of what the character himself feels." Not necessarily what he *is*, but what he feels: his anger and bitterness and sense of outrage have of course got to go into it to make it real.

Ben Kingsley: *Well, I think that as an actor I tend to clutter. I think I ought always to simplify, simplify, simplify. So I won't yet impose a character on these words. As an exercise I'll still try to allow these words to push me into some sort of shape. They should be more vigorous.*

Something that would launch you into the scene more would be to make an entrance. If you start static the speech will be static. So enter in outrage at what you've just seen.

Ben Kingsley: *Yes. All right, I'll try that.* (He does so.)

Nay, but this dotage of our general's
O'erflows the measure. Those his goodly eyes,
That o'er the files and musters of the war
Have glowed like plated Mars, now bend, now turn
The office and devotion of their view
Upon a tawny front. His captain's heart,
Which in the scuffles of great fights hath burst
The buckles on his breast, reneges all temper,
And is become the bellows and the fan
To cool a gypsy's lust.

Ben Kingsley: *It makes me shake, this language. It actually makes me shake. It is so strong that if I let it push me, it's like getting a little vial of something and whacking it into your arm. It works on you.*

Roger Rees: *Yes, the language made you angry.*

Good, the language made you angry. We did an interesting thing there, didn't we? We worked the wrong way round. We started with the language and then we went to the intentions. You solved it beautifully the second time because you came in under great pressure and with a great need to tell us about what you'd seen. And so you found your intention and it made the language come alive. I'm not saying that the character or the intention isn't important, only that occasionally it's valuable to start with the text and the language only.

Ben Kingsley: *Oh, for me it's the right and the only way. Otherwise I impose.*

Lisa Harrow: *If you turned it the other way round, and went only for the emotion and the situation and ignored the language, we probably wouldn't understand what you were saying. And then the play wouldn't get the right kickoff.*

I think there's a lesson in that.

Let's look now at a rather harder example. In *Henry V* the Lord Grandpré is describing to the French the condition of the English army. Listen to how curious and disturbing the language is.

GRANDPRÉ (*Patrick Stewart*): Why do you stay so long, my lords of
France?
Yon island carrions, desperate of their bones,
Ill-favouredly become the morning field . . .
Big Mars seems bankrupt in their beggared host,
And faintly through a rusty beaver peeps.
The horsemen sit like fixèd candlesticks
With torch-staves in their hand; and their poor jades
Lob down their heads, dropping the hides and hips,
The gum down-roping from their pale-dead eyes,
And in their pale dull mouths the gimmaled bit
Lies foul with chawed grass, still and motionless;
And their executors, the knavish crows,
Fly o'er them all, impatient for their hour.
Description cannot suit itself in words
To demonstrate the life of such a battle. *Henry V: IV.2.*

Clearly the function of this speech is also choric, isn't it? It is there to "demonstrate the life of such a battle." The things described obviously matter more than the character of the speaker. The language is so heightened and peculiar and quirky that it is clearly the most important thing. So maybe one should say character doesn't matter here? Or does it?

> Patrick Stewart: *Oh, surely yes. Character always matters. It's not enough to say that a speech is simply choric or descriptive. Although Shakespeare doesn't tell us what Grandpré had for breakfast or whether he was bottle-fed when he was a baby, he clothes the character in such rich text that an actor can find a variety of characters if he looks carefully enough.*

I agree entirely. You've put your finger on it. The text *is* the character. It fills him out and gives him his life. With a speech like this we have to ask what is the character reason why the old boy uses such extraordinary words and images.

I could spend the evening digging into the text of that one speech and anatomizing that strange old man. But it's time now to look at one or two longer examples. Here's a place where Shakespeare introduces a new character into a play in a very emotional and personal situation and yet gives her primarily a choric function. In *Julius Caesar,* Caesar's wife Calphurnia comes to tell him that the day is ominous. The actress who plays her mustn't fall into the trap of trying to play the heightened language up just because it's obviously heightened. Try to search out that language. Calphurnia is trying to find the meaning of all the images that she has seen and heard. What were they? Why did they happen? So *search* them rather than demonstrate them.

> CALPHURNIA (*Sinead Cusack*): What mean you, Caesar? Think you to
> walk forth?
> You shall not stir out of your house today.
> CAESAR (*David Suchet*): Caesar shall forth. The things that threatened me
> Ne'er looked but on my back; when they shall see
> The face of Caesar, they are vanishèd.

CALPHURNIA: Caesar, I never stood on ceremonies,
Yet now they fright me. There is one within
Besides the things that we have heard and seen,
Recounts most horrid sights seen by the watch.
A lioness hath whelpèd in the streets,
And graves have yawned and yielded up their dead;
Fierce fiery warriors fought upon the clouds
In ranks and squadrons and right form of war,
Which drizzled blood upon the Capitol;
The noise of battle hurtled in the air;
Horses did neigh, and dying men did groan,
And ghosts did shriek and squeal about the streets.
O Caesar, these things are beyond all use,
And I do fear them.   *Julius Caesar: II.2.*

I thought you did that beautifully because you found a happy balance between the character and the heightened text. You moved us by what you had seen as much as by your feelings about what you had seen. Now, let's look at Casca the conspirator, also in *Julius Caesar.* He is talking to Brutus and Cassius.

CASSIUS (*David Suchet*): Who offered him the crown?

CASCA (*Ben Kingsley*): Why, Antony.

BRUTUS (*Roger Rees*): Tell us the manner of it, gentle Casca.

CASCA: I can as well be hanged as tell the manner of it; it was mere foolery; I did not mark it. I saw Mark Antony offer him a crown; yet 'twas not a crown neither, 'twas one of these coronets; and as I told you, he put it by once; but for all that, to my thinking, he would fain have had it . . . And then he offered it the third time; he put it the third time by; and still as he refused it, the rabblement hooted, and clapped their chopped hands, and threw up their sweaty night caps, and uttered such a deal of stinking breath because Caesar refused the crown, that it had, almost, choked Caesar; for he swooned and fell down at it. And for mine own part, I durst not laugh, for fear of opening my lips and receiving the bad air.   *Julius Caesar: I.2.*

Prose: terse, reductive and cynical. Now listen to him sixty lines later. He is talking about the same supernatural storm which we've just heard Calphurnia describing.

> CASCA: Are not you moved, when all the sway of earth
> Shakes like a thing unfirm? O Cicero,
> I have seen tempests when the scolding winds
> Have rived the knotty oaks, and I have seen
> Th'ambitious ocean swell and rage and foam,
> To be exalted with the threatening clouds;
> But never till tonight, never till now,
> Did I go through a tempest dropping fire.
> Either there is a civil strife in heaven,
> Or else the world, too saucy with the gods,
> Incenses them to send destruction.   *Julius Caesar: I.3.*

Good. Now I think that every actor who plays Casca finds this switch from the worldly, down-to-earth prose scene to the hysterical verse scene a huge acting problem. He feels in the second that he is asked by Shakespeare to be choric rather than real. The two scenes seem not to connect. What do you think, Ben?

Ben Kingsley: *Yes, it is hard. But over the last two minutes while we were working on it, I had one of those gifts, those little revelations. You cannot have somebody who always exists on a hysterical level reacting to something extraordinary and still hope to move the audience. Because he's cried wolf. You would think "Oh well, it's Casca blowing his top again." But if it's somebody who is always laid back, always urbane, if nothing surprises him and nothing shocks him and yet you suddenly find him in a terrible state, I think that it will convey to his fellow characters and to the audience that there is something deeply disturbing going on. If Casca always used heightened verse, and if that were his plane of existence, I think that the scene wouldn't work. The audience wouldn't believe that something terrible was happening.*

David Suchet: *Shakespeare often does that, doesn't he? I mean he seems to go into bits of illogic.*

Yes, but I'm sure that the drastic change here is quite deliberate on Shakespeare's part. Because a normally cool man goes berserk, the storm becomes more real. It often pays off with Shakespeare to go for each scene as it comes and commit to it totally, rather than try to iron out the inconsistencies. After all, human beings are pretty inconsistent. Again and again Shakespeare writes seeming inconsistencies which are entirely deliberate. I think maybe this is the most important point to make about how Shakespeare builds up his characters. Actors shouldn't try to iron out these inconsistencies but rather embrace them. Let's look, for instance, at a bit of *The Merchant of Venice*. When Bassanio comes to choose between the gold, silver and lead caskets, Portia's first speech to him is fairly naturalistic.

> PORTIA (*Lisa Harrow*): I pray you tarry, pause a day or two
> Before you hazard, for in choosing wrong
> I lose your company. Therefore forbear awhile.
> There's something tells me, but it is not love,
> I would not lose you: and you know yourself
> Hate counsels not in such a quality.   *The Merchant of Venice: III.2.*

A little while after, when she bids him choose from among the caskets, her text becomes poetic and heightened:

> Away then, I am locked in one of them;
> If you do love me, you will find me out . . .
> Let music sound while he doth make his choice,
> Then if he lose he makes a swanlike end,
> Fading in music. That the comparison
> May stand more proper, my eye shall be the stream
> And watery deathbed for him. He may win,
> And what is music then? Then music is
> Even as the flourish when true subjects bow
> To a new-crownèd monarch. Such it is
> As are those dulcet sounds in break of day
> That creep into the dreaming bridegroom's ear
> And summon him to marriage. Now he goes,

With no less presence but with much more love
Than young Alcides when he did redeem
The virgin tribute paid by howling Troy
To the sea monster. I stand for sacrifice;
The rest aloof are the Dardanian wives,
With bleared visages come forth to view
The issue of th'exploit. Go, Hercules;
Live thou, I live. With much, much more dismay
I view the fight than thou that mak'st the fray.

There's a huge difference, isn't there? But in the second speech Portia isn't just switching into romantic language because Shakespeare felt like a spot of lyricism. She's trying to find the words she can to express her situation and make it bearable. Do you see what I'm doing here? I am going for the heightened language but I am trying to approach it via the intentions. That also embraces my earlier point about language and character being one. I believe that this is the only way our two traditions can come together.

Now let's sum up. We have been going for the heightened language, but I think that somewhere we maybe could all have gone a bit farther and been a bit more daring. What do you all think?

Ben Kingsley: *Well, it's limits, isn't it? I mean, art is limits. How far can you go before you've broken a limit and rendered it unintelligible?*

Personally I'd go very far. But of course it's the old question again of balance, isn't it?

David Suchet: *John, would you like to show how you yourself would go at it? You should do that speech in* Henry V.

Lisa Harrow: *The old French king.*

Roger Rees: *Yes, the list of the French knights.*

Lisa Harrow: *Sit in this chair.*

Well, I don't think I'll do it in Elizabethan English, but what I might try is to give you my idea of how an Elizabethan actor might have gone for a bit of tricky text. So, I may go a bit far with it and then you can all tell me.

Roger Rees: *Yes, this is your set.*

Ben Kingsley: *A modest little chair.*

A hot seat. This is perhaps a good speech to look at because on the surface it doesn't look particularly resonant. But I'll tend to pronounce every single sound within a word because I suspect that Elizabethan actors may have done that more than we do. So I'll overstress and overrelish the sounds and we'll see if it's useful.

Roger Rees: *Yes, do it like an Elizabethan actor.*

FRENCH KING (*John Barton*): Where is Mountjoy the Herald? Speed
              him hence,
 Let him greet England with our sharp defiance,
 Up, Princes, and with spirit of honour edged,
 More sharper than your swords, hie to the field!
 Charles Delabreth, High Constable of France,
 You Dukes of Orleans, Bourbon, and of Berri,
 Alençon, Brabant, Bar, and Burgundy,
 Jacques Chatillon, Rambures, Vaudemont,
 Beaumont, Grandpré, Roussi, and Faulconbridge,
 Foix, Lestrale, Bouciqualt, and Charolois,
 High Dukes, great Princes, Barons, Lords and Knights,
 For your great seats, now quit you of great shames.
 Bar Harry England, that sweeps through our land
 With pennons painted in the blood of Harfleur! . . .
 Go down upon him, you have power enough,
 And in a captive chariot into Rouen
 Bring him our prisoner.   *Henry V: III.5.*

Was that too far? Or not too far?

Lisa Harrow: *No, not at all.*

Ben Kingsley: *Not to my taste, not to my ear, no.*

Roger Rees: *It was like a fruitcake stuffed with lots of different ingredients.*

Lisa Harrow: *But there was this amazing thread that went right the way through from the beginning to the end. You never let it drop or let us flag for one second. You just kept on going like a huge relentless wave and that was marvelous.*

Did the text take you with it?

Ben Kingsley: *It never lets us off the hook when it's done that way. It swept us along.*

Roger Rees: *How did you say "Rouen"?*

I said "Roan": R-O-A-N. That's how it's spelled in the Folio and of course it makes a much better verse-line. "And in a captive chariot into Rouen" sounds a bit lame but "In a captive chariot into Roan" is much more resonant.

Roger Rees: *It's wonderful to hear something like that because so much of our literature and playwriting today seems to be obsessed with the lack of language. You know . . . the spaces and the pauses . . . the absence of text sometimes. To hear a bit of text so highly encrusted with all kinds of different shapes and movement in it and in the sounds is wonderful.*

Lisa Harrow: *It's energy, isn't it? It requires a huge amount of energy to use this language well. So much modern writing is thrown away and deflated. But a speech like that requires a fantastic drive, and that's something we need to hold on to and remember.*

It's as if Shakespeare means each name to stand for five thousand men. So by the end of the speech you've had the whole of the army: "Into a thousand parts divide one man/And make imaginary puissance."

What are the key points we should remember from this exploration? One is of course to go further with the language than we think we can. But it seems to me that the most important point is that the characters *need the language* to express their situation and their characters.

> Ben Kingsley: *Yes. Their language is never remotely incidental. It is them and that should be our starting point.*

But of course we have to keep this balance between the Elizabethan tradition and our tradition. Always that word "balance." Perhaps in one or two of our versions we may have gone a bit too far one way, perhaps in others we've gone too far another. Too naturalistic or too rhetorical. The melancholy truth is that in performance things are hardly ever perfect. There's no perfect answer.

> Ben Kingsley: *"Let your own discretion be your tutor."*

That's right. That's the way it goes. All we can say is that if the situation is right and the character is right, and if we find and fresh-mint the language, we won't be far off. So, as ever, the moral and the rule is, *make the words your own.*

CHAPTER FOUR

Using the Prose

Why Does Shakespeare Use Prose?

[The following actors took part in the program that
forms the basis of this chapter: TONY CHURCH, SINEAD CUSACK,
SUSAN FLEETWOOD, LISA HARROW, BEN KINGSLEY, JANE LAPOTAIRE,
BARBARA LEIGH-HUNT, MICHAEL PENNINGTON, ROGER REES,
NORMAN RODWAY, DAVID SUCHET.]

So far we've talked almost entirely about Shakespeare's verse.
We've looked at what goes on in it and we've tried to find out how it
works. I find his prose much harder to talk about. But why, you may
ask, should we worry about it at all? Surely it's much easier to manage than verse? Doesn't it look after itself? Well, in Shakespeare it
very often doesn't. His prose has very strong rhythms and if an actor
does not get in touch with them there will be a loss of definition and
energy and clarity. There's also an awful lot of it. It's worth quoting a
statistic: just over twenty-eight percent of the text of Shakespeare's
plays is in prose, over a quarter. So it's not a minor question, it's a
major challenge. The difficulty is that there are few rules and no
norm like the reassuring rhythm of blank verse: "de-dum, de-dum,
de-dum, de-dum, de-dum." Prose has no set rhythm, and is much
trickier to analyze. And yet the principle is still the same. The most
fruitful approach is, I believe, the same one as we used towards
Shakespeare's verse: look for the strong stresses and sense the
rhythm from that.

As ever, the best way to understand how Shakespeare's text works
is to look at a lot of examples, so as to gain a sense of how strong his
prose rhythms are. And I hope too that a lot of the passages we take
will make their point with a minimum of comment from me. Let's

start with an extreme example. In *Henry IV, Part One* Prince Hal and Falstaff have just met before the Battle of Shrewsbury. (*To Norman Rodway.*) Don't try to characterize it particularly. Go for the meaning and for the strong stresses and the rhythm.

> FALSTAFF (*Norman Rodway*): Hal, if thou see me down in the battle and bestride me, so. 'Tis a point of friendship.
> PRINCE (*Roger Rees*): Nothing but a Colossus can do thee that friendship. Say thy prayers, and farewell.
> FALSTAFF: I would 'twere bed-time, Hal, and all well.
> PRINCE: Why, thou owest God a death.
> FALSTAFF: 'Tis not due yet.

Verse so far, now comes the prose.

> FALSTAFF: I would be loath to pay him before his day. What need I be so forward with him that calls not on me? Well, 'tis no matter, honour pricks me on. Yea, but how if honour prick me off when I come on, how then? Can honour set to a leg? No. Or an arm? No . . . Honour hath no skill in surgery then? No. What is honour? A word. What is in that word honour? What is that honour? Air. A trim reckoning! Who hath it? He that died a' Wednesday. Doth he feel it? No. Doth he hear it? No. 'Tis insensible, then? Yea, to the dead. But will it not live with the living? No. Why? Detraction will not suffer it. Therefore I'll none of it. Honour is a mere scutcheon—And so ends my catechism.
>
> *Henry IV, Part One: V.1.*

You sensed the prose rhythm pretty well there, but I'd like to push you a bit further. I thought that you got all the details right but that you could have gone more with the sweep and drive and surge of the whole. The speech is so clear and the rhythm so strong that you needn't break it up much. I couldn't quite see the wood for the trees, so try to focus it more.

Norman Rodway: *Yes, I know what you mean. Shakespeare sets the speech up in antithesis to Hotspur's vision of honor. It's the first time in the play that honor has really been questioned.*

That's right. Just do the beginning bit—"Can honour set to a leg?"—again.

> FALSTAFF: Can honour set to a leg? No. Or an arm? No. Or take away the grief of a wound? No. Honour hath no skill in surgery then? No. What is honour? A word. What is in that word honour? What is that honour? Air.

You need to follow the rhythm of a prose speech just as much as a verse speech, and you certainly did so. "What is honour? A word. What is in that word honour?" The rhythm is if anything stronger here than it is in a lot of blank verse.

That's one surprising discovery. Another one is to find out where and how Shakespeare uses prose.

> Norman Rodway: *Would it be true to say that in certain plays like* Richard II, *when the text is formal and rhetorical, the entire play is in verse, whereas if you take a play like* Much Ado, *which is domestic and social, a great deal of it is in prose?*

Yes, that is true. But what I want you to concentrate more on this evening is the way Shakespeare keeps ringing the changes between the two within a given scene. I believe such changes often contain hints to an actor about character. So I want to ask why Shakespeare uses one or another in a given instance. I suppose we would expect him to use verse for romantic, heightened passages and prose for naturalistic and low-life ones. And indeed he often does so. But not always, as we shall see in a minute. So let's start asking why. There's always a good dramatic reason.

There is a very powerful change, for instance, at the end of *Antony and Cleopatra*. A country clown brings Cleopatra a basket of asps for her to kill herself. Their dialogue is in prose and we'll take a bit of it near the end of the scene.

> CLEOPATRA (*Jane Lapotaire*): Will it eat me?
> CLOWN (*Roger Rees*): You must not think I am so simple but I know the devil himself will not eat a woman. I know that a woman is a dish for the gods, if the devil dress her not. But truly, these same whoreson dev-

ils do the gods great harm in their women, for in every ten that they
make the devils mar five.

CLEOPATRA: Well, get thee gone; farewell.

CLOWN: Yes, forsooth. I wish you joy o' th' worm.

CLEOPATRA: Give me my robe; put on my crown; I have
Immortal longings in me.   *Antony and Cleopatra: V.2.*

Isn't the switch there from prose to verse terrific? From "Yes, forsooth. I wish you joy o' th' worm." To "Give me my robe; put on
my crown; I have/Immortal longings in me."

> Norman Rodway: *This is a splendid example of Shakespeare switch-
> ing from naturalistic prose to a romantic highly charged verse.*

But, alas, it's not always as simple as that. Many of his most heightened passages are in prose and much of his blank verse is naturalistic.

> David Suchet: *What is it that makes Shakespeare decide to use the
> one or the other at a particular moment?*

I'm afraid there are really no rules. Shakespeare isn't consistent. All
we can do is ask what he is up to in a given instance and usually it's
not hard to smell out the answer. Not always, of course, but usually
you can find a good dramatic and acting reason for it. In *Henry IV*
the political scenes are in verse and the low-life tavern scenes are in
prose. That is an obvious example and more or less self-explanatory.

> David Suchet: *But I suppose it can sometimes be the other way
> round. In* The Merchant of Venice, *for example, Shakespeare gener-
> ally uses prose for mercantile Venice, and verse for the romantic
> scenes in Belmont. And yet at the very start of the play he breaks the
> convention. The opening scene, which we've already looked at, is in
> verse although the scene is set in Venice.*

> Norman Rodway: *Yes, that's right. And when you get to Belmont,
> which you expect to be a romantic and blank verse scene, Nerissa
> and Portia talk in prose.*

Yes, I said Shakespeare wasn't consistent. But in a way you've both made the point. The first two scenes of the play have the contrast of verse and prose and so their ambience feels different. I think Shakespeare uses prose for Portia and Nerissa because their dialogue is full of verbal wit and he usually finds prose the best form to embody it. So let's look at their scene. It shows very clearly one important way in which Shakespeare's prose works. It is built centrally and basically on a verbal device we have already looked at: *antithesis*. Virtually everything that Portia and Nerissa say is based on antithesis and the setting of one word against another.

PORTIA (*Lisa Harrow*): By my troth, Nerissa, my little body is aweary of this great world.

NERISSA (*Jane Lapotaire*): You would be, sweet madam, if your miseries were in the same abundance as your good fortunes are; and yet for aught I see, they are as sick that surfeit with too much as they that starve with nothing. It is no mean happiness, therefore, to be seated in the mean; superfluity comes sooner by white hairs, but competency lives longer.

PORTIA: Good sentences, and well pronounced.

NERISSA: They would be better if well followed.

PORTIA: If to do were as easy as to know what were good to do, chapels had been churches, and poor men's cottages princes' palaces. It is a good divine that follows his own instructions. I can easier teach twenty what were good to be done than to be one of the twenty to follow mine own teaching. The brain may devise laws for the blood, but a hot temper leaps o'er a cold decree . . . But this reasoning is not in the fashion to choose me a husband. O me, the word 'choose'! I may neither choose who I would nor refuse who I dislike, so is the will of a living daughter curbed by the will of a dead father.

The Merchant of Venice: I.2.

If the antitheses are not played in that passage, it is very hard to follow. Pointed up like that, the text is clear as daylight. Now let's look at another passage where the antitheses are equally strong and obvious. If they're not brought out fully the sentences would seem long and sprawling. But if they're played to the hilt the speech will be buoyant and punchy. Coriolanus's mother Volumnia is trying to cheer up her son's wife while he is away at the wars.

> VOLUMNIA (*Barbara Leigh-Hunt*): I pray you, daughter, sing, or express yourself in a more comfortable sort. If my son were my husband, I should freelier rejoice in that absence wherein he won honour than in the embracements of his bed where he would show most love. When yet he was but tender-bodied and the only son of my womb, when youth with comeliness plucked all gaze his way, ... I, considering how honour would become such a person—that it was no better than picture-like to hang by th'wall, if renown made it not stir—was pleased to let him seek danger where he was like to find fame ... I tell thee, daughter, I sprang not more in joy at first hearing he was a man-child than now in first seeing he had proved himself a man.
>
> *Coriolanus: I.3.*

Perhaps after those two passages you may think that antithesis is somehow a literary thing and is something always reserved for Shakespeare's aristocratic characters. So look now at part of a prose conversation in *As You Like It* between the Clown and townsman Touchstone and the old, rural shepherd Corin.

> CORIN (*Tony Church*): And how like you this shepherd's life, Master Touchstone?
>
> TOUCHSTONE (*Ben Kingsley*): Truly, shepherd, in respect of itself, it is a good life; but in respect that it is a shepherd's life, it is naught. In respect that it is solitary, I like it very well; but in respect that it is private, it is a very vile life. Now in respect it is in the fields, it pleaseth me well; but in respect it is not in the court, it is tedious. As it is a spare life, look you, it fits my humour well; but as there is no more plenty in it, it goes much against my stomach. Hast any philosophy in thee, shepherd?
>
> CORIN: No more but that I know the more one sickens, the worse at ease he is, and that he that wants money, means, and content is without three good friends; that the property of rain is to wet and fire to burn; that good pasture makes fat sheep; and that a great cause of the night is lack of the sun; that he that hath learned no wit by nature nor art may complain of good breeding, or comes of a very dull kindred.

TOUCHSTONE: Such a one is a natural philosopher.
As You Like It: III.2.

A feast of rural antitheses. In each of these passages the antitheses articulate and define the sentences and hold them together. But there is also a very strong rhythm which an actor needs to go along with instinctively. It is clearly quite as strong as the rhythm of verse, so let's take one more example of a passage where a combination of strong stresses, antitheses and an overall driving rhythm give a prose speech great energy and panache. Don Armado, a fantastical Spaniard in *Love's Labour's Lost,* tells us he is in love with a country slut. Notice particularly that there's nothing naturalistic about it. Armado is affected and so his speech rhythm is affected too.

DON ARMADO (*David Suchet*): I do affect the very ground, which is base, where her shoe, which is baser, guided by her foot, which is basest, doth tread. I shall be forsworn, which is a great argument of falsehood, if I love. And how can that be true love which is falsely attempted? Love is a familiar; Love is a devil; there is no evil angel but Love. Yet was Samson so tempted, and he had an excellent strength; yet was Solomon so seduced, and he had a very good wit. Cupid's butt-shaft is too hard for Hercules' club, and therefore too much odds for a Spaniard's rapier . . . The passado he respects not, the duello he regards not. His disgrace is to be called boy, but his glory is to subdue men. Adieu, valour; rust, rapier; be still, drum; for your manager is in love; yea, he loveth. Assist me, some extemporal god of rhyme, for I am sure I shall turn sonnet. Devise, wit; write, pen; for I am for whole volumes in folio.
Love's Labour's Lost: I.2.

All the passages we have taken so far have, I think, something in common and make the same demand of an actor. They need a lot of verbal energy. If they were taken flatly or naturalistically they would be hard to follow and difficult to listen to. The key words have to be served up. This is especially true of prose *dialogue.* And it is even more true when the text contains a battle of wits. In such a dialogue each actor has to serve up the key words for the other to play off them. Here is an exchange between Beatrice and Benedick from

Much Ado About Nothing. Notice how each of them keeps picking up a word or idea of the other's and turning it round in some way. The first speaker has to set up a particular word for the second to play on and hit back with.

> BEATRICE (*Sinead Cusack*): I wonder that you will still be talking, Signor Benedick; nobody marks you.
>
> BENEDICK: (*Ben Kingsley*): What, my dear Lady Disdain! Are you yet living?
>
> BEATRICE: Is it possible disdain should die while she hath such meet food to feed it as Signor Benedick? Courtesy itself must convert to disdain, if you come in her presence.
>
> BENEDICK: Then is courtesy a turncoat. But it is certain I am loved of all ladies, only you excepted; and I would I could find in my heart that I had not a hard heart, for, truly, I love none.
>
> BEATRICE: A dear happiness to women; they would else have been troubled with a pernicious suitor! I thank God and my cold blood, I am of your humour for that; I had rather hear my dog bark at a crow than a man swear he loves me.
>
> BENEDICK: God keep your ladyship still in that mind! So some gentleman or other shall 'scape a predestinate scratched face.
>
> BEATRICE: Scratching could not make it worse, an 'twere such a face as yours were.
>
> BENEDICK: Well, you are a rare parrot-teacher.
>
> BEATRICE: A bird of my tongue is better than a beast of yours.
>
> BENEDICK: I would my horse had the speed of your tongue, and so good a continuer. But keep your way a God's name, I have done.
>
> BEATRICE: You always end with a jade's trick; I know you of old.
>
> *Much Ado About Nothing: I.1.*

Do you sense how the words bounce off one another? Maybe that's a useful phrase: the words must *bounce*. Here's another example of the same thing. In *Love's Labour's Lost,* Costard the Clown is being cross-examined about his sex life by the King.

> KING (*Ben Kingsley*): Sirrah, what say you to this?
>
> COSTARD (*Roger Rees*): Sir, I confess the wench.

KING: Did you hear the proclamation?

COSTARD: I do confess much of the hearing it, but little of the marking of it.

KING: It was proclaimed a year's imprisonment to be taken with a wench.

COSTARD: I was taken with none, sir; I was taken with a damsel.

KING: Well, it was proclaimed 'damsel'.

COSTARD: This was no damsel neither, sir; she was a virgin.

KING: It is so varied too, for it was proclaimed 'virgin'.

COSTARD: If it were, I deny her virginity. I was taken with a maid.

KING: This 'maid' will not serve your turn, sir.

COSTARD: This maid will serve my turn, sir.

KING: Sir, I will pronounce your sentence: you shall fast a week with bran and water.

COSTARD: I had rather pray a month with mutton and porridge.

Love's Labour's Lost: I.1.

I think that it could be made more of a verbal tennis match. Imagine the text is a ball and your wits are like two rackets. One of you serves the ball up and the other hits it back as hard as he can. It's a rally and one of you is going to ace the other at the end. The moral is once again that you have not only to look at the details but at the sweep and rhythm of the whole passage. By making it a tennis match you can make me sit up and live through it with you. And it will release the comic juices more.

> David Suchet: *But you still haven't explained why or on what principle Shakespeare decides to use prose instead of verse. You said he wasn't consistent. So is his choice arbitrary? Or is there a reason behind it which might be helpful for an actor to know about?*

I think there's always a specific reason in a given instance, though it's almost impossible to define it or make general rules about it. One must simply ask why Shakespeare switches from one to the other at a particular point. Usually it's not too hard to find the answer. I think the best way to explain it is to look at some individual examples and ask what sort of effect he is after in each of them. We'll find, just as we did when we analyzed his verse, that such switches in the text contain useful hints to the actor about how to play the scene. In particular we should look at the way in which verse gives way to prose and prose is followed by verse within particular scenes.

Let us assume one thing. The change is never arbitrary but Shakespeare the director is telling us something thereby. First, we'll take another bit of Portia from *The Merchant of Venice* towards the end of a long scene between her and Bassanio, whom she loves. The news has come that Antonio the Merchant cannot pay Shylock the money he owes him and so the Jew is going to claim his pound of flesh. The scene has all been inverse and the language has been romantic and heightened. But at the end Bassanio reads Portia the letter he has received from Antonio and it is in prose.

PORTIA (*Lisa Harrow*):   Come away,
For you shall hence upon your wedding day.
Bid your friends welcome, show a merry cheer;
Since you are dear bought, I will love you dear.
But let me hear the letter of your friend.

Verse, and what's more, rhymed verse. Now follows the prose.

BASSANIO (*Michael Pennington*): 'Sweet Bassanio, my ships have all miscarried, my creditors grow cruel, my estate is very low, my bond to the Jew is forfeit. And since in paying it, it is impossible I should live, all debts are cleared between you and I if I might but see you at my death. Notwithstanding, use your pleasure. If your love do not persuade you to come, let not my letter.'   *The Merchant of Venice: III.2.*

Prose, undemonstrative, the emotion held back. The flat, down-to-earth rhythm of this letter at the end of the scene undercuts the previous three hundred buoyant, joyous verse-lines. The dramatic point is obvious: reality breaks in on romance.

Now let's look at what is probably the supreme example of Shakespeare switching to prose after a long passage of lyric and romantic verse. In *Troilus and Cressida* the two lovers have finally come together and swear their everlasting faith. That's the verse section. Then their uncle Pandarus interrupts and urges them to go to bed together. He does so in prose. Troilus and Cressida each have a romantic and highly lyrical speech here, but Pandarus's prose provides the scene's climax. He is earthy and carnal and undercuts the poetry and idealism of the lovers' verse. Once again, crude reality breaks in with the prose.

> TROILUS (*Michael Pennington*): True swains in love shall in the world
> to come
> Approve their truths by Troilus. When their rhymes,
> Full of protest, of oath, and big compare,
> Want similes, truth tired with iteration—
> 'As true as steel, as plantage to the moon,
> As sun to day, as turtle to her mate,
> As iron to adamant, as earth to th'centre'—
> Yet, after all comparisons of truth,
> As truth's authentic author to be cited,
> 'As true as Troilus' shall crown up the verse
> And sanctify the numbers.
> CRESSIDA: Prophet may you be!
> If I be false, or swerve a hair from truth,
> When time is old and hath forgot itself,
> When waterdrops have worn the stones of Troy,
> And blind oblivion swallowed cities up,
> And mighty states characterless are grated
> To dusty nothing, yet let memory,
> From false to false, among false maids in love,
> Upbraid my falsehood! When they've said 'as false
> As air, as water, wind, or sandy earth,
> As fox to lamb, or wolf to heifer's calf,
> Pard to the hind, or stepdame to her son',
> Yea, let them say, to stick the heart of falsehood,
> 'As false as Cressid'.

Now comes the prose.

> PANDARUS (*Tony Church*): Go to, a bargain made. Seal it, seal it. I'll be the witness. Here I hold your hand; here my cousin's. If ever you prove

false one to another, since I have taken such pains to bring you together, let all pitiful goers-between be called to the world's end after my name—call them all Pandars: let all constant men be Troiluses, all false women Cressids, and all brokers between Pandars. Say 'amen'.

TROILUS: Amen.

CRESSIDA: Amen.

PANDARUS: Amen. Whereupon I will show you a chamber with a bed; which bed, because it shall not speak of your pretty encounters, press it to death. Away! And Cupid grant all tongue-tied maidens here bed, chamber, pandar, to provide this gear!   *Troilus and Cressida: III.2.*

There's not much doubt about the whys and wherefores of that, is there? In acting terms the verse and the prose are clearly right for the three different characters in the scene.

But let's look now at a switch-around which is the opposite to what we would expect. In this example the change is from prose to verse. In *Othello* the norm is for Othello, the romantic, to speak verse and for Iago, who destroys him, to relish prose. But when Iago finally persuades Othello that his wife is unfaithful and Othello breaks down in a fit, the very opposite happens. Othello himself goes into broken prose and Iago uses triumphant and easy verse.

OTHELLO (*David Suchet*): Hath he said anything?

IAGO (*Norman Rodway*): He hath, my lord; but be you well assured, No more than he'll unswear.

OTHELLO: What hath he said?

IAGO: Faith, that he did—I know not what he did.

OTHELLO: What? What?

IAGO: Lie—

OTHELLO: With her?

IAGO: With her, on her; what you will.

OTHELLO: Lie with her? Lie on her? We say lie on her when they belie her. Lie with her! Zounds, that's fulsome! Handkerchief—confession—handkerchief! To confess and be hanged for his labour. First to be hanged, and then to confess! I tremble at it. Nature would not invest herself in such shadowing passion without some instruction. It is not

words that shakes me thus! Pish! Noses, ears, and lips! Is't possible?—
Confess? Handkerchief! O devil!

IAGO: Work on,
My medicine, work! Thus credulous fools are caught,
And many worthy and chaste dames even thus,
All guiltless, meet reproach.   *Othello: IV.1.*

In this context the reasons for Othello's prose and Iago's verse are surely clear enough. Othello breaks down here, mentally and physically. His normal speech is noble and inclined to rhetoric, so the stabbing, half-articulate prose helps the actor who plays him to show how utterly he has changed. Iago's verse on the other hand here gives him the rhetorical ascendant.

It is quite common for Shakespeare to keep ringing the changes between verse and prose within a scene, sometimes from speech to speech and quite often from line to line. Here's a good example from *Romeo and Juliet.* The prose speaker in this passage is Mercutio who continually sends up Romeo's romanticism. Here, in what is basically a verse scene, he still sticks at the moment of his death to prose. He has just been mortally wounded and is speaking to Romeo and Benvolio. Editors of the text determine differently what is verse and what is prose here, but I think my general point holds.

> MERCUTIO (*Michael Pennington*):   I am hurt.
> A plague a' both your houses! I am sped.
> Is he gone and hath nothing?
> BENVOLIO (*Roger Rees*):   What, art thou hurt?

Verse so far, now a prose line.

> MERCUTIO: Ay, ay, a scratch, a scratch. Marry, 'tis enough.

Now back to verse.

> MERCUTIO: Where is my page? Go, villain, fetch a surgeon.
> ROMEO: Courage, man. The hurt cannot be much.

Now prose again.

> MERCUTIO: No, 'tis not so deep as a well, nor so wide as a church door.
> But 'tis enough. 'Twill serve. Ask for me tomorrow, and you shall find
> me a grave man. I am peppered, I warrant, for this world. A plague a'
> both your houses! Zounds, a dog, a rat, a mouse, a cat, to scratch a man
> to death! A braggart, a rogue, a villain, that fights by the book of arith-
> metic! Why the devil came you between us? I was hurt under your arm.
> ROMEO: I thought all for the best.
> MERCUTIO: Help me into some house, Benvolio, or I shall faint. A
> plague a' both your houses! They have made worms' meat of me. I have
> it, and soundly too. Your houses!
>
> (*He is taken out.*)

Now verse again.

> ROMEO: This gentleman, the Prince's near ally,
> My very friend, hath got this mortal hurt
> In my behalf—my reputation stained
> With Tybalt's slander—Tybalt, that an hour
> Hath been my cousin. O sweet Juliet,
> Thy beauty hath made me effeminate,
> And in my temper softened valour's steel! *Romeo and Juliet: III.1.*

Once again it's clear enough how the prose works. It has to do with
the grim reality of death. Listen again to one line: "Ask for me
tomorrow and you shall find me a grave man." Let's do as we did
when we were looking at Shakespeare's verse and ask how many
strong stresses there are. I would argue that there are six strong
stresses in the last seven words: "You shall find me a grave man."
Seven slow monosyllables, slow as monosyllabic lines usually are in
Shakespeare. It is a good rhythm for Mercutio here, who is sardonic,
self-mocking and tough. And it is characteristic of Romeo that
he should revert to verse as soon as Mercutio is taken out. Here,
the verse romanticizes and emotionalizes while the prose uses flat
simple words and deflates emotion. Or perhaps I should say it
heightens it.

I want to look at two or three more passages where the changes between verse and prose are at first sight much more puzzling. In the Forum scene in *Julius Caesar*, which follows Caesar's assassination, there are two orations. One, by Antony, is in verse. The other, which precedes it, is by Brutus and is in prose. Yet nowhere else in the play does Brutus use prose. The part is entirely in verse except for this one speech. Ben, come and do Brutus and then, Roger, you do Antony. Remember that you are in a public Forum, with thousands of people listening. Here, for the first time, we see Brutus's public persona.

> BRUTUS (*Ben Kingsley*): Romans, countrymen and lovers, hear me for my cause, and be silent, that you may hear. Believe me for mine honour, and have respect to mine honour, that you may believe. Censure me in your wisdom, and awake your senses, that you may the better judge. If there be any in this assembly, any dear friend of Caesar's, to him I say that Brutus' love to Caesar was no less than his. If then that friend demand why Brutus rose against Caesar, this is my answer: Not that I loved Caesar less, but that I loved Rome more. Had you rather Caesar were living, and die all slaves, than that Caesar were dead, to live all free men? As Caesar loved me, I weep for him; as he was fortunate, I rejoice at it; as he was valiant, I honour him; but, as he was ambitious, I slew him. There is tears for his love; joy for his fortune; honour for his valour; and death for his ambition. Who is here so base that would be a bondman? If any, speak; for him have I offended. Who is here so rude that would not be a Roman? If any, speak; for him have I offended. Who is here so vile that will not love his country? If any, speak; for him have I offended. I pause for a reply. *Julius Caesar: III.2.*

You can hear once again the strong rhythm of the prose, and it is all the stronger because of Brutus's absolutely obsessive use of antitheses. That's clear and palpable. But why prose? Ben, why do you think Brutus, or rather Shakespeare, uses prose here?

Ben Kingsley: *Well, I think it's complicated at first sight because one always, perhaps mistakenly, thinks of prose as being the language that has the common touch. It may be rather patronizing of Brutus to use it, but he's consciously mobilized his language in a particular way which he thinks has warmth and familiarity. But in fact it is so studied and so mechanical with its levers and pulleys that it's like an engine. It's not human. Its built-in antitheses and rhythms strike me as not spontaneous and therefore not moving. They are preconceived packages of information. He tells his audience (a) to listen and (b) to listen carefully and (c) to shut up while he's talking. He lacks the common touch. He delivers this meticulously balanced speech and then says at the end "If you've got anything to say, say it." It's intellectually arrogant and preconceived and practiced. Practiced art.*

Yes, you've put your finger on it: it's studied and not spontaneous. But I suppose that's exactly what Shakespeare is after. He makes the speech stylized and formal and rhetorical. The antitheses are so labored that it all sounds prepared, as if Brutus has conned it in the study in front of his mirror. So it's a deliberate contrast to the easy, natural human verse-rhythm of Antony. So now, Roger, let's listen to Antony. 'Friends, Romans, countrymen' is a famous speech, but try starting it quite simply and modestly. Antony is feeling his way, so feel your way with the speech also. In contrast to Brutus make the verse as informal, spontaneous and unrhetorical as you can.

ANTONY (*Roger Rees*): Friends, Romans, countrymen, lend me your ears;
I come to bury Caesar, not to praise him.
The evil that men do lives after them,
The good is oft interrèd with their bones;
So let it be with Caesar. The noble Brutus
Hath told you Caesar was ambitious.
If it were so, it was a grievous fault,
And grievously hath Caesar answered it.
Here, under leave of Brutus and the rest—
For Brutus is an honourable man;
So are they all, all honourable men—
Come I to speak in Caesar's funeral.
He was my friend, faithful and just to me;
But Brutus says he was ambitious,

And Brutus is an honourable man.
He hath brought many captives home to Rome,
Whose ransoms did the general coffers fill;
Did this in Caesar seem ambitious?
When that the poor have cried, Caesar hath wept;
Ambition should be made of sterner stuff.
Yet Brutus says he was ambitious,
And Brutus is an honourable man.   *Julius Caesar: III.2.*

Of course, there is an infinity of things one might say about so famous a speech as Antony's but let's just stick to what we're looking at in this session. His verse here is simple and down-to-earth and above all, human. Later on in his oration it does get more rhetorical, but here it's almost naturalistic. So the switch from prose to verse gives us a terrific character contrast between the two speakers.

Roger Rees: *It seems strangely intimate when you think Antony's addressing thousands of people.*

That's because he very cleverly decides to undercut Brutus, isn't it? Brutus is rhetorical and pompous, so Antony just says very simply, "Friends, Romans, countrymen, lend me your ears." The stage tradition which makes the speech big and rhetorical and heroic is surely wrong.

Sometimes this alternation between verse and prose is more subtle and surprising, and the text changes in the one direction or the other from speech to speech. In *Othello,* Othello's wife Desdemona and her maid Emilia are talking about men. They start in verse. Desdemona is idealistic and romantic and sad and Emilia is down-to-earth. She teases Desdemona and tries to cheer her up.

DESDEMONA (*Lisa Harrow*):   O, these men, these men!
Dost thou in conscience think—tell me, Emilia—
That there be women do abuse their husbands
In such gross kind?
EMILIA (*Jane Lapotaire*):   There be some such, no question.
DESDEMONA: Wouldst thou do such a deed for all the world?

EMILIA: Why, would not you?
DESDEMONA: No, by this heavenly light!

Verse so far but now we go to prose.

EMILIA: Nor I neither by this heavenly light; I might do't as well i'th' dark.

Emilia's prose deflates Desdemona's verse, but Desdemona answers with another verse-line.

DESDEMONA: Wouldst thou do such a deed for all the world?
EMILIA: The world's a huge thing: it is a great price for a small vice.
DESDEMONA: In troth, I think thou wouldst not.

Surprisingly, Desdemona has suddenly gone into prose.

EMILIA: In troth I think I should; and undo't when I had done it. Marry, I would not do such a thing for a joint ring, nor for measures of lawn, nor for gowns, petticoats, nor caps, nor any petty exhibition. But for the whole world! Ud's pity, who would not make her husband a cuckold, to make him a monarch? I should venture purgatory for't.
DESDEMONA: Beshrew me, if I would do such a wrong for the whole world!
EMILIA: Why, the wrong is but a wrong i'th' world; and having the world for your labour, 'tis a wrong in your own world, and you might quickly make it right.
DESDEMONA: I do not think there is any such woman.
EMILIA: Yes, a dozen: and as many to th' vantage as would store the world they played for.

Now a very surprising thing happens. Emilia goes into verse.

EMILIA: But I do think it is their husbands' faults
If wives do fall. Say that they slack their duties,
And pour our treasures into foreign laps;
Or else break out in peevish jealousies,

Throwing restraint upon us, or say they strike us,
Or scant our former having in despite—
Why, we have galls, and though we have some grace,
Yet have we some revenge. Let husbands know
Their wives have sense like them: they see and smell,
And have their palates both for sweet and sour
As husbands have. What is it that they do,
When they change us for others? Is it sport?
I think it is. And doth affection breed it?
I think it doth. Is't frailty that thus errs?
It is so too. And have not we affections,
Desires for sport, and frailty, as men have?
Then, let them use us well: else let them know
The ills we do, their ills instruct us so.
DESDEMONA: Good night, good night. God me such uses send,
Not to pick bad from bad, but by bad mend!   *Othello: IV.3.*

Why do you think Emilia goes into verse there?

Jane Lapotaire: *Well, I think it's because this is the first time she's ever
thought about the subject of marriage. In the early part of the scene
she's tried to jolly Desdemona out of her mood. But when she says
"But I do think it is their husbands' faults/If wives do fall," she suddenly has to think about* why *she said that and so she goes into herself. When she says "What is it that they do/When they change us for
others?" I think she completely forgets that Desdemona is there. She
is talking about her own situation and following her own thoughts.*

Lisa Harrow: *I think the change to verse tells us something very
important about the scene and the nature of the relationship
between the two women. Up till now things have been rather
strained and difficult between them. Then suddenly Emilia sees
Desdemona here at her most vulnerable and decides to reveal something about herself. So for the first time Desdemona sees a side of
Emilia she didn't know existed, vulnerability and pain and wisdom.
That is marvelous. So I think the change from prose into verse is a
very fine character point and marks a change in their relationship.*

By asking that one question, "Why verse?" "Why prose?", you have discovered more about the characters and their relationship. Here again we find that, if you dig into the text, Shakespeare himself will start to direct you.

So we've seen here how the text frequently changes from verse to prose and back again, sometimes from line to line. But Shakespeare quite often blurs the boundaries between the two so that the conventional division between verse and prose virtually disappears. This need not be confusing, provided that the actors still feel instinctively for the rhythm. So let's look now at a passage in which the text is only partly in blank verse but where the rhythms are very, very strong. It's hard to say in places what is prose and what is verse. In *As You Like It* the pairs of lovers, Rosalind and Orlando, and Silvius and Phebe, try to find words to express their love. It starts in verse.

> PHEBE (*Lisa Harrow*): Good shepherd, tell this youth what 'tis to love.
> SILVIUS (*Roger Rees*): It is to be all made of sighs and tears,

Now it goes into prose, but strongly rhythmic prose.

> SILVIUS: And so am I for Phebe.
> PHEBE: And I for Ganymede.
> ORLANDO (*Michael Pennington*): And I for Rosalind.
> ROSALIND (*Susan Fleetwood*): And I for no woman.
> SILVIUS: It is to be all made of faith and service,
> And so am I for Phebe.
> PHEBE: And I for Ganymede.
> ORLANDO: And I for Rosalind.
> ROSALIND: And I for no woman.

Now it goes back to verse again.

> SILVIUS: It is to be all made of fantasy,
> All made of passion, and all made of wishes,
> All adoration, duty and observance,
> All humbleness, all patience, and impatience,

All purity, all trial, all obedience;
And so am I for Phebe.

PHEBE: And so am I for Ganymede.

ORLANDO: And so am I for Rosalind.

ROSALIND: And so am I for no woman.

PHEBE (*to Rosalind*): If this be so, why blame you me to love you?

SILVIUS (*to Phebe*): If this be so, why blame you me to love you?

ORLANDO: If this be so, why blame you me to love you?

ROSALIND: Why do you speak too 'Why blame you me to love you?'

ORLANDO: To her that is not here, nor doth not hear.

ROSALIND: Pray you no more of this, 'tis like the howling of Irish wolves against the moon.   *As You Like It: V.2.*

Good. I didn't interrupt to point out all the changes between verse and prose there because I hope you could hear the difference for yourselves. But it's worth pointing out that this passage seems naturalistic on the surface but also has a heightened quality and, though I hesitate to use the word, a *poetic* resonance. I have stressed already that with Shakespeare an actor often has to combine and marry the naturalistic and the heightened. And that is true of prose just as much as verse. Indeed it's not uncommon to find that there is as much, and perhaps more, poetry in a prose passage as there is in some verse ones. It's vital for an actor to realize this.

Let's end with a dialogue between Falstaff, old and tired and depressed, and his whore, Doll Tearsheet. It's prose, and on the surface it's naturalistic prose. But ask yourselves if it isn't somehow a poetic scene as well. But as so often happens with Shakespeare, it isn't obvious poetry. The passage also has some interruptions and asides from Prince Hal and Poins who are watching in disguise. Music is playing.

DOLL (*Jane Lapotaire*): Thou whoreson little tidy Bartholomew boar-pig, when wilt thou leave fighting a days and foining a nights, and begin to patch up thine old body for heaven?

FALSTAFF (*Norman Rodway*): Peace, good Doll, do not speak like a death's-head; do not bid me remember mine end.

DOLL: Sirrah, what humour's the Prince of?

FALSTAFF: A good shallow young fellow. 'A would have made a good pantler; 'a would ha' chipped bread well.

DOLL: They say Poins has a good wit.

FALSTAFF: He a good wit? Hang him, baboon! His wit's as thick as Tewkesbury mustard. There's no more conceit in him than is in a mallet.

DOLL: Why does the Prince love him so, then?

FALSTAFF: Because their legs are both of a bigness, and 'a plays at quoits well, and eats conger and fennel, and drinks off candles' ends for flap-dragons, and rides the wild mare with the boys, and jumps upon joint-stools, and swears with a good grace, and wears his boots very smooth like unto the sign of the leg, and breeds no bate with telling of discreet stories, and such other gambol faculties 'a has, that show a weak mind and an able body, for the which the Prince admits him . . .

PRINCE (*Roger Rees*): Would not this nave of a wheel have his ears cut off?

POINS (*Ben Kingsley*): Let's beat him before his whore.

PRINCE: Look whe'er the withered elder hath not his poll clawed like a parrot.

POINS: Is it not strange that desire should so many years outlive performance?

FALSTAFF: Kiss me, Doll . . . Thou dost give me flattering busses.

DOLL: By my troth, I kiss thee with a most constant heart.

FALSTAFF: I am old, I am old.

DOLL: I love thee better than I love e'er a scurvy young boy of them all.

FALSTAFF: What stuff wilt have a kirtle of? I shall receive money a-Thursday; shalt have a cap tomorrow. A merry song! Come, it grows late; we'll to bed. Thou'lt forget me when I am gone.

DOLL: By my troth, thou'lt set me a-weeping an thou sayst so. Prove that ever I dress myself handsome till thy return. Well, hearken a'th'end.   *Henry IV Part Two: II.4.*

Music makes all the difference. But the text itself: "'A plays at quoits well, and eats conger and fennel, . . . and rides the wild mare with the boys"—isn't that poetic? Heightened? Resonant? An old man envying youth. The prose here is as precise and as charged as any poem is. You can't change a word or a syllable. And when an actor speaks it he needs to relish the words quite as much as in a heightened verse speech. So you see, he needs to approach Shakespeare's prose in very much the same way that we've suggested he should approach the verse. He must beware of being too naturalistic. He must go for the strong stresses and the rhythm. He must point up the antitheses and he must relish the words. He must do justice to the heightened language. But as ever in doing so, he must find the intentions and the character. And he must be *real*.

➤➤ ◄◄

Set Speeches and Soliloquies

Taking the Audience with You

[The following actors took part in the program that
forms the basis of this chapter: TONY CHURCH, SINEAD CUSACK,
JUDI DENCH, SUSAN FLEETWOOD, LISA HARROW, ALAN HOWARD,
JANE LAPOTAIRE, BARBARA LEIGH-HUNT, RICHARD PASCO,
MICHAEL PENNINGTON, DONALD SINDEN, PATRICK STEWART,
DAVID SUCHET.]

So far we've talked of what an actor needs to look for in Shakespeare's text to help him. The same point could be made by looking at things a different way round. What must the actor do if he is to help and hold his audience? Let me take you back to something that I said at the beginning. I don't believe that most audiences really listen to a complex text unless the actor makes them do so. I know I don't; I know that my attention wanders if the actors don't hold me. I suspect that many of you in our audience would say the same. I believe that when this happens the main reason is that the actor is what I would call *generalizing,* i.e. playing the general mood or emotion which the speech suggests to him. It's so easy to play a kind of *summary* of a speech and not to discover it line by line as it is spoken.

This problem arises particularly with soliloquies and long or set speeches. Both actors and audience have to work harder with them than they do with dialogue. That's because a dialogue contains an obvious story or argument or clash or confrontation. One character persuades, another character resists and so on. That is relatively easy to follow. But with a set speech it's very easy for the play to lose its momentum and for the story to become becalmed. You can almost hear the audience switching off when an actor launches into some long tirade. The brutal fact is that a set speech in theater can easily be boring. I don't know which is the greater enemy to long purple passages in performance, boredom or excessive reverence. All actors dread what sometimes happens with a set speech. Voices in the audience join in, and the speech becomes not a living, fresh thing but a repeated litany.

So, what's to be done? How can an actor make the audience feel the story is still moving forward in a long speech and is therefore worth listening to? Here, even more than elsewhere, he must be deeply inside the situation. As we stressed at the very beginning, he must *find* the language and make his listeners feel the words are coming out for the very first time. If he does so, the audience will feel that the play is moving on and going somewhere. And so they will go with him. You see, though our theme is set speeches, I'm starting by talking about something very down-to-earth and practical. I am not stressing golden language or high astounding words. I am acknowledging a crude fact of life in the theater. An audience's attention wanders if an actor does not hold it, and the blame often lies with the actor as much as the audience.

So how to proceed? I should like to use this session for demonstrating some commonsense points, rather than for discussing details as we've done so far. Partly because we are looking at territory about which most actors are agreed; and partly because it's time to consider more sustained passages than we have looked at so far. We'll start with a famous set speech, marred for us only by being so much quoted in anthologies. Portia's "The quality of mercy is not strained" speech seems to preexist because we know it so well. Actually in context it's a spontaneous outburst triggered by Shylock's aggression to her in the court.

PORTIA (*Sinead Cusack*): Is your name Shylock?
SHYLOCK (*David Suchet*):   Shylock is my name.
PORTIA: Of a strange nature is the suit you follow,
Yet in such rule that the Venetian law
Cannot impugn you as you do proceed.
(*To Antonio*) You stand within his danger, do you not?

ANTONIO: Ay, so he says.
PORTIA: Do you confess the bond?
ANTONIO: I do.
PORTIA: Then must the Jew be merciful.
SHYLOCK: On what compulsion must I? Tell me that.
PORTIA: The quality of mercy is not strained,
It droppeth as the gentle rain from heaven
Upon the place beneath. It is twice blest . . .

The Merchant of Venice: IV.1.

Hold it there for a moment: we've got a bit too gentle. And it's to do with you, David, not pressurizing Portia enough. The little dialogue at the beginning is the trigger for her spontaneous outburst. If you don't press on her, she can't bounce back at you. Take me literally, if you will.

PORTIA: Is your name Shylock?
SHYLOCK: Shylock is my name.
PORTIA: Of a strange nature is the suit you follow,
Yet in such rule that the Venetian law
Cannot impugn you as you do proceed.
(*To Antonio*) You stand within his danger, do you not?
ANTONIO: Ay, so he says.
PORTIA: Do you confess the bond?
ANTONIO: I do.
PORTIA: Then must the Jew be merciful.
SHYLOCK: On what compulsion must I? Tell me that.
PORTIA: The quality of mercy is not strained,
It droppeth as the gentle rain from heaven
Upon the place beneath. It is twice blest,
It blesseth him that gives and him that takes:
'Tis mightiest in the mightiest, it becomes
The thronèd monarch better than his crown.
His sceptre shows the force of temporal power,
The attribute to awe and majesty,
Wherein doth sit the dread and fear of kings;
But mercy is above this sceptred sway,

It is enthronèd in the hearts of kings;
It is an attribute to God himself,
And earthly power doth then show likest God's
When mercy seasons justice. Therefore, Jew,
Though justice be thy plea, consider this:
That in the course of justice none of us
Should see salvation. We do pray for mercy,
And that same prayer doth teach us all to render
The deeds of mercy.   *The Merchant of Venice: IV.1.*

The famous lines came out really spontaneously then. They arose out of the situation and didn't preexist. Now I said a set speech must move and take the audience along with it. But how does the actor achieve this? Most set speeches break into three. They pick up something in the immediate situation and respond to it, they then explore the situation which makes up the bulk of the speech, and they then resolve what's been explored and either come to some conclusion or perhaps decide that there is no conclusion. An obvious example is Jacques' "All the world's a stage." I suppose it's the most obvious set speech of all. The first two lines respond to something the Duke has said. The bulk of the speech explores the subject and the last sentence resolves it.

DUKE (*Tony Church*): This wide and universal theatre
Presents more woeful pageants, than the scene
Wherein we play in.
JACQUES (*Richard Pasco*):   All the world's a stage,
And all the men and women merely players;
They have their exits and their entrances;
And one man in his time plays many parts,
His Acts being seven ages. At first the infant,
Mewling and puking in the nurse's arms;
Then the whining schoolboy, with his satchel
And shining morning face, creeping like snail
Unwillingly to school; and then the lover,
Sighing like furnace, with a woeful ballad
Made to his mistress' eyebrow; then, a soldier,

Full of strange oaths, and bearded like the pard,
Jealous in honour, sudden and quick in quarrel,
Seeking the bubble reputation
Even in the cannon's mouth; and then the justice,
In fair round belly, with good capon lined,
With eyes severe, and beard of formal cut,
Full of wise saws and modern instances,
And so he plays his part; the sixth age shifts
Into the lean and slippered pantaloon,
With spectacles on nose, and pouch on side,
His youthful hose, well saved, a world too wide
For his shrunk shank, and his big manly voice,
Turning again toward childish treble, pipes
And whistles in his sound; last Scene of all,
That ends this strange eventful history,
Is second childishness, and mere oblivion,
Sans teeth, sans eyes, sans taste, sans everything.   *As You Like It: II.7.*

You certainly made me feel I hadn't heard that before.

Richard Pasco: *Very broken up though, wasn't it?*

Very broken up. But you made me feel I was hearing it for the first
time and you certainly made me listen.

Now let's look at another problem. Some long speeches are written very rhetorically and formally. They have such a strong rhythm
that it can take over and make the speech sound unreal. Listen to a
bit of *Richard III* where the old Queen Margaret, banished and
broken, exults over the miseries of Queen Elizabeth who succeeded
her. Try and get both the sweep of the verse and the human details
within it.

ELIZABETH (*Lisa Harrow*): O, thou didst prophesy the time would
come
That I should wish for thee to help me curse
That bottled spider, that foul bunch-back'd toad!
MARGARET (*Barbara Leigh-Hunt*): I called thee then vain flourish of
my fortune;

I called thee then poor shadow, painted queen,
The presentation of but what I was,
The flattering index of a direful pageant,
One heaved a-high to be hurled down below,
A mother only mocked with two fair babes,
A dream of what thou wast, a breath, a bubble,
A sign of dignity, a garish flag
To be the aim of every dangerous shot;
A queen in jest, only to fill the scene.
Where is thy husband now? Where be thy brothers?
Where are thy two sons? Wherein dost thou joy?
Who sues and kneels and says, 'God save the Queen'?
Where be the bending peers that flattered thee?
Where be the thronging troops that followed thee?
Decline all this, and see what now thou art:
For happy wife, a most distressed widow;
For joyful mother, one that wails the name;
For one being sued to, one that humbly sues;
For queen, a very caitiff crowned with care;
For she that scorned at me, now scorned of me;
For she being feared of all, now fearing one;
For she commanding all, obeyed of none.
Thus hath the course of justice wheeled about
And left thee but a very prey to time . . .   *Richard III: IV.4.*

Our old friend Time again. I thought that was a good balance between going with the flow and the sweep of the verse and getting a lot of variety out of individual lines. The problem is how to do justice to the rhetoric and yet to keep it human. Shakespeare often explores a single emotional moment and situation with text that at first blush seems *literary*. The speaker seems much more articulate than he could possibly be if he was really in that actual situation.

In *Titus Andronicus,* for instance, Titus has just seen his daughter, Lavinia, with her hands and her tongue cut off. She has been mutilated and ravished, and Titus himself has just had his hand cut off also. As extreme a situation as any you'll find in Shakespeare. The obvious problem of such a speech is that in real life the emotion of the speaker would be much greater than his power to articulate that emotion in words. So it's very understandable if an actor confronted with such a speech recoils from the literary content, tries to express the emotion to the full, and so leaves the words to take care of themselves. Try it that way to start with.

> TITUS (*Patrick Stewart*): O, here I lift this one hand up to heaven,
> And bow this feeble ruin to the earth,
> If any power pities wretched tears,
> To that I call! (*To Lavinia*) What, wouldst thou kneel with me?
> Do then, dear heart, for heaven shall hear our prayers,
> Or with our sighs we'll breathe the welkin dim,
> And stain the sun with fog . . .
> MARCUS (*John Barton*): But yet let reason govern thy lament.
> TITUS: If there were reason for these miseries,
> Then into limits could I bind my woes:
> When heaven doth weep, doth not the earth o'erflow?
> If the winds rage, doth not the sea wax mad,
> Threat'ning the welkin with his big-swoln face?
> And wilt thou have a reason for this coil?
> I am the sea; hark, how her sighs doth blow.
> She is the weeping welkin, I the earth:
> Then must my sea be movèd with her sighs,
> Then must my earth with her continual tears
> Become a deluge, overflowed and drowned:
> For why? My bowels cannot hide her woes,
> But like a drunkard I must vomit them.   *Titus Andronicus: III.1.*

Bravely done. Now what happened? We got a powerful sense of Titus's feelings but did we follow what he was saying? Or did we listen? Or did the emotion take over and in a sense replace the text? Was it generalized?

> Patrick Stewart: *Frankly, yes.*

But of course you didn't do it like that when you actually played the part onstage. Perhaps the key here is Titus asking in an earlier speech, "What shall we *do?*" It's a question once again of intentions.

I suspect that the only way to the speech, and to make an audience both listen to and feel with it, is for Titus to try to *come to terms* with the incredible and the impossible. He needs the words to deal with reality, partly to accept it and partly to shut it out. So try it again, and this time find each image with as much difficulty as you can. Use the words to try to cope with as much as to express the emotions.

(*Patrick Stewart does so.*)

That was a very different thing. It was much, much more something I could go along with and it also moved me more.

Let's take another speech where the emotion of the speaker may also get on top of what's being said. In *Henry IV,* Hotspur's widow, Lady Percy, is trying to persuade his father, Northumberland, not to raise another rebellion. Northumberland didn't join his son in the battle in which he was killed, so he's largely responsible for Hotspur's death. Now the difficulties here are similar to those in the speech from Titus. A balance has to be found between Lady Percy's need to express her grief, her anger with Northumberland, and her wish to persuade him not to go to war. If she lets her emotions carry her away, she may put his back up and he may not listen. The emotions must be there fully, but you must channel them to get what you want.

> LADY PERCY (*Lisa Harrow*): O, yet for God's sake, go not to these wars!
> The time was, father, that you broke your word
> When you were more endeared to it than now,
> When your own Percy, when my heart's dear Harry,
> Threw many a northward look to see his father
> Bring up his powers. But he did long in vain.
> Who then persuaded you to stay at home?
> There were two honours lost, yours and your son's.
> For yours, the God of heaven brighten it!
> For his, it stuck upon him as the sun
> In the grey vault of heaven, and by his light
> Did all the chivalry of England move
> To do brave acts. He was indeed the glass

Wherein the noble youth did dress themselves.
He had no legs that practised not his gait;
And speaking thick, which nature made his blemish,
Became the accents of the valiant;
For those that could speak low and tardily
Would turn their own perfection to abuse,
To seem like him. So that in speech, in gait,
In diet, in affections of delight,
In military rules, humours of blood,
He was the mark and glass, copy and book,
That fashioned others. And him,—O wondrous him!
O miracle of men!—him did you leave,
Second to none, unseconded by you,
To look upon the hideous god of war
In disadvantage, to abide a field
Where nothing but the sound of Hotspur's name
Did seem defensible: So you left him.
Never, O never, do his ghost the wrong
To hold your honour more precise and nice
With others than with him! Let them alone.
The Marshal and the Archbishop are strong;
Had my sweet Harry had but half their numbers,
Today might I, hanging on Hotspur's neck,
Have talked of Monmouth's grave.   *Henry IV Part Two: II.3.*

Lisa Harrow: *I got a bit lost somewhere in that. I thought it should have been driven more.*

I thought you found the right mixture of passionate feeling and clarity of thought. If you had driven it more it would have become a nag. Of course the verse helped you, especially those sentences which start at the half-line. They kept the speech moving forward. You made us listen and you certainly moved me. I shall come back to this question of balancing text and emotion later. The point I want to make here is that in a set speech the actor always needs to go for the *argument* if he is to take his audience with him.

Let's take an extreme example, a real monster. Let's look at the

Archbishop of Canterbury. He's explaining to King Henry V that the English claim to the French throne is lawful. It's a solemn situation with the council all around, and yet the speech is in part comic. So, go first for the tortuous argument and see if you can make us follow it clearly. But keep a balance. You must keep two balls in the air, political seriousness and character comedy. I don't want to say too much about it, but there are two other important points to remember. First, you'll need variety, because monotony or sticking to one tempo in a long speech is fatal. And, secondly, you mustn't be too quick or too slow but you must *think quickly*. If you do, you'll find the natural tempo.

HENRY V (*Michael Pennington*): My learnèd lord, we pray you to
                                                        proceed,
And justly and religiously unfold
Why the law Salic that they have in France
Or should or should not bar us in our claim . . .
ARCHBISHOP (*Tony Church*): Then hear me, gracious sovereign, and
                                                        you peers,
That owe yourselves, your lives, and services,
To this imperial throne. There is no bar
To make against your highness' claim to France
But this, which they produce from Pharamond:
'*In terram Salicam mulieres ne succedant*'
'No woman shall succeed in Salic land';
Which Salic land the French unjustly gloze
To be the realm of France, and Pharamond
The founder of this law and female bar.
Yet their own authors faithfully affirm
That the land Salic is in Germany,
Between the floods of Sala and of Elbe;
Where Charles the Great, having subdued the Saxons,
There left behind and settled certain French,
Who, holding in disdain the German women
For some dishonest manners of their life,
Established then this law: to wit, no female
Should be inheritrix in Salic land;

Which Salic, as I said, 'twixt Elbe and Sala,
Is at this day in Germany called Meisen.
Then doth it well appear the Salic law
Was not devisèd for the realm of France;
Nor did the French possess the Salic land
Until four hundred one-and-twenty years
After defunction of King Pharamond,
Idly supposed the founder of this law,
Who died within the year of our redemption
Four hundred twenty-six; and Charles the Great
Subdued the Saxons, and did seat the French
Beyond the river Sala, in the year
Eight hundred five. Besides, their writers say,
King Pepin, which deposèd Childeric,
Did, as heir general, being descended
Of Blithild, which was daughter to King Clothair,
Make claim and title to the crown of France.
Hugh Capet also,—who usurped the crown
Of Charles the Duke of Lorraine, sole heir male
Of the true line and stock of Charles the Great—
To find his title with some shows of truth,
Though in pure truth it was corrupt and naught,
Conveyed himself as th'heir to th'Lady Lingare,
Daughter to Charlemain, who was the son
To Lewis the Emperor, and Lewis the son
Of Charles the Great. Also King Lewis the Tenth,
Who was sole heir to the usurper Capet,
Could not keep quiet in his conscience,
Wearing the crown of France, till satisfied
That fair Queen Isabel, his grandmother,
Was lineal of the Lady Ermengare,
Daughter to Charles the foresaid Duke of Lorraine;
By the which marriage the line of Charles the Great
Was re-united to the crown of France.
So that, as clear as is the summer's sun,
King Pepin's title, and Hugh Capet's claim,
King Lewis his satisfaction, all appear

To hold in right and title of the female
So do the kings of France unto this day.
Howbeit they would hold up this Salic law
To bar your highness claiming from the female,
And rather choose to hide them in a net
Than amply to imbare their crookèd titles
Usurped from you and your progenitors.   *Henry V: I.2.*

You did just what I asked, so I won't make any comment.

There's one particular kind of set speech which many actors find the hardest problem of all. What should they do with a soliloquy? A situation in which a character is almost always alone and seems to be talking to himself. Should such a speech be done to oneself, or should it be shared with the audience? There are very few absolute rules with Shakespeare, but I personally believe that it's right ninety-nine times out of a hundred to share a soliloquy with the audience. I'm convinced it's a grave distortion of Shakespeare's intention to do it to oneself. If the actor shares the speech it will work. If he doesn't it'll be dissipated, and the audience won't listen properly. And yet soliloquies are very often done the other way. So which is better? Let's take some test cases. I'm not trying to find a definitive way of doing a soliloquy. There's no such thing. So are there in fact any rules here? Only our basic points. The speech must arise out of a situation, it must have a story and it must be spontaneous. And it must be real. So once again the actor must make the language his own.

Let us look at a bit of Cressida. The soliloquy comes at the end of a long scene in *Troilus and Cressida* in which her uncle Pandarus has tried to persuade her to go to bed with Troilus. Try a bit to yourself first and let's see what happens.

CRESSIDA (*Jane Lapotaire, looking at herself in a mirror*): Words, vows,
                          gifts, tears, and love's full sacrifice,
He offers in another's enterprise;
But more in Troilus thousandfold I see
Than in the glass of Pandar's praise may be.
Yet hold I off: women are angels, wooing:
Things won are done—joy's soul lies in the doing . . .

Hold it there. You see what happened? For the first line or two we got interested in Cressida's vanity and her self-absorption, but when Jane went on playing the same thing the speech didn't go anywhere and got stuck. It became a generalized comment on her vanity rather than an invitation to us to listen and to share her thoughts.

So go now to the opposite extreme and share it totally with your audience. Show off and flaunt to them. Show them how clever you are.

> CRESSIDA (*Jane Lapotaire, to the audience*): Words, vows, gifts, tears,
> and love's full sacrifice,
> He offers in another's enterprise;
> But more in Troilus thousandfold I see
> Than in the glass of Pandar's praise may be.
> Yet hold I off: women are angels, wooing:
> Things won are done—joy's soul lies in the doing.
> That she beloved knows naught that knows not this:
> Men prize the thing ungained more than it is.
> That she was never yet that ever knew
> Love got so sweet as when desire did sue.
> Therefore this maxim out of love I teach:
> 'Achievement is command; ungained, beseech'.
> Then though my heart's content firm love doth bear,
> Nothing of that shall from mine eyes appear. *Troilus and Cressida: I.2.*

That was beautifully shared. The first version got stuck and constipated. The second time, by sharing totally, Jane took us along and we went with her. And so the story moved on also. What do you think?

> Jane Lapotaire: *I think if you're doing a speech on an empty stage, why are you doing it? I mean, you can't be telling yourself things that you already know, so the whole point must be to share it with the audience. To let them in on the character's private story as opposed to her function in the whole story of the play.*

So the moral is that, just as you share your thoughts with another character when you're playing a scene, so that process of sharing has to go on when you're left alone.

Jane Lapotaire: *Yes, it's a wonderful way of getting one-up on everybody else. It's just you and the audience and you're saying, "Look, this is what I'm really thinking. And this is the way I'm going to behave after I've finished this speech. So you're all going to be in on what my innermost thoughts are."*

That's right. So you keep the suspense going.

Jane Lapotaire: *Yes, yes. Hopefully.*

I feel I am making a point here which is glaringly obvious, and yet I have seen soliloquies so often tackled the other way, on film, on television and in the theater, that perhaps I deceive myself. But I don't think so.

Let's go on with looking at this question of sharing. Here's a bit of early Shakespearean verse which we used at the very beginning of the book. Here again there is a strong rhetorical rhythm, yet the speaker needs to be very simple and very human. Henry VI is brooding on his situation while his army is fighting a battle with the Yorkists.

HENRY VI (*Alan Howard*): This battle fares like to the morning's war,
When dying clouds contend with growing light
What time the shepherd, blowing of his nails,
Can neither call it perfect day nor night.
Now sways it this way, like a mighty sea
Forced by the tide to combat with the wind;
Now sways it that way, like the self-same sea
Forced to retire by fury of the wind.
Sometime the flood prevails, and then the wind;
Now one the better, then another best;
Both tugging to be victors, breast to breast,
Yet neither conqueror nor conquerèd;
So is the equal poise of this fell war . . .
O God! Methinks it were a happy life
To be no better than a homely swain;
To sit upon a hill, as I do now;

To carve out dials quaintly, point by point,
Thereby to see the minutes how they run:
How many makes the hour full complete,
How many hours brings about the day,
How many days will finish up the year,
How many years a mortal man may live.
When this is known, then to divide the times:
So many hours must I tend my flock, . . .
So many hours must I contemplate,
So many hours must I sport myself,
So many days my ewes have been with young,
So many weeks ere the poor fools will ean,
So many years ere I shall shear the fleece.
So minutes, hours, days, months, and years,
Passed over to the end they were created,
Would bring white hairs unto a quiet grave.
Ah, what a life were this! How sweet! How lovely!
Gives not the hawthorn bush a sweeter shade
To shepherds looking on their silly sheep
Than doth a rich embroidered canopy
To kings that fear their subjects' treachery?
O yes, it doth; a thousand-fold it doth.   *Henry VI Part Three: II.5.*

The splendid thing there was that Alan went totally with the rhetorical rhythm of the verse and yet had great spontaneity and humanity. We find over and over when playing Shakespeare that it is perfectly possible to do two seemingly opposite things with a speech at the same time. Shakespeare wants that, and when it happens it is very exciting. The speech we've just heard could easily become soporific but Alan kept it specific and so we went with him.

Now let's look at a soliloquy which at first sight seems very hard to follow. It is also in rhyme, which we haven't looked at yet. In *A Midsummer Night's Dream,* Helena is lamenting the complexities of her love life. She dotes on Demetrius but unfortunately he's in love with her best friend, Hermia. The actress needs to make the argument here as clear as possible and to relish the rhymes.

HELENA (*Susan Fleetwood*): How happy some o'er other some can be!
Through Athens I am thought as fair as she.
But what of that? Demetrius thinks not so;
He will not know what all but he do know.
And as he errs, doting on Hermia's eyes,
So I, admiring of his qualities.
Things base and vile, holding no quantity,
Love can transpose to form and dignity.
Love looks not with the eyes, but with the mind,
And therefore is winged Cupid painted blind.
Nor hath love's mind of any judgement taste;
Wings and no eyes figure unheedy haste.
And therefore is love said to be a child
Because in choice he is so oft beguiled.
As waggish boys in game themselves forswear,
So the boy love is perjured everywhere;
For ere Demetrius looked on Hermia's eyne
He hailed down oaths that he was only mine,
And when this hail some heat from Hermia felt,
So he dissolved, and showers of oaths did melt.
I will go tell him of fair Hermia's flight.
Then to the wood will he tomorrow night
Pursue her; and for this intelligence
If I have thanks it is a dear expense.
But herein mean I to enrich my pain,
To have his sight thither, and back again.

A Midsummer Night's Dream: I.1.

You were half using the script and that helped you to work it out as
you went. It's the sort of speech that is so easy to start generalizing
with once you know it well. But you took your audience with you
because you really worked it out. And as you did so, we worked it
out with you. That's something which is easy to forget sometimes.

Susan Fleetwood: *It would be quite fun to have done it traveling. To
have been walking across the stage and meaning to go off much earlier and then being caught and having to talk to the audience.*

Yes. It would have helped because you would have felt more in a situation. But you still made it very clear.

Now let's look at a different point. What does the actor do if a soliloquy seems to be partly to the audience, partly to himself and partly to someone else? Let's take Othello's soliloquy before he kills his wife Desdemona. Two points. First, something I've hardly mentioned before. This speech is very *monosyllabic,* and when a Shakespearean speech is in monosyllables it's always good counsel not to rush it. Each word needs to breathe, so take your time. (*To Donald Sinden:*) Try also to make it very clear whether you're talking to Desdemona or to the audience or to yourself or to your friend there, the candle.

> OTHELLO (*Donald Sinden, speaking slowly and carefully*):
> It is the cause, it is the cause, my soul
> Let me not name it to you, you chaste stars!
> It is the cause. Yet I'll not shed her blood,
> Nor scar that whiter skin of hers than snow,
> And smooth as monumental alabaster:
> Yet she must die, else she'll betray more men.
> Put out the light, and then put out the light:
> If I quench thee, thou flaming minister,
> I can again thy former light restore,
> Should I repent me; but once put out thy light,
> Thou cunning'st pattern of excelling nature,
> I know not where is that Promethean heat
> That can thy light relume. When I have plucked thy rose,
> I cannot give it vital growth again,
> It needs must wither. I'll smell it on the tree.
> O balmy breath, thou dost almost persuade
> Justice to break her sword! One more, one more.
> Be thus when thou art dead and I will kill thee,
> And love thee after. One more, and this the last . . .
> > She wakes.   *Othello: V.2.*

Good, you took your time. I want to stress here this matter of the monosyllables. It's extraordinary how many there are in this speech.

It contains 169 words and 146 of them are monosyllables. It just doesn't work if you take a monosyllabic line quickly. It sounds unreal and it's almost impossible to do. Think of trying to say, "It is the cause, it is the cause, my soul" quickly. In Shakespeare such lines are almost always packed and loaded, although it is easy to overlook their importance because the words themselves are so short and simple. Again and again characters use them at moments of great stress or importance, and the short simple words have a poetic resonance. I am not saying that an actor should try initially to *make* them poetic. What he needs to go for is the simplicity and the humanity. The poetry will then begin to work of its own accord. So if an actor gives the words air the poetic resonance will follow. But if he clips or rushes them, there will be a kind of thinning-out, both of poetry and of humanity.

The soliloquies we've looked at so far have a strong and clear through-line and argument. But sometimes the situation which a soliloquy explores is much more muddled. And sometimes its cross-currents may be a terrific mixture of, say, comedy and seriousness. Let's have a look at Viola's ring soliloquy. She's disguised as a boy. Malvolio has brought her a ring from Olivia, who has fallen in love with her. (*To Judi Dench:*) So what were your main feelings when you came to act this soliloquy long ago?

> Judi Dench: *Well, it's another wonderful opportunity just to share with the audience and show what a dilemma she's in. She can speak directly to them and say, "This is the situation I'm in. And how would you all react if you were in such a situation?"*

Yes, as ever, our word is "share." So go for the mixture and share both the funny side of the situation and the horrors of it. Give us a mixture throughout of the comedy and the pain. Here comes Malvolio with the ring from Olivia.

> MALVOLIO (*Donald Sinden*): Were not you even now with the Countess Olivia?
> VIOLA (*Judi Dench*): Even now, sir: on a moderate pace I have since arrived but hither.

MALVOLIO: She returns this ring to you, sir. You might have saved me
my pains, to have taken it away yourself. She adds, moreover, that you
should put your lord into a desperate assurance she will none of him;
and one thing more, that you be never so hardy to come again in his
affairs—unless it be to report your lord's taking of this. Receive it so.

VIOLA: She took the ring of me, I'll none of it.

MALVOLIO: Come, sir, you peevishly threw it to her, and her will is it
should be so returned. If it be worth stooping for, there it lies, in your
eye; if not, be it his that finds it. (*Exit.*)

VIOLA: I left no ring with her; what means this lady?
Fortune forbid my outside have not charmed her!
She made good view of me, indeed so much
That—methought—her eyes had lost her tongue,
For she did speak in starts, distractedly.
She loves me, sure, the cunning of her passion
Invites me in this churlish messenger.
None of my lord's ring? Why, he sent her none.
I am the man! If it be so—as 'tis—
Poor lady, she were better love a dream.
Disguise, I see thou art a wickedness
Wherein the pregnant enemy does much.
How easy is it for the proper false
In women's waxen hearts to set their forms.
Alas, our frailty is the cause, not we,
For such as we are made, if such we be.
How will this fadge? My master loves her dearly,
And I, poor monster, fond as much on him;
And she, mistaken, seems to dote on me.
What will become of this? As I am man,
My state is desperate for my master's love.
As I am woman—now, alas the day,
What thriftless sighs shall poor Olivia breathe!
O time, thou must entangle this, not I!
It is too hard a knot for me t' untie.   *Twelfth Night: II.2.*

A very hard knot to untie indeed. Yet in one way this is an easy soliloquy. It very clearly does what I spoke of earlier. It has a strong story

line. It responds to, explores and tries to solve a difficult situation. What is not so easy is the mixture of moods within it. A balance has to be kept between making it either too agonized or too jokey. Often Shakespeare requires an actor to play two or more different moods at once. I think you did just that, so you kept us on tenterhooks, not knowing quite how to respond. Good.

Now, we mustn't dodge it any longer. What about the most famous soliloquy of all? With "To be or not to be" there are an infinite number of possibilities, but I think that if we're in doubt there's one very good rule to follow. In acting and, yes, in directing, we must see the complexities, but we must always try to be *simple*. So much has been said and written about *Hamlet*. It seems at times to bring out a special madness in whoever writes or talks about it. I'm not getting at the best literary criticism, but listen for a moment to a passage from one of the world's leading theatrical magazines which is supposed to cater to theatrical people.

> *David Suchet:* "This ambiguity is one of the significant aesthetic coun- terparts of the broad philosophic drift defining the modern age . . . In theatre, *Hamlet* predicts this epistemologic tradition . . . The execution of the deed steadily loses way to a search for the personal modality of the deed—a search for Hamlet's character within the various mandates of his social position . . . The conflict is not a conflict of equal and con- tending social proprieties . . . Scripture fades in *Hamlet* against the incandescence of its hero's characterological vitality . . . This . . . exem- plifies the leading aesthetic problem of the actor in modern theatre— the interpretation of action through characterologic nuance and rarefaction."
>
> Donald M. Kaplan: *Tulane Drama Review,* 1966/67

Michael, come and follow that. But where to begin? Why don't you also start by taking it at first to yourself? Let's go through the process again of seeing how that works.

> HAMLET (*Michael Pennington, to himself*):
> To be, or not to be—that is the question;
> Whether 'tis nobler in the mind to suffer

The slings and arrows of outrageous fortune
Or to take arms against a sea of troubles
And by opposing end them . . .

Once again we see and we observe him, but we don't share. We see someone generally under stress, but I don't believe we go along with his thoughts. Now try it the other way and share it with us. Everything we've said tonight comes up here. You must take us with you, you must work it out as you go, and you must not go at it too emotionally. Of course you must have emotions, but your intention is to make sense of them. Imagine that the words have never been said or thought by any actor ever before. Give us a taste of your rarefaction.

HAMLET (*Michael Pennington, very simply*):
To be, or not to be—that is the question;
Whether 'tis nobler in the mind to suffer
The slings and arrows of outrageous fortune
Or to take arms against a sea of troubles
And by opposing end them. To die, to sleep . . .
To sleep—perchance to dream. Ay, there's the rub.
For in that sleep of death what dreams may come
When we have shuffled off this mortal coil
Must give us pause. There's the respect
That makes calamity of so long life.
For who would bear the whips and scorns of time,
Th'oppressor's wrong, the proud man's contumely,
The pangs of despised love, the law's delay,
The insolence of office, and the spurns
That patient merit of th'unworthy takes,
When he himself might his quietus make
With a bare bodkin? Who would fardels bear,
To grunt and sweat under a weary life,
But that the dread of something after death,
The undiscovered country, from whose bourn
No traveller returns, puzzles the will.
And makes us rather bear those ills we have
Than fly to others that we know not of?

Thus conscience does make cowards of us all;
And thus the native hue of resolution
Is sicklied o'er with the pale cast of thought,
And enterprises of great pitch and moment
With this regard their currents turn awry
And lose the name of action. *Hamlet: III.1.*

I think the great thing there also was that Michael moved the speech forward and took us with him as if he was telling a *story*. He didn't come on and issue a statement about his state of mind. He opened himself to us and worked it out with us, and it was deeply felt. Yet the thought was always in control of the feelings, so he made us think with him.

Well, there are obviously an infinite number of ways of handling a set speech. Even so I believe that some general conclusions can be drawn from what we've looked at. They are mostly matters of common sense rather than of interpretation. It's dangerous to do a long speech too solemnly, for instance. And it doesn't work if the audience stands back and observes the character thinking. The actor must open himself to his audience, and make them think with him because he needs to share his problems. In dialogue a character reaches out to another character and in a soliloquy a character reaches out to the audience. There's no great difference between the two. The moral is simple. An actor must make the audience listen and follow the story line of the thoughts. There will be no danger then of people switching off till the dreaded long speech is over. Provided that he shares. Yes, provided that he *shares.*

➤➤ ◄◄

CHAPTER SIX

Using the Sonnets

Going Over Some Old Ground

[The following actors took part in the program that
forms the basis of this chapter: TONY CHURCH,
MIKE GWILYM, SHEILA HANCOCK, LISA HARROW,
BARBARA LEIGH-HUNT, MICHAEL WILLIAMS.]

We've crammed so many points into the previous sessions that it's perhaps a good idea to go over some of them again as a recap and reminder. But we're going to raise them in rather a different context. We've already looked at a few of Shakespeare's sonnets and now we're going to look at them in some detail. First, I ought perhaps to say what a sonnet is. It's based on the same meter as blank verse and the normal rhythm of each line goes "de-dum, de-dum, de-dum, de-dum, de-dum": ten syllables. But a sonnet is also rhymed and it is fourteen lines long. First there are four lines which rhyme alternately, than another four lines that do the same and then another four. Finally it ends with a couplet that sums up what has been explored in the first twelve lines and often reaches some surprising conclusion.

But why, you may ask, are we going to work on nondramatic bits of text when our theme is acting in Shakespeare's plays? Well, sonnets can be excellent exercise pieces for actors. Most of the textual and verbal points that come up in working on the plays appear in the sonnets in concentrated form. We've often found that it's better to use them when we have a session on Shakespeare's text than to take a speech or speeches from a particular play. Speeches are often too long to work on in detail and they always trigger off questions about the speaker's character and the rest of the play that they are part of. This may be a distraction from coming to terms with purely textual challenges. Sonnets can help to take the pressure off. They are compact and complete in themselves and they can be treated as situations for which the only evidence is the sonnet itself. They are like little self-contained scenes, fourteen lines long. Yet they have the same basic ingredients as all scenes or long speeches. A situation is reacted to, explored, and at the end in some way resolved. Sometimes the speaker is talking to someone he loves and sometimes he is exploring a situation by himself. In other words he has a little soliloquy. Let me make it clear that we're not concerned here with the question of what's the best way to speak sonnets in public and at, say, some poetry recital. That's quite a different challenge. The question of how much they should or should not be acted in that context is disputed territory. I don't want to go into it here because we're not trying to show how a sonnet should be spoken, only how some selective exercise work on them can help put an actor more at ease when he comes to act in Shakespeare's plays.

More at ease: that is the crux. I'd like to bring into the open here something we have skirted round once or twice without articulating it clearly. I am sure that the greatest obstacle an actor has to overcome with Shakespeare's verse is simply fear. Fear that it is all too difficult and that he can never master it. This fear seems to me quite natural and understandable. Yet, as is the way with fear, it often leads to an actor becoming hostile or defensive. And so he rationalizes his fear by saying that if he worries about the verse he will become unreal and unspontaneous. He perhaps points to other actors who do care about the verse and says, "Look how unreal they are." The answer probably is that they are not unreal because of the verse but because they have fallen into the trap of playing qualities rather than intentions. Or maybe they are not very good actors. Yet I believe this kind of fear is less common than it used to be. It is certainly less overt, but it is apt to take the more insidious form of an actor paying lip service to the verse on the surface but being still inhibited by it internally.

So how can that fear be eased? In rehearsal it is often too late. Hence the idea of exercise-work outside the pressures of rehearsal, and hence the sonnets now. The ones we are going to work on are mostly what I would call "I" sonnets. They are all in the first person, and because Shakespeare is first and foremost a playwright they are essentially dramatic. Each actor will therefore imagine that he or she is in the particular situation which the sonnet explores, and that he is finding the words he needs to articulate or handle that situation. That will be the general acting intention. All we need to know about the background is that the sonnets are all about either a beautiful young man or a dark lady who is a wanton. Shakespeare loved both and they betrayed him with one another. I am simplifying of course but I needn't say more than that here. For our purposes the questions of whom he wrote them to and how much they are autobiographical are largely irrelevant. But we might as well start by letting Shakespeare speak for himself in a sonnet which disposes frankly of the age-old question of whether Shakespeare was homosexual or not.

> *Tony Church:* "A woman's face with nature's own hand painted
> Hast thou, the master-mistress of my passion;
> A woman's gentle heart, but not acquainted
> With shifting change as is false women's fashion;
> An eye more bright than theirs, less false in rolling,
> Gilding the object whereupon it gazeth;
> A man in hue all hues in his controlling,
> Which steals men's eyes and women's souls amazeth.
> And for a woman wert thou first created,—
> Till nature, as she wrought thee fell a-doting,
> And by addition me of thee defeated,
> By adding one thing to my purpose nothing.
>> But since she prick'd thee out for women's pleasure,
>> Mine be thy love, and thy love's use their treasure." *Sonnet 20*

This seems clear enough, although it's dangerous to think the sonnets will give us a lot of factual details about Shakespeare himself. That's not to say they don't tell us a lot about how his mind works and how he expresses himself. He likes verbal complexity but is often simple and direct. His thoughts naturally shape themselves antithetically, as his characters' thoughts so often do in his plays. He loves ambiguity and paradox. He delights in the sheer act of expressing himself and in handling seemingly impossible situations. And though he's writing sonnets, over and over his instinct as a dramatist is at work. The convention he writes in may be literary but the contents are dramatic and often cry out to be spoken. That's why they provide such good acting exercises. Let's look now at a sonnet we used earlier—one which consists of only one sentence. We picked it before as an example of how Shakespeare's verse can help to phrase a very long sentence, which would be unmanageable if treated as prose. The verse-line helps the actor to shape and clarify the thoughts. Now with such a sentence it's vital to pick out what is most important and what is less important. It starts with lots of little subclauses which lead up to the main thought, the main clause at the end. The acting trap is to break it up too much. These clauses mustn't be treated as self-sufficient sentences by themselves. You need to keep the whole long sentence going. And though you seem in a sad mood at the start, you must of course beware of being overtaken and swamped by your sadness. The whole point of the sonnet is that when you're low you think of your love and then you're joyful. Play it as if it is you yourself who are in the situation and try to laugh at yourself a little.

> *Sheila Hancock:* "When, in disgrace with Fortune and men's eyes,
> I all alone beweep my outcast state,
> And trouble deaf heaven with my bootless cries,
> And look upon myself and curse my fate—
> Wishing me like to one more rich in hope,
> Featur'd like him, like him with friends possess'd,
> Desiring this man's art, and that man's scope,
> With what I most enjoy contented least;
> Yet in these thoughts myself almost despising
> Haply I think on thee, and then my state,
> Like to the lark at break of day arising
> From sullen earth, sings hymns at heaven's gate:
>   For thy sweet love remember'd such wealth brings
>   That then I scorn to change my state with kings." *Sonnet 29*

Now let's look at another sonnet which is also a single fourteen-line sentence. It contains a further challenge because it is a terrific exercise in our old friends *alliteration* and *antithesis*. With this kind of exercise work it is good to take the text more slowly than one would speak it in performance. The sonnets are verbally packed and it is easy for an actor to take them faster than he can in fact think them. When that happens the language remains something existing on a page rather than something which the speaker has found and made his own. So feel your way.

> *Barbara Leigh-Hunt:* "When I do count the clock that tells the time,
> And see the brave day sunk in hideous night;
> When I behold the violet past prime,
> And sable curls o'er-silver'd all with white;
> When lofty trees I see barren of leaves,
> Which erst from heat did canopy the herd,
> And summer's green all girded up in sheaves
> Borne on the bier with white and bristly beard:
> Then of thy beauty do I question make
> That thou among the wastes of time must go,
> Since sweets and beauties do themselves forsake,
> And die as fast as they see others grow;
> And nothing 'gainst Time's scythe can make defence
> Save breed to brave him when he takes thee hence." *Sonnet 12*

Do you notice here how particular words and phrases are once again set against one another? "And see the brave day sunk in hideous night": a double antithesis. "Brave" is set against "hideous," and "day" is set against "night." Words work on words, qualifying and changing the direction of the thought. One phrase is set up so that it can be knocked down by another. So if you set up "brave day" brightly you can attack and destroy it with "sunk in hideous night." The actual sounds of the words must work on one another. The sound of the words "brave day" is brave in itself, and the consonants in "sunk in hideous night" are destructive and ugly. The same thing happens again in the fourth line:

And sable curls o'er-silver'd all with white

And also in the fifth line:

> When lofty trees I see barren of leaves

Can you hear the same thing happening? In the second of these lines, "barren" is the key word, and its importance is reinforced because it is put in a contrapuntal position in the verse-line. Instead of the normal rhythm, "de-dum, de-dum, de-dum, de-dum, de-dum," we get "de-dum, de-dum, de-dum, dum-dum, de-dum." So the word "barren" breaks into the line destructively. Here is another example of some verbal contrasts:

> And summer's green all girded up in sheaves
> Borne on the bier with white and bristly beard

The same sort of thing again. A lyric image, "summer's green," is set up and then deflated and wiped out by "white and bristly beard," and "borne on the bier" should perhaps suggest the sound of a bell tolling. Finally at the end of the sonnet the vital word "Time" crops up once again. In the midst of the rich language around it that word always needs to be picked out and stressed in Shakespeare. In the penultimate line it is also given added stress by being put in the contrapuntal position in the verse-line:

> And nothing 'gainst Time's scythe can make defence

"Time's scythe": dum-dum.

A common error with heightened and lyric text is to take it too solemnly. I believe that is quite as bad as throwing it away. It's easy for an actor to overlook the hidden ingredients of wit and humor, both in Shakespeare's sonnets and in his plays. Let's take a lighter sonnet now where the speaker is partly mocking his own poetry and partly teasing the person he loves. Once again, you should imagine that it's you yourself and not Shakespeare in the situation.

> *Michael Williams:* "Who will believe my verse in time to come?
> If it were fill'd with your most high deserts—
> Though yet heaven knows it is but as a tomb

Which hides your life and shows not half your parts,—
If I could write the beauty of your eyes,
And in fresh numbers number all your graces,
The age to come would say: 'This poet lies;
Such heavenly touches ne'er touch'd earthly faces.'
So should my papers, yellow'd with their age,
Be scorn'd, like old men of less truth than tongue,
And your true rights be term'd a poet's rage,
And stretchèd metre of an ántique song.
    But were some child of yours alive that time,
    You should live twice—in it and in my rhyme."   *Sonnet 17*

Now let's take a much sadder and darker sonnet. I want to concentrate on three things in it. First, the way in which once again the blank verse norm is again and again broken into by harsh contrapuntal stresses: "dum-dum" rather than "de-dum." Eight of the fourteen lines in the sonnet begin like that. Secondly, the word "Time" turns up once again and is crucially important. And thirdly, listen to the way that the movement of the verse and the actual sound and timbre of the words give the feeling of waves breaking remorselessly on the seashore. The text is rich in onomatopoeia. But of course you mustn't let the textual points make you overlook why you are saying it all and what you are after.

Mike Gwilym: "Like as the waves make towards the pebbled shore,
So do our minutes hasten to their end;
Each changing place with that which goes before
In sequent toil all forwards do contend.
Nativity, once in the main of light,
Crawls to maturity, wherewith being crown'd,
Crookèd eclipses 'gainst his glory fight,
And Time that gave doth now his gift confound.
Time doth transfix the flourish set on youth,
And delves the parallels in beauty's brow,
Feeds on the rarities of nature's truth,
And nothing stands but for his scythe to mow.
    And yet to times in hope my verse shall stand,
    Praising thy worth, despite his cruel hand."   *Sonnet 60*

The text is richer and more obviously poetic than the previous one, so I'd like to push you a bit further with the timbre and resonance of the language. Give us the feel and the sound of the sea. Take the opening lines again and make us hear the remorseless drive of waves across the beach.

> Like as the waves make towards the pebbled shore,
> So do our minutes hasten to their end;
> Each changing place with that which goes before
> In sequent toil all forwards do contend.

The onomatopoeia is very powerful there, isn't it? "Each changing place," "In sequent toil all forwards do contend": those words capture the swish and chafing of the sea as it sweeps over the shingle. Often in Shakespeare the rhythm and timbre of the language constitute the most important element of the thought, and they clearly do so here. But of course these are dangerous words. It won't work if an actor just makes sea noises. He can't and mustn't just play the poetry and hope for the best. What I am urging is that he should marry the onomatopoeia with clear intentions and great humanity.

But I want to go back to the question of offbeat stresses. They are very, very important because they help make a text vigorous and tough rather than smooth and bland. Listen to a key example. It is a famous sonnet and much could be said of it, but I want to stick here to this one key point only. It begins like this:

> *Lisa Harrow:* "Let me not to the marriage of true minds
> Admit impediments: love is not love
> Which alters when it alteration finds . . ." *Sonnet 116*

The opening 'Let me not' has great emphasis because the verse is broken with two extra stresses at the beginning: "Let me not." In acting terms I think these stresses can perhaps tell us something about the situation which the text is exploring. It is as if this sonnet is answering some other speech about how full of alteration love is. Just take those three lines again:

Let me not to the marriage of true minds
Admit impediments: love is not love
Which alters when it alteration finds . . .

If you make this a passionate answer to someone, "Love is not love"
scans as "dum-dum, dum-dum." Four stresses in four words. Once
again the extra stresses help you to drive the point home. Now look
at the whole sonnet and let's see if we can spot the other place where
there's extra stressing.

Let me not to the marriage of true minds
Admit impediments: love is not love
Which alters when it alteration finds,
Or bends with the remover to remove.
Oh no! it is an ever-fixèd mark
That looks on tempests and is never shaken;
It is the star to every wandering bark,
Whose worth's unknown although his height be taken.
Love's not Time's fool, though rosy lips and cheeks
Within his bending sickle's compass come;
Love alters not with his brief hours and weeks,
But bears it out even to the edge of doom.
    If this be error and upon me prov'd,
    I never writ, nor no man ever lov'd.   *Sonnet 116*

The phrase with the extra stresses stands out, doesn't it? "Love's not
Time's fool": the four stresses packed together give the statement a
terrific insistence. And notice also how Shakespeare puts the two
most important words, "Love" and "Time," in the contrapuntal
position. It's worth noting also how their impact is reinforced by
there being some quite regular verse-lines beforehand. Let's take
some of the lines again:

Oh no! it is an ever-fixèd mark
That looks on tempests and is never shaken;
It is the star to every wandering bark,
Whose worth's unknown although his height be taken.
Love's not Time's fool . . .

That's something which is very common in Shakespeare. He writes a few lines which scan regularly and then he suddenly breaks that rhythm with an arresting contrapuntal stress:

Love alters not with his brief hours and weeks,
But bears it out even to the edge of doom.

And then, having made his point, he rounds off the sonnet with a couplet containing further extra stresses which reinforce the conviction of the closing sentence:

If this be error, and upon me prov'd,
I never writ, nor no man ever lov'd.

Do you see how it works? These offbeat stresses make us sit up because they break the norm and give us a jolt. When Lisa read that sonnet I thought she was absolutely within the situation and was really talking to someone, and yet the rhythm and surge and drive of the verse heightened and intensified what she felt. I hope it doesn't sound as if I'm saying something rather theoretical and abstract, because what I'm urging is that the verse actually helps make the speech more alive and human. What do you think?

> Lisa Harrow: *That sonnet is my favorite. I believe passionately in what it's saying and I know it inside out. So maybe the moral is that you need to know a piece of text like that really well. Shakespeare puts real passion into the sonnet form, and we as interpreters need to enter that passion. We have to contain it because of the shape of the sonnet form. Yet at the same time we have to embrace it as well.*

That's why I was saying at the beginning, take these sonnets from inside yourselves. I know that they don't necessarily relate to you autobiographically, but the value of this sort of exercise lies in learning how to make a piece of literary text your own and how to bring it alive at the moment you speak it. You need to surprise us by surprising yourself. It's my old point about coining or fresh-minting the words, and I make no apology for repeating it so often.

It's perhaps the most important point of all about handling heightened text.

Let's look now at a sonnet which is built on surprises, but they are
surprises in the actual images used by the speaker. We loosely expect
a sonnet to praise the beloved with lyric and romantic comparisons.
But this whole sonnet's life springs from its confounding the conventional expectation of love sonnets.

> *Michael Williams:* "My mistress' eyes are nothing like the sun;
> Coral is far more red than her lips' red;
> If snow be white, why then her breasts are dun;
> If hairs be wires, black wires grow on her head:
> I have seen roses damask'd, red and white,
> But no such roses see I in her cheeks;
> And in some perfumes is there more delight
> Than in the breath that from my mistress reeks.
> I love to hear her speak, yet well I know
> That music hath a far more pleasing sound;
> I grant I never saw a goddess go,—
> My mistress when she walks treads on the ground.
>   And yet by heaven I think my love as rare
>   As any she belied with false compare." *Sonnet 130*

I thought that Mike took that with a fine balance between textual relish and a personal humanity. Of course when this balance is
right we don't notice. We only notice if the balance goes wrong and
if a speech is either taken with an excess of textual relish or too casually. It would be interesting to take a few lines and push them to
these two opposite extremes. You could go further with the textual
colors, for instance, by contrasting a goodly colored thing with an
ugly thing. You could set "If snow be white," a lyric image, more
strongly against "her breasts are dun," a shitty image. Or you could
push the comedy by being more flip and naturalistic. So first of all go
further in setting the texture and colors of the words against each
other.

(*Michael Williams does so.*)

My mistress' eyes are nothing like the sun;
Coral is far more red than her lips' red;
If snow be white, why then her breasts are dun;
If hairs be wires, black wires grow on her head . . .

Let's keep that in mind and see what happens if you're very flip and outrageous and free with it:

(*Michael Williams does so.*)

My mistress' eyes are nothing like the sun;
Coral is far more red than her lips' red;
If snow be white, why then her breasts are dun;
If hairs be wires, black wires grow on her head . . .

That should serve to remind us that all questions of handling Shakespeare's text are to do with *balances* between various extremes, which in this case could be an excess of textual relish or an excess of naturalistic throwaway. We are sometimes drawn to these extremes but we rightly suspect them. It seemed to me that Mike started with a wonderful balance between the two. What do you all feel about that?

> Tony Church: *Well, the question is always with you, isn't it? Each time you do a speech it goes too far one way or the other. It's like walking on a tightrope all the time. Yet if it's not, then there's something wrong: you're not playing dangerously enough.*

Yes, Tony's quite right. However much we may analyze the text as we're doing now, when you actually come to it you're not going to know quite which way that balance will go, not if you are genuinely fresh-minting it. Do you have any preference about which way you should take that sonnet?

> Michael Williams: *Well, no. The first way I did it was the way I believe it should be done. But if I was playing it to an audience, which of course is not the purpose of this exercise, I would probably feel and guess how outrageously I could do it.*

That's right, because with comedy the response of the audience starts to direct you.

Now let's go on to a crucial textual challenge. We've touched on it already this session but now I want really to hammer it home. I said earlier that if I was only allowed to give one piece of counsel to an actor new to Shakespeare, I would probably choose to say "Look out for the *antitheses* and play them." Over and over, not only simple sentences, but whole speeches are built on them, sometimes perhaps whole scenes. Look at this example. If you stress the antitheses the text will be totally clear. If not, it will be muddy and cloudy. Shakespeare is talking of how the man and the woman he loves are having an affair together.

> *Tony Church:* "Two loves I have, of comfort and despair,
> Which like two spirits do suggest me still:
> The better angel is a man right fair,
> The worser spirit a woman colour'd ill.
> To win me soon to hell, my female evil
> Tempteth my better angel from my side,
> And would corrupt my saint to be a devil,
> Wooing his purity with her foul pride.
> And whether that my angel be turn'd fiend
> Suspect I may, yet not directly tell;
> But being both from me, both to each friend,
> I guess one angel in another's hell.
> Yet this shall I ne'er know, but live in doubt
> Till my bad angel fire my good one out."   *Sonnet 144*

Tony played the antitheses up to the hilt there, and the meaning came through very clearly and brightly. So let me raise another point. This is a good example of text in which an uneasy situation and thoughts are coped with by the speaker, by the use of wit and humor. Tony *needed* the words and the humor there to make the situation bearable. The ingenuity of the thought worked on the unpleasant experience and thereby eased and relieved him. If we were to work more on that sonnet I would want to try pushing Tony further in two seemingly opposite directions. Perhaps there could be both more inner pain and yet more surface humor, so there would be a greater inner tension. That's something Shakespeare is always demanding of his actors: to play two or three quite contradictory attitudes at once. These sonnets are rich in that kind of clash, humor and pain, clarity and confusion, double meanings and contradictions. This is another reason why sonnets are such good exercise pieces. I reckon that if an actor can handle the *ambiguity* of a sonnet then he is ready to unlock anything in the text of the plays.

We've been looking at various verbal complexities and I seem to be suggesting that the sonnets and indeed the whole text of Shakespeare are a minefield of problems for an actor. But of course Shakespeare's text is often not at all convoluted. So as I have stressed antithesis and ambiguity and double meanings, it's perhaps time to take a sonnet which is much more direct and upbeat and buoyant. Maybe it tells us something about Shakespeare that, though the sonnets are fantastically rich and varied, relatively few of them are purely happy and set in a major key. There's usually crisis and ambiguity and sorrow somewhere in them but here is one which is a rare exception. The scansion is more regular here because the thought is joyful and direct and the feeling is clear-cut. The verbal detail must of course be brought out, but I think the most important thing here is the sweep and bravery of the whole.

> *Barbara Leigh-Hunt:* "Not marble, nor the gilded monuments
> Of princes shall outlive this powerful rhyme;
> But you shall shine more bright in these contents
> Than unswept stone besmear'd with sluttish time.
> When wasteful war shall statues overturn,
> And broils root out the work of masonry,
> Nor Mars his sword nor war's quick fire shall burn
> The living record of your memory.
> 'Gainst death and all oblivious enmity
> Shall you pace forth: your praise shall still find room
> Even in the eyes of all posterity
> That wear this world out to the ending doom.
>   So, till the judgement that yourself arise,
>   You live in this, and dwell in lovers' eyes."   *Sonnet 55*

It's easier than some of the other sonnets we've considered. If there's a pitfall here, I suppose it's that it could become sentimental. I want to go through and pick out some of the most important textual points, because it provides a good context for summarizing the kind of thinking I've been urging. In the middle there are of course a number of extra contrapuntal stresses:

> When wasteful war shall statues overturn,
> And broils root out the work of masonry,
> Nor Mars his sword nor war's quick fire shall burn
> The living record of your memory.
> 'Gainst death and all oblivious enmity
> Shall you pace forth . . .

And so on up to the final line, "You live in this." This sonnet is also full of vivid adjectives which need fresh-minting. It is only too easy to treat an adjective and its noun as one simple thought unit and to miss the way in which the adjective qualifies the noun or brings out some surprising contrast. "*Gilded* monuments," "this *powerful* rhyme," "*unswept* stone," "war's *quick* fire," "the *living* record" and "*all oblivious* enmity." Each of these phrases is in some way surprising, and if you find them at the moment you speak them they will have life and freshness. And then there are the verbs. It is easy to overlook them, but here they are especially vital and active. "You shall *shine*," "*besmear'd* with sluttish time," "When broils *root out*," "nor war's quick fire shall *burn*," "Shall you *pace forth*," and so on. Each of these verbs should perhaps surprise us also.

But above all, go for the *alliteration*. That's something we've not yet mentioned, but this sonnet is packed with it:

> Not marble, nor the gilded monuments
> Of princes shall outlive this powerful rhyme . . .

And so on. Barbara, I won't go through them all because I don't want to overload your mind with too much detail. Go for the spirit of what I'm saying as much as for the details. Go for the joy of utterance and the joy of braving Time. So far we've done each sonnet sitting down and it's perhaps made us a bit too reverent. So as an exercise and to help change the mood, try standing and opening it up to the audience. Keep what you did with it the first time but be bolder with the language. Ride those images and those words as if you were out in the open air and on some fiery steed. Open yourself and try to go over the top.

(*Barbara Leigh-Hunt does so.*)

"Not marble, nor the gilded monuments
Of princes shall outlive this powerful rhyme;
But you shall shine more bright in these contents
Than unswept stone besmear'd with sluttish time.
When wasteful war shall statues overturn,
And broils root out the work of masonry,
Nor Mars his sword nor war's quick fire shall burn
The living record of your memory.
'Gainst death and all oblivious enmity
Shall you pace forth: your praise shall still find room
Even in the eyes of all posterity
That wear this world out to the ending doom.
  So, till the judgement that yourself arise,
  You live in this, and dwell in lovers' eyes."
                                                Sonnet 55

Text as rich as this can be pushed in many directions. Though it is of course really said to the person you love, I think it was good to open it to the audience because it gave you a largeness and a sweep and a vigor which released you. It's a sonnet that seems to cry out for the theater.

Barbara Leigh-Hunt: *Yes, it has a greater conviction than a lot of his sonnets do. Most of them are contemplative and full of uncertainty but this one can be interpreted as an emotional outcry.*

In case you think that we've been straying too far from our brief of how to act Shakespeare's *plays,* I think we should end our exploration by looking at two sonnets which actually are part of one of those plays. In *Romeo and Juliet* the Prologue is actually written in sonnet form. Make your audience sit up and excite them about what's going to happen. Start by grabbing their attention with that extra stress at the very beginning.

> PROLOGUE (*Sheila Hancock*): Two households, both alike in dignity
> In fair Verona, where we lay our scene,
> From ancient grudge break to new mutiny,
> Where civil blood makes civil hands unclean.
> From forth the fatal loins of these two foes
> A pair of star-crossed lovers take their life;
> Whose misadventured piteous overthrows
> Doth with their death bury their parents' strife.
> The fearful passage of their death-marked love
> And the continuance of their parents' rage,
> Which, but their children's end, naught could remove,
> Is now the two hours' traffic of our stage;
> The which if you with patient ears attend,
> What here shall miss, our toil shall strive to mend.
>
> *Romeo and Juliet: Prologue*

There is a family resemblance between the sonnet form and ordinary blank verse because they both use the iambic pentameter, our old friend "de-dum, de-dum, de-dum, de-dum, de-dum." That's another reason why I think that sonnets make such good exercise pieces. Let's look finally at a sonnet that is actually a dialogue and part of the text of a scene. It's also from *Romeo and Juliet*. When the two lovers first meet they share a sonnet between them. Yes, their dialogue is actually in sonnet form. It is also the first time that we hear them speak to one another. (*To Mike Gwilym and Lisa Harrow.*) The text is full of metaphor, so find it because you need it and can feel your way with it towards your first kiss. Listen to how the movement of the sonnet provides the momentum towards that kiss.

> ROMEO (*Mike Gwilym*): If I profane with my unworthiest hand
> This holy shrine, the gentle sin is this.
> My lips, two blushing pilgrims, ready stand

To smooth that rough touch with a tender kiss.
JULIET (*Lisa Harrow*): Good pilgrim, you do wrong your hand too
                                                              much,
Which mannerly devotion shows in this.
For saints have hands that pilgrims' hands do touch,
And palm to palm is holy palmers' kiss.
ROMEO: Have not saints lips, and holy palmers too?
JULIET: Ay, pilgrim, lips that they must use in prayer.
ROMEO: O, then, dear saint, let lips do what hands do!
They pray: grant thou, lest faith turn to despair.
JULIET: Saints do not move, though grant for prayers' sake.
ROMEO: Then move not while my prayer's effect I take.

Romeo and Juliet: I.5.

What is the moral there? It's something else I've not yet talked about: how should we play metaphor? The whole of that discussion is built on wordplay about prayers and saints and palmers. So if the first metaphor and image, "this holy shrine," is not set up, we will get a little bit lost with the way that metaphor is developed. So it has to be put into inverted commas and underlined by Romeo, if what follows is to be clear to the audience. The next religious image we get is "my lips, two blushing pilgrims, ready stand," and then Juliet picks that image up and, as it were, hands it back to him. If the actors don't hand the metaphor on to each other, the text will be hard to follow. Of all forms of heightened language, metaphor and simile must be freshly found the most. That's very important.

But it's time now to sum up. You may think that the kind of points I've been urging are very subjective, and you may ask, how can he be sure that they are so? Isn't he reading more into the text than is objectively there? Well, I don't think I am. I think that I have been pointing to what is palpably there and objectively there. There's no mystery about them. In later sessions I will freely admit that what I shall urge will often be subjective. But here I would claim that all these textual points are plain as a pikestaff once you spot them.

So although our title has been "The Sonnets," what we've really been doing is to look once again at how Shakespeare's text works dramatically. Never mind whether we always get it right, so long as we learn to look for the clues and hidden stage directions which Shakespeare puts into his text. As ever, they can help and feed the actor, provided he doesn't on the one hand worry too much about them, or on the other become too solemn and earnest. I always fear when I hear myself saying, "Stress this," "stress that," "go further," that I may be getting a bit earnest and loading an actor with too many details. There always comes a point in rehearsal when the director or the actors say, "Let's forget everything we've said. It will still work upon us but we mustn't get tied down by it." And that is right. Let me stress once again that an actor must never never become bound or bogged down by such work. Yet if he can find his way through it and make friends with the text he will become, not bound, but more *free*. As I began by talking about fear, let me end by making a plea for having fun. Acting is hard work, but I believe that it's no accident that the alternative word we have for it is "playing." Playing Shakespeare is at bottom to do with playing with words, just as we have heard Romeo and Juliet doing. Yes, playing in every sense of playing: playing a game, being zestful, using our wits, spending energy and enjoying oneself. If the actor enjoys the word games, the audience will enjoy them too.

PART TWO

✦➤ ◄✦

Subjective Things

CHAPTER SEVEN

✦

Irony and Ambiguity

Text That Isn't What It Seems

[The following actors took part in the program that forms the basis of this chapter: TONY CHURCH, MIKE GWILYM, ALAN HOWARD, BEN KINGSLEY, JANE LAPOTAIRE, RICHARD PASCO, MICHAEL PENNINGTON, NORMAN RODWAY.]

I said earlier that perhaps the actor's most difficult problem in Shakespeare was the handling of soliloquies. Well, I was wrong. There's something more difficult and that is how to handle irony. It may sound surprising to give a whole session over to irony, but Shakespeare uses it over and over again, and an actor who cannot handle it will keep missing out a vital element in the character he is building. I believe it is as important a subject as any we are raising in this series. But it is difficult to talk about and a much more subjective question than any we've looked at so far.

Today we're not very good at irony. Most of us use it rarely, if at all. The best people at handling irony in Shakespeare that I've ever come across have been New York drama students. That's because irony is part of their natural idiom and they use it daily. But on the whole we don't. Sardonic humor, maybe. Sending up, certainly, but irony: not very oft. Perhaps we'd even be pushed to say what irony is. I suppose the simplest way of defining it is to say that it involves saying one thing while meaning something else. Something that is opposite to the surface meaning. It's commonly humorous but it may at the same time be deadly serious. The speaker enjoys it, sometimes wryly at his own expense. One of the reasons why irony is difficult is that it's often halfway between thought and feeling. Basic emotions like joy and hate and fear and greed come easily to an actor. He knows what they mean and he can tap them somewhere inside himself. But irony? (*To the actors.*) If I say, play it ironically, how do all of you respond? Do you know what I mean? Do you know what to do?

Ben Kingsley: *What you've said is very clear. The difficulty about irony is that it doesn't leap off the page and it's very easy to overlook. In a sense you cannot write irony down. The words on the page seem to hold either one meaning or another. That is why it's so dangerous to give an ironic answer to a question that an interviewer asks you. The printed word does not convey your full meaning. One cannot write ironically. The actor has to interpret ironically.*

Yes. So what Shakespeare does is to write down one word or group of words which are, as you say, just one set of words, but he wants us to find two meanings to it.

A word I haven't used much yet, though it obviously comes up in the context of this program, is *ambiguity*. A double meaning in a single word or phrase. Irony always involves ambiguity. So that's what we've got to dig into and see if we can find out how to handle it. I think that perhaps a useful starting point is to say that irony involves the speaker in being at once inside and outside the situation in which he finds himself. If an actor can achieve that, I think he'll find his way towards solving the problem.

But, of course, before he does that, he must begin by finding the right intention. That's crucial. But a certain special *tone* is involved with irony. That's what I think we'll find hard to define. Let's look at some examples, both simple and complex. First, let's listen to Mark Antony in the forum in *Julius Caesar*.

MARK ANTONY (*Mike Gwilym*): Friends, Romans, countrymen, lend
me your ears;
I come to bury Caesar, not to praise him.
The evil that men do lives after them,
The good is oft interrèd with their bones;
So let it be with Caesar. The noble Brutus
Hath told you Caesar was ambitious . . .
And Brutus is an honourable man.   *Julius Caesar: III.2.*

"Brutus is an honourable man" is about as simple and clear a piece of irony as anything in Shakespeare. But I thought, Mike, you could go further with it. One way of making the irony clear to the audience is by putting the ironic words in inverted commas. Or, if you prefer it, by giving them capital letters. I think you could have treated "Brutus is an honourable man" like that.

That's an obvious example. The irony is as overt as Antony dares to make it. But sometimes Shakespeare's characters are more subtle. In the deposition scene in *Richard II,* the king looks at his face in a mirror and says to Bolingbroke, who has deposed him:

> RICHARD II (*Richard Pasco*): A brittle glory shineth in this face.
> As brittle as the glory is the face,
>   (*Breaks mirror.*)
> For there it is, cracked in a hundred shivers.
> Mark, silent King, the moral of this sport:
> How soon my sorrow hath destroyed my face.
> BOLINGBROKE (*Norman Rodway*): The shadow of your sorrow hath destroyed
> The shadow of your face.
> RICHARD II: Say that again!
> 'The shadow of my sorrow'—ha, let's see.   *Richard II: IV.1.*

"The shadow of your sorrow hath destroyed/The shadow of your face." This sentence is both ironic and ambiguous. The situation seems to be about the grief and the emotions of the king, but the key sentence is Bolingbroke's. What he says goes to the very heart of Richard II's nature. I believe that Richard is a player king in the sense that he plays at kingship. His emotions are often mere emotional indulgences which make a kind of play out of the reality around him. He turns the situation he finds himself in into a cue for emotional and dramatic display. But here, when he does so, Bolingbroke catches him at it. When the king breaks the mirror and says, "Mark ... how ... my sorrow hath destroyed my face," it is a dramatic and striking gesture, but Bolingbroke sees through it. So when he says "The shadow of your sorrow," he really means "the unreality of your sorrow." "The shadow of your sorrow hath destroyed/The shadow of your face:" i.e. your false sorrow has destroyed your false, playerly face. Bolingbroke is telling Richard that his sorrow is as unreal as the rest of his public persona. Dickie, you played this part famously many years ago. How does that passage strike you coming back to it?

> Richard Pasco: *I think that the way I saw Richard's tragedy was that he never actually discovered himself. Even in moments like this, he doesn't really understand. He's in a state of almost perpetual bewilderment. In the first few scenes of the play we concentrated very much on the player king, as you were saying. The show-off, the demonstrator. Yet he does sometimes try genuinely to know himself. And there are glimpses of his search for himself and his internal reality perhaps as early on as the return from Ireland.*

Yes, of course there are moments when the king has that self-knowledge and then he is ironic about himself. We'll look at one later.

> Norman Rodway: *But I don't really think that the little sequence we've just done is what you say it is. I wouldn't describe it as an example of either irony or ambiguity. If you're being ironical then you're being disingenuous and saying something meaning the reverse of what you say. In this particular case Bolingbroke means exactly what he says. I think it's nearer to gentle sarcasm than to irony.*

I think it's irony because it does have the double meaning of irony. I can't be certain, but I think that to Richard the remark seems to be a sympathetic remark, and so he takes up its surface meaning. But actually Bolingbroke means something else. That's why he's making an ironic joke because he knows the king won't understand it.

> Norman Rodway: *Well, in that case I did it wrong.*

> Richard Pasco: *Where does sarcasm end and where does irony begin?*

> Norman Rodway: *I didn't play irony, I played gentle sarcasm.*

It is irony because you are saying a surface thing which Richard thinks he understands, but you are really voicing a criticism of him which he doesn't understand.

Norman Rodway: *Well, then I should have said it as a surface thing.*

Both as a surface thing and an ironic thing. You've got to play *both* meanings, haven't you? Ambiguity.

Norman Rodway: *Right, try again.*

RICHARD II: For there it is cracked in a hundred shivers.
Mark, silent King, the moral of this sport:
How soon my sorrow hath destroyed my face.
BOLINGBROKE: The shadow of your sorrow hath destroyed
The shadow of your face.   *Richard II: IV.1.*

Good, got it. I thought the double meaning was very clear. As soon as we dig into irony this conversation always comes up: "how much is it overt and how much is it hidden?" This is a very good example of text which requires that it be both at once.

Now let's look at a particularly tricky sonnet. It is full of irony but the irony isn't at first apparent. It is also a terrific exercise in our old friends, *antithesis* and *stressing the key words.* If an actor doesn't plant and stress them this particular sonnet will be incomprehensible. Let's see what happens if Jane starts by taking the text unstressed. Then we'll see how we make it clearer by the stressing.

Jane Lapotaire: "Those parts of thee that the world's eye doth view
Want nothing that the thought of hearts can mend;
All tongues (the voice of souls) give thee that due,
Uttering bare truth, even so as foes commend . . ."

O.K. point made. If it's unstressed, it's gibberish and impossible to follow. Now go for the stresses and the antithetical words.

Those parts of thee that the world's éye doth view
Want nothing that the thought of heárts can mend;

All tongues (the voice of soúls) give thee that due,
Uttering bare truth, even so as foes commend . . .

Good, that's stage two. You're beginning to make it clear to us and
we can begin to follow the argument. But now let's bring in the
irony, because it isn't clear yet what the speaker is actually doing.
Remember that you're mocking somebody. You are pretending to be
on his side but you are actually criticizing him.

Those parts of thee that the world's eýe doth view
Want nothing that the thought of hearts can mend;
All tongues (the voice of soúls) give thee that due,
Uttering baŕe tŕuth, even so as foes commend.
Thine outẃard thus with outẃard praise is croẃn'd;
But those same tongues that give thee so thine own
In other accents do this praise coñfound
By seeing farther than the eýe hath shown
They look into the beauty of thy mind,
And that, in guess, they measure by their deéds;
Then, chúrls, their thoughts, although their eyés were kind
To thy fair flówer add the ránk sméll of weéds.
But why thy odóur matcheth not thy shów,
The sóil is this—that thou dost coḿmon grow.   *Sonnet 69*

Good. The antitheses ran right through it. You also put the antithetical words into inverted commas, so the irony was apparent.
    Now let's take one thing further. Do that couplet at the end again.
Go deeper, not only into the irony, but into the ambiguity about
what you mean by "soil" and "common."

Jane Lapotaire: *It's sexual ambiguity.*

Yes. "Soil" means the earth and "common" means a common land.
But "soil" also means sexually soiled and "common" means sexually
common. Just those two lines.

But why thy odour matcheth not thy show,
The *soil* is this—that thou dost *common* grow.

Once again you captured that double meaning by putting the words into inverted commas.

Jane Lapotaire: You have to signal to the audience in a way.

You have to play with the words to give the audience the right information.

Ben Kingsley: So that the audience has to be an active listener, not a passive listener. If you are serving them with ambiguous words they cannot just sit there. They must listen positively. They must be involved.

That's right. So even though Jane played the speech to one person, she actually shared it with the audience as well.

Let's now go on to an easier sonnet that makes the same point. Ben, "When my love swears that she is made of truth" is also an ironic sonnet, but this time there's a different situation. You're not actually talking to your mistress. You're telling us about your love. So share it with us.

> *Ben Kingsley:* "When my love swears that she is made of truth
> I do believe her, though I know she lies,
> That she might think me some untutor'd youth
> Unlearnèd in the world's false subtleties.
> Thus vainly thinking that she thinks me young,
> Although she knows my days are past the best,
> Simply I credit her false-speaking tongue:
> On both sides thus is simple truth suppress'd.
> But wherefore says she not she is unjust?
> And wherefore say not I that I am old?
> Oh, love's best habit is in seeming trust,
> And age in love loves not to have years told.
>   Therefore I lie with her, and she with me,
>   And in our faults by lies we flatter'd be."   *Sonnet 138*

All our old points come up, don't they? Plenty of antitheses like "When my love swears that she is made of truth/I do believe her though I know she lies." And there's a lot of ambiguity too. A number of words there mean two things, like "*vainly* thinking" and "I lie with her." And I think we've also stumbled here on another kind of irony, irony against oneself. Shakespeare always enjoys that. Take the obvious ambiguity or pun, "Therefore I *lie* with her, and she with me/And in our faults by *lies* we flattered be." No actor is going to miss the double meaning here in the word "lie." Perhaps the only problem is to decide which is the surface meaning and which is the undermeaning. Let's take a third sonnet which is just as rich in ambiguity and double meanings, but first and foremost it's another terrific exercise in antithesis. (*To Norman Rodway.*) So, Norman, start by going for the meaning and for all the key antitheses. You're discussing your sex life with your mistress.

> *Norman Rodway:* "Love is too young to know what conscience is,—
> Yet who knows not conscience is born of love?
> Then, gentle cheater, urge not my amiss
> Lest guilty of my faults thy sweet self prove.
> For, thou betraying me, I do betray
> My nobler part to my gross body's treason:
> My soul doth tell my body that he may
> Triumph in love: flesh stays no farther reason,
> But rising at thy name doth point out thee
> As his triumphant prize. Proud of this pride,
> He is contented thy poor drudge to be,
> To stand in thy affairs, fall by thy side.
>   No want of conscience hold it that I call
>   Her 'love' for whose dear love I rise and fall."   *Sonnet 151*

Thank you, you played the surface meanings very clearly. So, having got the antitheses and the argument, let's feed in one crucial piece of information which affects the meaning and tone of the whole sonnet. "Conscience" here is ambiguous. The Elizabethans used it not only in the moral sense as we do, but also in the sense of carnal knowledge. So do it again and bring out all the sexual innuendoes. "To stand in thy affairs" and so on. And as Ben did, mock both your mistress and yourself.

(*Norman Rodway takes the sonnet again.*)

Very rich in ambiguity. This sonnet is very tricky verbally, which is why I want to unravel it bit by bit. We've got the antitheses and we've got the double meanings, but now let's take it one step further. The thing we haven't brought out fully yet is the irony. It's like the sonnet Ben did: the irony is largely against yourself. Mock yourself for being your mistress's sexual slave, and share your thoughts with your audience as much as with her. Be outrageous and go as far as you can in relishing the ironic and ambiguous words.

(Norman Rodway takes the sonnet again.)

Good. Very ambiguous and very ironic. Now I want to make a digression. What about the *rhymes* in these sonnets? And indeed what about the many rhyming couplets in the plays themselves? What should an actor do about them? Should he play them or should he ignore them? I've heard both points of view argued, but personally I'm sure that he should play them because they are there in the text. To dodge them is a cop-out and a textual distortion. They need to be relished consciously. Our old point about finding or fresh-minting the language comes up again here. After all, rhyme *is* a form of heightened language. The actor (or rather the character) needs, as it were, to make the rhymes up himself. They must not just be rhymes that happen to be in the text, but *his* rhymes. And there must be an intention behind them. Perhaps he coins them deliberately, or perhaps he is showing off or trying to score or stress a point. Or maybe he's just trying to round something off at the end of a speech.

I suppose we'd agree that though we may be clear about the nature of irony, it still doesn't necessarily enable us always to communicate it. An actor can't just say or even stress the words. He clearly has to do something with them. Norman, for instance, was rightly using, relishing and savoring the words. The most practical advice I can offer therefore about irony is to keep stressing what I've briefly said already. The actor must put the word in quotes or give it a capital letter or both. That's what we've actually been doing: "Brutus is an 'honourable' man" in quotes. "Brutus is an HONOURABLE man": capital letters. Of course I'm exaggerating but I think my point holds. So let's look now at a very familiar speech which brings it out very strongly. King Richard II has heard his land is in arms against him and so he laments his downfall.

> RICHARD II (*Richard Pasco*): For God's sake let us sit upon the ground
> And tell sad stories of the death of kings—
> How some have been deposed, some slain in war,
> Some haunted by the ghosts they have deposed,
> Some poisoned by their wives, some sleeping killed,
> All murdered. For within the hollow crown
> That rounds the mortal temples of a king
> Keeps death his court; and there the antic sits,
> Scoffing his state and grinning at his pomp,
> Allowing him a breath, a little scene,
> To monarchize, be feared, and kill with looks,
> Infusing him with self and vain conceit,
> As if this flesh which walls about our life
> Were brass impregnable; and humoured thus,
> Comes at the last, and with a little pin
> Bores through his castle wall, and—farewell, king!   *Richard II: III.2.*

Now what I want to push further here is once again the element of the self-mockery. Irony that is against oneself. It involves sending up all the noble concepts in the speech: "kings," "crown," "state," "monarchize." Push that as far as you can. The vital thing is to set the whole thing up at the start, and the crux is in the first two lines. "For God's sake let us sit upon the ground/And tell sad stories of the death of kings." Don't pity yourself. Enjoy seeing through the hollowness of kingship. Inflate and so deflate the word "kings." Say to the audience, "This is going to be great, telling the story of the death of *kings.*" If you find that trigger you'll be away for the whole speech. But if you go totally into your grief you'll lose the idea of standing outside yourself and yet luxuriating in the situation. Just go for those two lines.

> For God's sake let us sit upon the ground
> And tell sad stories of the death of kings.

That's right. "It's delicious, it's going to be glorious. We're going to have fun." Now let's skip a few lines for a moment and come to the famous bit, "For within the hollow crown/That rounds the mortal temples of a king." Play your *enjoyment* of discovering that the crown is hollow, not the *grief* of the crown's weight and greatness. And when you talk of rounding "the mortal temples of a king," enjoy the discovery that you are mortal. Don't play the woe of it, but enjoy seeing through the surface splendor of the crown.

> For within the hollow crown,
> That rounds the mortal temples of a king
> Keeps death his court; and there the antic sits,
> Scoffing his state and grinning at his pomp.

That line about Death "scoffing his state and grinning at his pomp," is the clue to the speech, isn't it? You realize Death is mocking you, and so you enjoy mocking yourself. Why don't you try it all through again? And take it a bit quicker, because then you will find more lightness and humor.

(*Richard Pasco takes the speech again.*)

I think you showed beautifully there something that I touched on earlier. You managed both to be inside the character and yet to *stand outside yourself* at the same time. That's the double vision which lies at the heart of irony. It's not easy to do both at once but you certainly did so then.

Richard Pasco: *Can you define it a bit more? When you're directing an actor, you often say, "Be more wry." Do you link wryness with irony? It is the same thing or is there a tinge of difference between irony and wryness?*

Wryness is simpler, isn't it? We talk about "wry humor" but that's not ambiguous. Irony usually has humor in it too but it also always has this double vision. That's why it's more difficult. I realize we've strayed here beyond something which is demonstrably and objectively present in the text to something much more subjective. I know a lot of people wouldn't agree with me about this speech. And so often with Shakespeare it's at first sight arguable whether irony is there at all. Perhaps you may think, "Surely the surface meaning is the whole meaning?" But Shakespeare's whole habit of mind led him to relish double-think. No one was keener on puns, sometimes in grim contexts, and it's in those contexts that irony and ambiguity are easy to overlook. Particularly in Shakespeare's political plays. Over and over he gives his politicians bits of hidden irony as part of their political persona. They have a surface urbanity and an inner malice and bitterness, but it's very easy for an actor to miss it.

Let's take one very simple example. In *Henry IV, Part I* the rebel Worcester comes to a parley with the king.

> WORCESTER (*Tony Church*):   I protest
> I have not sought the day of this dislike.
> HENRY IV (*Norman Rodway*): You have not sought it? How comes it,
>   then? . . .
> WORCESTER: It pleased your majesty to turn your looks
> Of favour from myself, and all our house,
> And yet I must remember you, my lord.   *Henry IV Part I: V.i.*

Hold it there. Let's ask ourselves why there's that little superfluous "my lord" in the third line. There's already been a "your majesty" in the first line and Shakespeare doesn't usually pad out a line. I am sure that both "your majesty" and "my lord" are ironic here because Worcester is reminding Henry that he's a usurper and not really a king.

> Tony Church: *Well, yes, it's either that they're both ironic or that one's right and the other's wrong, isn't it? I don't know. But they're set against each other anyway.*

That's right. He thinks he is "his majesty," but you, as Worcester, don't.

> Tony Church: *All right, let's see if we can get all that out of two words.*

WORCESTER: I protest
I have not sought the day of this dislike.
HENRY IV: You have not sought it? How comes it, then? . . .
WORCESTER: It pleased *your majesty* to turn your looks
Of favour from myself, and all our house,
And yet I must remember you, *my lord.*

Good, very ironic. It's the little words of irony that are often the
easy ones to overlook, but those were very clearly defined. I think
one vital element in this kind of irony is enjoyment. It's an odd sort
of enjoyment and in this case it's a kind of enjoyment of one's own
bitterness. Hamlet is full of that. It's often a mistake with Shakespeare just to act bitter. There has to be a zest in verbalizing the bitterness.

Now let's look at yet another problem. What happens when a
character *hides* his irony from the person he's speaking to but has
obliquely to *reveal* it to the audience? When his mother persuades
Coriolanus to desert the Volscians and spare Rome, the Volscian
leader, Tullus Aufidius, says nothing for nearly two hundred lines.
When he finally speaks, he only says four words. Here is Coriolanus
talking to his mother.

CORIOLANUS (*Mike Gwilym*):   O my mother, mother! O!
You have won a happy victory to Rome.
But for your son—believe it, O believe it—
Most dangerously you have with him prevailed,
If not most mortal to him. But let it come.
Aufidius, though I cannot make true wars,
I'll frame convenient peace. Now good Aufidius,
Were you in my stead, would you have heard
A mother less? Or granted less, Aufidius?
AUFIDIUS (*Ben Kingsley*): I was moved withal.   *Coriolanus: V.3.*

Aufidius's reply is so brief that it's hard to be certain of his intention.
Clearly it's very ambiguous. He was moved, but he puts it dryly and
stands outside his own emotion, as Ben did then. The whole content
of the scene tells us that he's thinking here about the implications of

Coriolanus's betrayal. So the surface meaning is true: he was indeed moved. But Ben also caught wonderfully the ironic undermeaning which contradicts it.

Let's look a bit more at the way in which irony may be at work where it doesn't seem to be. Let's take another political speech. Montjoy, the French herald, is threatening King Henry V.

> MONTJOY (*Alan Howard*): Thus says my King: 'Say thou to Harry of England, Though we seemed dead, we did but sleep. Advantage is a better soldier than rashness. Tell him we could have rebuked him at Harfleur, but that we thought not good to bruise an injury till it were full ripe. Now we speak upon our cue, and our voice is imperial.
>
> *Henry V. III.6.*

Hold it there. You played that threateningly, and it certainly seems to go with the way it's written. But now let's try it in a different way. Montjoy's intention is clear: he is out to humiliate Henry V in front of all his soldiers. So let's imagine he does it with great gentleness and surface sympathy for Henry. As if he's saying, "My dear old fellow, I'm terribly worried about you; I'm sorry for you and I'm on your side." So try sending him up by mock sympathy.

> MONTJOY (*Alan Howard, with great sympathy*): Thus says my King: 'Say thou to Harry of England, Though we seemed dead, we did but sleep. Advantage is a better soldier than rashness. Tell him we could have rebuked him at Harfleur, but that we thought not good to bruise an injury till it were full ripe. Now we speak upon our cue, and our voice is imperial: England shall repent his folly, see his weakness, and admire our sufferance. Bid him therefore consider of his ransom, which must proportion the losses we have borne the subjects we have lost, the disgrace we have digested; which in weight to re-answer, his pettiness would bow under. For our losses, his exchequer is too poor; for th'effusion of our blood, the muster of his kingdom too faint a number; and for our disgrace, his own person kneeling at our feet but a weak and worthless satisfaction. To this add defiance: and tell him for conclusion, he hath betrayed his followers, whose condemnation is pronounced.' So far my King and master; so much my office.
>
> *Henry V: III.6.*

That is a kind of irony, isn't it? But the technique is different. The mocking is inverted. It masquerades as sympathy but I think the way Alan did it is much more devastating. But of course I am being subjective. As Ben said earlier, in a way irony can't be written down. How can I be sure the surface bullying by Montjoy isn't the whole meaning here? Well, I can't be absolutely sure. But if we agree that Montjoy's intention is to humiliate Henry then the second way that Alan did it surely achieves that much more than the first. I suppose what I'm really saying is that it's healthy with Shakespeare to be continually on the lookout for irony in unlikely places. It can make a performance much richer and can prevent the text being taken too solemnly. Of course when I urge that we look for more humor, I am not necessarily thinking of jolly humor. It's the dark, wry, bitter, sardonic humor that irony can so well reveal.

Let's end by looking at one further piece of political irony and ambiguity. In *Troilus and Cressida* the Trojan hero Hector meets Ulysses, the Greek politician. They like each other and are very courteous, but the courtesy is loaded and ironic. They are looking at the walls of Troy.

> ULYSSES (*Tony Church*): I wonder now how yonder city stands,
> When we have here her base and pillar by us.
> HECTOR (*Michael Pennington*): I know your favour, Lord Ulysses, well.
> Ah, sir, there's many a Greek and Trojan dead,
> Since first I saw yourself and Diomed
> In Ilion, on your Greekish embassy.
> ULYSSES: Sir, I foretold you then what would ensue.
> My prophecy is but half his journey yet;
> For yonder walls, that pertly front your town,
> Yon towers, whose wanton tops do buss the clouds,
> Must kiss their own feet.
> HECTOR: I must not believe you.
> There they stand yet; and modestly I think
> The fall of every Phrygian stone will cost
> A drop of Grecian blood. The end crowns all;
> And that old common arbitrator, Time,
> Will one day end it.

ULYSSES: So to him we leave it.

Troilus and Cressida: IV.5.

I think you would get the irony going further here if you actually played the surface courtesy and chivalry more, like Alan did in the Montjoy speech.

Tony Church: *We were being a bit too beady, were we?*

Yes, a bit too obviously beady. I think Hector and Ulysses both play the surface game of diplomatic courtesies. You've met before and maybe you actually quite like and respect each other, so there's an umbilical cord of human friendliness.

Tony Church: *They did actually try to stop the war happening, didn't they?*

Yes, Ulysses went on an embassage to try to stop the war, and so they formed a bond. But within that bond the barbs can here become more loaded. When Ulysses says, "base and pillar," you did put it in inverted commas. You sent him up. But if you did so with courtesy, the mockery might get more dangerous.

Tony Church: *Perhaps the answer is initially just to play the courtesy and see what happens. Play it more Chinese.*

(*They take the dialogue again.*)

That worked, didn't it? The irony did come out more through the courtesy.

Tony Church: *Because if we do it that way, the irony is a shared irony and not one that's against each other. We both know the score and what's going to happen, so it isn't actually a scene of opposition at all. It's about two experienced men regretfully looking into the future.*

Excellent. Shared irony is a new kind of irony that we've found.

Michael Pennington: *There's also a third character in the scene, isn't there? And that's the city. Which makes it possible for us not necessarily to be in contact. There's always the city to look at and to play off.*

That's true.

Tony Church: *And there's a fourth character in the scene. There's old Time as well.*

Yes, we've certainly got to get more out of our old friend Time, haven't we? "That old common arbitrator, Time." What does the word mean here? There's its literal surface meaning, but in Hector's mind it also means death, maybe to the Greeks and maybe to the Trojans. So Hector is saying "We're all doomed and we're all equal." The words have got to have, not irony, but ambiguity and resonance. I also want to push further the sudden switches from irony to direct statement. They're very powerful here. I think that the irony goes on up to the point were Hector breaks it by saying, "I must not believe you." Mike, take that very courteously also. And then say with complete simplicity and romantic love of your city, "There it is, *Troy.*" That's the nonironic bit and it will come over the more strongly after the irony. I thought you could make a bigger change there. And you, Tony, could help it by putting more irony into "Yonder walls and towers." Say to him, "O they're wonderful, those towers, they're splendid." And then Hector can undercut your mockery. Try it again.

(*They do so.*)

We've spent a whole session on irony, not merely because it's important and difficult, but because it comes up in Shakespeare so often. There's so much more of it than people realize. The strange thing is that I can actually think of no sustained long passage where Shakespeare gives irony to women. Odd moments, yes, but never for very long. The only bit I found suitable was that sonnet which, strictly speaking, should be spoken by a man. That is why we've only worked on men's speeches. Perhaps that tells us something about Shakespeare, or perhaps it tells us something about irony.

We have strayed into thorny areas. That is, as I've said, because we've moved on from what is objective to what is subjective. Talking about irony has led us inexorably to talking about interpretation and in the remaining sessions of this series we shall go further that way. I hope you won't think that I'm trying to push my interpretations as something authoritative or absolute. I'm more concerned with suggesting a way of thinking than with trying to say this is the *only* way a particular speech can be done. I believe that it is always fruitful to open this subject up. If an actor is on the lookout for irony he will find more richness of *character* thereby. But as I said at the very outset, we'll find that there are many knotty questions here and few certain answers. So we must always go on searching.

CHAPTER EIGHT

⇥ ⇤

Passion and Coolness

A Question of Balance

[The following actors took part in the program that
forms the basis of this chapter: TONY CHURCH, SUSAN FLEETWOOD,
MIKE GWILYM, SHEILA HANCOCK, LISA HARROW, BEN KINGSLEY,
BARBARA LEIGH-HUNT, MICHAEL PENNINGTON,
DONALD SINDEN, PATRICK STEWART.]

LEAR (*Donald Sinden, full out*):
Blow, winds, and crack your cheeks! Rage! Blow!
You cataracts and hurricanoes, spout
Till you have drenched our steeples, drowned the cocks!
You sulphurous and thought executing fires . . . !   *King Lear: III.2.*

*H*old it there a moment.

Donald Sinden: *I was just beginning to enjoy myself.*

Sit down a moment and let's talk about our theme for this session.
Passion, pain, emotion and extremes. We're going to look at the
question of how an actor marries the emotional and intellectual
demands of the text. Once again we'll find we're talking about balance. Very crudely, if we go too far one way, we will find that we
need to go a bit in the opposite direction. It's the same principle as
that which we've already found with heightened language. If actors
start working the text too hard, it may be healthy to take a speech or
scene more naturalistically and not to relish the words quite so
much. And vice versa. I said in our last program that we should be

venturing now into more subjective areas. But I'll try to be as selective as possible and concentrate on problems which relate peculiarly and chiefly to Shakespeare. You can of course find them in other dramatists, but not, I think, in so concentrated a form. What did Shakespeare himself think the balance between passion and coolness should be? As it's generally agreed that he's expressing his own view when he has Hamlet advise the Players about acting, let's listen to some of that advice once again.

> Speak the speech, I pray you, as I pronounced it to you, trippingly on the tongue. But if you mouth it as many of our players do, I had as lief the town crier spoke my lines. Nor do not saw the air too much with your hand, thus . . . But use all gently. For in the very torrent, tempest, and as I may say, whirlwind of your passion, you must acquire and beget a temperance that may give it smoothness.   *Hamlet: III.2.*

"Trippingly on the tongue," "mouth it," "gently," It's pretty clear where Shakespeare's sympathies lie. Hamlet asks for what we call coolness in playing passion. But he too is aware that there must be a balance.

> Be not too tame neither. But let your own discretion be your tutor. Suit the action to the word, the word to the action, with this special observance, that you o'erstep not the modesty of nature.   *Hamlet: III.2.*

I think the key phrase here is "o'erstep not the modesty of nature." This is Shakespeare's way of saying we must be natural and not false or grotesque. So let's explore this balance now and see how far we should go.

First I'd like to make an experiment. It's sometimes pointed out that if an actor gets himself too emotionally involved in a passionate speech, he will actually move the audience less than if he is less carried away. If he actually weeps, for instance, it may flatten out his voice and somehow cut off communication. So let's take one or two speeches and see what we think. Sometimes the balance between thought and emotion goes wrong because of an excess of naturalistic thinking. In *Henry IV Part I*, Hotspur and Prince Hal fight, according to the text, "a long hour by Shrewsbury clock." So clearly they must be pretty exhausted. Finally Hal gives Hotspur a mortal wound and Hotspur makes a dying speech. Let's see what happens if the actor plays it with his exhaustion and his wound and his pain uppermost in his mind.

> HOTSPUR (*Mike Gwilym does so*):
> O Harry, thou hast robbed me of my youth!
> I better brook the loss of brittle life
> Than those proud titles thou hast won of me.
> They wound my thoughts worse than thy sword my flesh . . .
>
> *Henry IV Part 1: V. 4.*

Now that's what I call the naturalistic fallacy.

> Mike Gwilym: *I was just getting into it.*

Getting into the feelings and the pain, but of course the text got strangulated and cut off. That often happens. Shakespeare himself wants to do something else with the speech, doesn't he? He makes Hotspur say, "They wound my thoughts worse than thy sword my flesh." That's quite a useful piece of direction by Shakespeare. I think that Hotspur's pain is in the mind rather than in his body.

> Mike Gwilym: *Pain's relative anyway, isn't it? I've known an actor fracture a bone onstage during a fight and not feel the pain until he gets off. It depends what you're concentrating on. If I, as Hotspur, determine to put my life in order, as it were, before I die, that will supplant the pain.*

That's right. One can almost always find a psychological or naturalistic reason for doing a speech in such a way that you can also release the poetic juices of it. So let's do it again, not necessarily feeling the pain but the wonder of dying: "God, what is happening to me?" Take a clue from the fact that you prophesy in the speech.

> HOTSPUR (*Mike Gwilym*): O Harry, thou hast robbed me of my youth!
> I better brook the loss of brittle life

Than those proud titles thou hast won of me.
They wound my thoughts worse than thy sword my flesh.
But thoughts the slave of life, and life, time's fool
And time, that takes survey of all the world,
Must have a stop. O, I could prophesy,
But that the earthy and cold hand of death
Lies on my tongue. No, Percy, thou art dust
And food for ... (*Dies*)
PRINCE HAL (*Michael Pennington*): For worms, brave Percy. Fare thee
                                        well, great heart!
                                        Henry IV Part 1: V.4.

Good, that way the text can begin to work upon us and stir us, which it can't do when the physical life's on top of it. Maybe you got too cool then, but I was more moved that way than I was the first time. I think we've stumbled here on our old problem of a speech which is partly choric. Hotspur in part stands outside his own dying. What he says about thoughts and life and time seems at first blush out of character. But it is exciting how a man who has lived so much in the moment should see clearly beyond that moment.

Let's look now at another passage where the choric element is even more striking. In *Hamlet,* when Gertrude brings the news of Ophelia's suicide, she says nothing to show her own feelings directly. The speech consists entirely of description.

GERTRUDE (*Barbara Leigh-Hunt*):
There is a willow grows aslant the brook,
That shows his hoar leaves in the glassy stream.
Therewith fantastic garlands did she make
Of crowflowers, nettles, daisies and long purples,
That liberal shepherds give a grosser name,
But our cold maids do dead-men's fingers call them.
There on the pendent boughs her crownet weeds
Clambering to hang, an envious sliver broke,
When down her weedy trophies and herself
Fell in the weeping brook. Her clothes spread wide,
And mermaid-like awhile they bore her up;

Which time she chanted snatches of old tunes, . . .
Or like a creature native and indued
Unto that element. But long it could not be
Till that her garments, heavy with their drink,
Pulled the poor wretch from her melodious lay
To muddy death.   *Hamlet: IV.7.*

I think you're absolutely right to keep Gertrude's feelings in check.
Clearly the choric function is dominant in the sense that the thing
described matters rather more than the feelings of the speaker. And
yet that's not quite true. It's still possible to find out what Gertrude
is feeling and trying to do inside herself while she speaks. I think you
did that. You didn't lack feelings, but you kept them in check and
had a surface coolness. What do you think about it?

> Barbara Leigh-Hunt: *Well, I think there's probably a great deal of
> guilt there. Gertrude probably feels she's partly responsible for what
> has taken place previously and is partly to blame for this girl's death.
> In the next scene she reveals that she loved her very much and hoped
> she would be the wife of her only son. I think that is probably strug-
> gling inside her all the time.*

Right. So there's a lot of subtext going on underneath inside, which
you can play as Gertrude, even if on the surface you seem just to be
playing the description. We've seen already how Shakespeare very
often requires an actor to show emotions and at the same time to
stand outside those emotions. He asks for passion and a degree of
detachment, if not coolness, at the same time. Actors need to
embrace that, as both you and Mike did.

Let's stick with this point and take a sonnet which, if taken as an
exercise piece, lends itself to many kinds of emotional interpretation.
One thing about it however is clear; it is emotionally dense and
highly charged. Sue, you're talking about your sex life. See if you can
look at it in three quite different ways. You are talking about lust.
You say in the course of the sonnet that lust is "A bliss in proof and
prov'd, a very woe;/Before, a joy propos'd, behind a dream." First of
all, try playing the enjoyment of the joy proposed. There's your bed,
your lover is coming.

Susan Fleetwood (with much lust):
"The expense of spirit in a waste of shame
Is lust in action: and till action, lust
Is perjur'd, murderous, bloody, full of blame,
Savage, extreme, rude, cruel, not to trust;
Enjoy'd no sooner but despisèd straight . . ."   *Sonnet 129*

Point made: very lustful. Let's imagine now that you've done it and you're getting out of bed and dressing. You are deeply disgusted with yourself for what you've just done.

(Susan Fleetwood takes the text disgustedly.)

Now both those versions were extreme in their emotion. First, lust and secondly, revulsion. Now let's do what we've been doing already in the program. See what happens this time if, still with a mixture of disgust and sexual excitement, you stand outside yourself and have a good wry, sardonic look at what you've done.

Susan Fleetwood: "The expense of spirit in a waste of shame
Is lust in action; and till action, lust
Is perjur'd, murderous, bloody, full of blame,
Savage, extreme, rude, cruel, not to trust;
Enjoy'd no sooner but despisèd straight;
Past reason hunted; and no sooner had,
Past reason hated, as a swallow'd bait
On purpose laid to make the taker mad,—
Mad in pursuit, and in possession so,
Had, having, and in quest to have, extreme;
A bliss in proof; and prov'd, a very woe;
Before, a joy propos'd; behind a dream.
    All this the world well knows; yet none knows well
    To shun the heaven that leads men to this hell."   *Sonnet 129*

Good. You were both in it and standing outside it. So you caught the characteristic Shakespearean mixture of feeling and experience. Once an actor achieves that, the text begins to do more work. If he goes for passion only he will almost certainly be overlaying something on top of that text. "Experience" is, I think, the word that best sums up and brings together this mixture of thought and emotion which we're after. It is to do with both having emotional experiences and with learning from them.

Very often an emotional speech in Shakespeare is to do with learning something. Particularly if the character who speaks it is highly articulate, as Shakespeare's characters usually are. And if he is so, and especially if he talks in heightened language and images, similes or metaphors, we can be pretty sure he is to some extent standing outside his own emotions. Hamlet is the supreme example of this. The old phrase about poetry being "emotion recollected in tranquillity" is perhaps worth remembering here. So also is another sentence from Hamlet's advice to the Players: "In the very . . . tempest and . . . whirlwind of your passion you must acquire and beget a temperance that may give it smoothness." A *temperance.* But please understand that I'm not trying to cry down or run away from expressing emotion. What I am saying is that an actor needs to be sure when it predominates and when it's mixed with the intellectual capacity to stand outside and handle those emotions.

Let's look at something easier to grasp but also easy to overlook. Shakespeare loves to give his characters sudden changes between passages where the mind or where the passions are uppermost. It is easy for an actor to fall into the trap of ironing these changes out, but very often a character changes hugely from the one to the other from speech to speech. Or indeed within a speech. In *Julius Caesar,* where Brutus contemplates Caesar's murder and meets his fellow conspirators, his emotional and intellectual balance keeps on changing. He's volatile and he's variable. He prides himself on being cool. But how cool is he? And how much of a mixture? Let's take four speeches, the first of which is a soliloquy.

BRUTUS (*Ben Kingsley*): It must be by his death; and for my part,
I know no personal cause to spurn at him,
But for the general.—He would be crowned.
How that might change his nature, there's the question.

It is the bright day that brings forth the adder,
And that craves wary walking. Crown him!—that!
And then, I grant, we put a sting in him
That at his will he may do danger with.
Th'abuse of greatness is when it disjoins
Remorse from power; and, to speak truth of Caesar,
I have not known when his affections swayed
More than his reason. But 'tis a common proof,
That lowliness is young ambition's ladder,
Whereto the climber-upward turns his face;
But when he once attains the upmost round,
He then unto the ladder turns his back,
Looks in the clouds, scorning the base degrees
By which he did ascend: so Caesar may;
Then, lest he may, prevent. And, since the quarrel
Will bear no colour for the thing he is,
Fashion it thus: that what he is, augmented,
Would run to these and these extremities;
And therefore think him as a serpent's egg
Which, hatched, would, as his kind, grow mischievous,
And kill him in the shell.   *Julius Caesar: II.1.*

Rational, exploratory, intellectual. Brutus is feeling his way and deliberately pushing down his feelings for Caesar. His thoughts dominate his emotions here. He's trying to justify himself, to elevate himself and to kid himself. But a little later on we get a glimpse of his true feelings.

BRUTUS: Since Cassius first did whet me against Caesar,
I have not slept.
Between the acting of a dreadful thing
And the first motion, all the interim is
Like a phantasma or a hideous dream:
The genius and the mortal instruments
Are then in council; and the state of man,
Like to a little kingdom, suffers then
The nature of an insurrection.   *Julius Caesar: II.1.*

This betrays his inner turmoil. But Brutus expresses his unease in brooding generalizations. He doesn't speak directly or openly of his own human feelings. But when the conspirators come to visit him, he's assured and very much the public man. When Cassius urges them all to swear their resolution, he opens out.

> BRUTUS: No, not an oath. If not the face of men
> The sufferance of our souls, the time's abuse—
> If these be motives weak, break off betimes,
> And every man hence to his idle bed;
> So let high-sighted tyranny range on
> Till each man drop by lottery. But if these,
> As I am sure they do, bear fire enough
> To kindle cowards and to steel with valour
> The melting spirits of women, then, countrymen,
> What need we any spur but our own cause
> To prick us to redress? . . . but do not stain
> The even virtue of our enterprise,
> Nor th'insuppressive mettle of our spirits,
> To think that or our cause or our performance
> Did need an oath; when every drop of blood
> That every Roman bears, and nobly bears,
> Is guilty of a several bastardy,
> If he do break the smallest particle
> Of any promise that hath passed from him.   *Julius Caesar: II.1.*

Do you hear how different the verse is? It's rhetorical and ringing and more regular. Brutus can give vent to his feelings here because he feels on safe ground. The speech needs to be as passionate as his first speech is cool. Later he has one other long speech to the conspirators which is triggered by Cassius urging that Mark Antony be assassinated as well as Caesar.

> BRUTUS: Our course will seem too bloody, Caius Cassius,
> To cut the head off and then hack the limbs,
> Like wrath in death and envy afterwards;
> For Antony is but a limb of Caesar.

Let us be sacrificers, but not butchers, Caius,
We all stand up against the spirit of Caesar,
And in the spirit of men there is no blood.
O, that we then could come by Caesar's spirit,
And not dismember Caesar! But, alas,
Caesar must bleed for it. And, gentle friends,
Let's kill him boldly, but not wrathfully;
Let's carve him as a dish fit for the gods,
Not hew him as a carcass fit for hounds.   *Julius Caesar: II.1.*

Brutus seems to me very emotional again here. Yet there's also something of the rationalizing and self-deception and elevation of murder which we saw in the first soliloquy. He's at great pains to stress his humanity. But how much is he humane and how much a politician paying lip service to humanity? How emotional is he and how much is he simply working on the conspirators' emotions? I suppose it's a bit of both. He's using his feelings to work up feelings in his listeners. What do you think?

Ben Kingsley: *Well, I think that all those hypotheses that you've just posed, all those questions, are the very source of Brutus's dilemma and his energy. And he must hand those questions over to an audience. That is his predicament in the play. On a first reading, of course, he seems to be fraught with contradictions and . . . what's your word for it?*

Ambiguity?

Ben Kingsley: *Ambiguities, contradictions. Things that are set antithetically against one another. Brutus's inconsistencies are only a microcosm of the whole play. If you try and iron out these inconsistencies in order to make the part playable, you will in fact anesthetize the energy within the lines. The energy of the character and the predicament of the character are only available to the audience if the tension between the opposing forces is observed, relished and played. But of course that's all theory. It's very difficult to spread-eagle oneself inside the giant silhouette of Brutus and remain faithful to all these seemingly contradictory elements. Each one has to be played to the full.*

In a way, the contradictions *are* the character.

Now here's a fearfully difficult passage for a woman. In *King John* Constance laments for her dead son Arthur. There's no doubt here about the degree of her passion.

> CONSTANCE (*Susan Fleetwood, passionately*): O that my tongue were in
> the thunder's mouth!
> Then with a passion would I shake the world . . .   *King John: III.4.*

Let's take this passage, much cut, and see what we can learn from it. The French king Philip and Cardinal Pandulph are trying to comfort her.

> KING PHILIP (*Tony Church*): Patience, good lady. Comfort, gentle
> Constance.
> CONSTANCE: No, I defy all counsel, all redress,
> But that which ends all counsel, true redress—
> Death! Death! O amiable, lovely death!
> Thou odoriferous stench! Sound rottenness! . . .
> Come, grin on me, and I will think thou smilest
> And buss thee as thy wife. Misery's love,
> O come to me!
> KING PHILIP: O fair affliction, peace!   *King John: III.4.*

I think that the question of variety comes up here as much as the question of balance. Constance is distracted and wild but it's dangerous to take the whole passage that way, because the way she luxuriates in her grief could become monotonous or generalized. So let's see what happens if we go on with the speech and say, "Go as far as you like in some places and hold back in others." I think probably that's the way Shakespeare wrote it.

> Susan Fleetwood: *Yes, I think she's striving for order in the next bit, in that she puts her woes into the form of a list. This seems to indicate the amount of control that she has. But I also think on the other hand that where Shakespeare puts an "O," it is some indication of emotional release. I find that quite helpful.*

Yes, that's very good counsel: Shakespeare's "O"s. I think one other bit of advice might be useful. It's important that, however distressed you are, part of you *enjoys* the speech in the sense of enjoying the emotional release. Constance needs the words to give herself that release; so, as ever, use them as much as you can. Go on from where we got to.

> CARDINAL PANDULPH (*Donald Sinden*): Lady, you utter madness, and
> not sorrow.
>
> CONSTANCE: Thou are not holy to belie me so!
> I am not mad. This hair I tear is mine.
> My name is Constance. I was Geoffrey's wife.
> Young Arthur is my son, and he is lost!
> I am not mad—I would to heaven I were,
> For then 'tis like I should forget myself!
> O, if I could, what grief should I forget!
> Preach some philosophy to make me mad,
> And thou shalt be canonized, Cardinal . . .
> CARDINAL: You hold too heinous a respect of grief.
> CONSTANCE: He talks to me that never had a son.
> KING PHILIP: You are as fond of grief as of your child.
> CONSTANCE: Grief fills the room up of my absent child,
> Lies in his bed, walks up and down with me,
> Puts on his pretty looks, repeats his words,
> Remembers me of all his gracious parts,
> Stuffs out his vacant garments with his form;
> Then have I reason to be fond of grief?
> Fare you well. Had you such a loss as I,
> I could give better comfort than you do . . .
> O Lord! My boy, my Arthur, my fair son! . . .
> My life, my joy, my food, my all the world!
> My widow-comfort, and my sorrows' cure!   *King John: III.4.*

The feeling was all there. Yet because you took it lightly, the words and the language worked on me as well. Constance is very articulate here, and you didn't let feelings get between you and the meaning.

Susan Fleetwood: *Yes, I think I could have inflected more and had more variation.*

You're right to raise the question of inflection here. There is always a danger with such a speech that the passion cuts off inflection and so makes it hard for us really to listen to and follow what is being said. I don't mean that an actor should just, as it were, put on inflections. That would be false and forced. But a lack of inflection is very often a symptom of a lack of communication. So what should an actor do about it? I think it's quite simple. He must play the meaning of the thoughts as strongly as the feelings, and in particular the key words have to be stressed and picked out.

Now let's go back to another speech where there's no doubt whatever of the emotional intensity of the speaker. Lear is going mad and he is on the heath in the storm. Donald, take us back to the speech we heard at the beginning. Go full out at first.

> LEAR (*Donald Sinden*): Blow, winds, and crack your cheeks! Rage! Blow!
> You cataracts and hurricanoes, spout
> Till you have drenched our steeples; drowned the cocks!
> You sulphurous and thought-executing fires,
> Vaunt-curriers of oak-cleaving thunderbolts,
> Singe my white head! And thou all-shaking thunder,
> Strike flat the thick rotundity o' the world,
> Crack Nature's moulds, all germens spill at once
> That makes ingrateful man! *King Lear: III.2.*

Powerful stuff. But of course if you do it as flat-out as that in a small studio it can be too much. It's a bit like a dinosaur sitting on a teacup. I must confess that I don't quite know how I think this speech should be done. Part of me does question the full-blooded, busting-a-gut version which you were going for. It could be that when you do it like that it's an overlay on Shakespeare rather than a realization of the text and indeed of the emotions. As ever, it seems to me that the text should do a great deal of the work. If your emotions don't get on top of it maybe the text itself will resonate more.

Donald Sinden: *You would like me to do a version over the top then?*

No, I don't think so: I don't think the roof and the lights and the cameras would stand it. Let's try an exercise and an experiment. Don't bash it this time: just breathe it and whisper it as quietly as you can. Don't try to shout the elements down, but imagine that there's a dip in the storm and that you're out of breath and that you're very, very old and you haven't got a big voice. And remember Hamlet's advice to the Players: "Speak the speech . . . trippingly on the tongue, but if you mouth it, I had as lief the town crier spoke my lines." Have a go.

Donald Sinden: *I do think here that Lear is asking for a storm actually, rather than shouting at one that's already there.*

Good counsel.

LEAR (*Donald Sinden, speaking very quietly*): Blow, winds, and crack
                                        your cheeks! Rage! Blow!
You cataracts and hurricanoes, spout
Till you have drenched our steeples, drowned the cocks!
You sulphurous and thought-executing fires,
Vaunt-curriers of oak-cleaving thunderbolts,
Singe my white head! And thou all-shaking thunder,
Strike flat the thick rotundity o' the world . . .   *King Lear: III.2.*

I thought you were getting much more richness out of it, both of feeling and of text, than when you brought the roof down.

Let's stick with the same point and look now at Mistress Quickly describing the death of Falstaff. (*To Sheila Hancock.*) Try it first in the same way: be very moved and carried away by what you're saying.

BARDOLPH (*Tony Church*): Would I were with him, wheresome'er he is, either in heaven or in hell!
MISTRESS QUICKLY (*Sheila Hancock*): Nay, sure, he's not in hell: he's in Arthur's bosom, if ever man went to Arthur's bosom. 'A made a finer

end, and went away an it had been any christom child; 'a parted e'en just between twelve and one, e'en at the turning o'th'tide; for after I saw him fumble with the sheets, and play with flowers, and smile upon his fingers' ends, I knew there was but one way ...   *Henry V: II.3.*

Sheila Hancock: *I think that's enough of that, don't you?*

Yes, though within the brief I set you I thought you did it very well. Now hold in your feelings because they're so painful, and try to describe exactly what it's like in Falstaff's bedroom. Try to make sense of what you've seen.

> BARDOLPH: Would I were with him, wheresome'er he is, either in heaven or in hell!
> MISTRESS QUICKLY: Nay, sure, he's not in hell: he's in Arthur's bosom, if ever man went to Arthur's bosom. 'A made a finer end, and went away an it had been any christom child; 'a parted e'en just between twelve and one, e'en at the turning o'th'tide; for after I saw him fumble with the sheets, and play with flowers, and smile upon his fingers' ends, I knew there was but one way; for his nose was as sharp as a pen, and 'a babbled of green fields. 'How now, Sir John?' quoth I, 'What, man, be o'good cheer!' So 'a cried out, 'God, God, God!' three or four times. Now I, to comfort him, bid him 'a should not think of God—I hoped there was no need to trouble himself with any such thoughts yet. So 'a bade me lay more clothes on his feet; I put my hand into the bed, and felt them, and they were as cold as any stone; then I felt to his knees, and so up'ard and up'ard, and all was as cold as any stone.
>   *Henry V: II.3.*

There's no doubt, is there, which way was best? And that example brings up another question I raised earlier. How much is the speech about Mistress Quickly and how much is it about Falstaff? Well, obviously it's about both. But my experience of it in the theater is that the balance is often wrong. The speech becomes too much about Mistress Quickly and her grief and her sentimentality, where what it's really there for is to make us see Falstaff on his deathbed. It is more moving to learn that Falstaff babbled of green fields than it is to serve up Mistress Quickly's feelings when she speaks of it. In other words there is once again a choric function here, though I'm not suggesting for a moment that it should consciously be played chorically. The moral is that it's sometimes more important to make the text resonate than to be moved oneself.

But these are dangerous words. I sound as if I'm suggesting that an actor, given half a chance, will always tend to indulge his emotions at the expense of his text. That does sometimes happen, but on the whole the reason the balance goes wrong is something quite different. It's very often simply to do with the size of the theater. In a rehearsal room actors can work quickly and lightly, and it's much easier for them to maintain the balance. But when they have to fill a big auditorium they naturally feel they have to project and make both their voices and emotions bigger. And of course they are quite right.

But very often they lose something thereby. Through no fault of the actor a speech which he has taken lightly but movingly in the rehearsal room can become forced. In our present context, a small intimate studio, we don't have the pressure of a big space to fill.

Let's look now at this difference. (*To Lisa Harrow.*) Do Portia's speech when Bassanio has chosen the right casket. She knows at last that she will be able to marry him. Go absolutely full out as if you were in the big theater at Stratford.

> PORTIA (*Lisa Harrow*): How all the other passions fleet to air:
> As doubtful thoughts, and rash-embraced despair,
> And shudd'ring fear, and green-eyed jealousy.
> O love, be moderate, allay thy ecstasy,
> In measure rain thy joy, scant this excess.
> I feel too much thy blessing, make it less
> For fear I surfeit.   *The Merchant of Venice: III.2.*

Now see what happens if you just breathe it and whisper it. (*She does so.*) What do you feel about those two extremes and possibilities?

Lisa Harrow: *Well, the first way you just need to express the huge joy that Portia is feeling and also the release of enormous tension.*

The tension of years of waiting for this casket to be chosen by the right person. So you have to use the language to push that emotion up and out. It's like one huge great sigh, isn't it? One huge cry of joy and relief and of amazement. In a big theater you need to be as out-going as possible and to push the emotion out. Yet Shakespeare has actually written "aside" against this speech. So when you're in a small space and very close to the person that's playing Bassanio, who isn't meant to hear, you have to bring it right in and contain it. You could whisper it, which you couldn't possibly do in a big house.

And which do you prefer?

Lisa Harrow: *Well, obviously I prefer the latter. But mostly we have to do the former.*

I think most actors would say the same thing. I realize that I seem to be coming down rather strongly on the side of cool Shakespeare. If so, it's not because I'm fighting shy of the emotions, but because I believe that I'm talking about the way to make the scene or a character or a speech *more* moving. What I'm really saying is that Shakespeare's language should be made to work on an audience as powerfully as an actor's emotions can. A heightened, poetic text has the power to do that, but the playing of emotions can sometimes strangulate that power. That at least is my experience. I don't for a moment mean that the actor shouldn't have emotions, but that they need to be channeled and controlled like the rest of his performance. I suppose that Hamlet is the supreme example in Shakespeare of a part which continually contains a mixture of passionate feeling and intense intellectual thought at the same time.

HAMLET (*Michael Pennington*): How all occasions do inform against me,
And spur my dull revenge! What is a man,
If his chief good and market of his time
Be but to sleep and feed? A beast, no more.
Sure He that made us with such large discourse,
Looking before and after, gave us not

That capability and godlike reason
To fust in us unused. Now, whether it be
Bestial oblivion, or some craven scruple
Of thinking too precisely on th'event—
A thought which, quartered, hath but one part wisdom
And ever three parts coward—I do not know
Why yet I live to say, "This thing's to do,"
Sith I have cause, and will, and strength, and means
To do't.   *Hamlet: IV.4.*

Michael Pennington: *This speech always seems to me like somebody going down for the third time. It comes at a point where Hamlet's life seems to have spun more than ever out of his control. After a bewildering series of catastrophes, he's become an exile and a murderer, but of the wrong man. The borderline between his assumed madness and his real disturbance has become very, very thin indeed. It seems to me he is trying here in one final attempt to assert his capability and godlike reason. He is trying to understand the volcanic emotions that he feels. He is hanging on by his fingers' ends, and Hamlet's fingers' ends are his exceptional ability to rationalize and reflect on his emotions.*

You could say that saves his reason, though it ultimately destroys his life. But he comes up against a sort of blank wall which is expressed in these four extraordinary lines of monosyllables: "I do not know/Why yet I live to say 'This thing's to do',/Sith I have cause, and will, and strength, and means/To do't." They are like a banner-headline that comes blazing off the script at an actor as he scans the text for clues.

What is very interesting indeed is the actor's need to control the flood tide of emotion and to discipline it mentally and technically. The means is the language through which, and only through which, that emotion can be fed. That is the essential eye of the needle. It coincides in a very peculiar way with the character's need to understand and rationalize his emotions. So that not for the first or last time in the play, the borderlines between the actor of Hamlet and the character of Hamlet begin to coincide, and a truly theatrical metaphor is set up.

And the borderline between passion and coolness, our theme this evening: the two are intense and locked together here, aren't they?

Michael Pennington: *Yes. A lot of the language in the play is terrifically wrought and elaborate. And it is possible through an excess of feeling to distort that language instead of working through it.*

Let's end by taking a passage without any further comment from myself. We can't do it full justice here because it's much cut and it needs the theater. Yet to me at any rate it is one of the most moving things in the canon. All the characters are full of passion but notice how practical the lines are as well. I want it to move you as it always moves me. I always weep when Shakespeare handles the theme of a lost thing found.

And at the end of *The Winter's Tale*, King Leontes thinks that he's killed his wife Hermione, and for fifteen years he's been grieving for her. But she's actually still alive, and at the end of the play Paulina presents her to him as if she were a dead statue. A fairy-tale situation. A thing full of wonder.

(*Lisa Harrow stands for Hermione, and Patrick Stewart as Leontes and Sheila Hancock as Paulina look at her.*)

PAULINA: I like your silence: it the more shows off
Your wonder. But yet speak: first you, my liege.
Comes it not something near?

LEONTES: Her natural posture!
Chide me, dear stone, that I may say indeed
Thou art Hermione; . . .
                                                   O thus she stood
Even with such life of majesty—warm life,
As it now coldly stands—when first I wooed her!
I am ashamed! Does not the stone rebuke me
For being more stone than it? . . .
Would I were dead, but that methinks already . . .
Would you not deem it breathed? and that those veins
Did verily bear blood? . . .
The fixture of her eye has motion in't,

As we are mocked with art.

PAULINA: I'll draw the curtain . . .
He'll think anon it lives.

LEONTES: O sweet Paulina,
Make me to think so twenty years together! . . .

PAULINA: I could afflict you farther.

LEONTES: Do, Paulina:
For this affliction has a taste as sweet
As any cordial comfort. Still methinks
There is an air comes from her. What fine chisel
Could ever yet cut breath? Let no man mock me,
For I will kiss her.

PAULINA: Good my lord, forbear.
You'll mar it if you kiss it; . . .

                              Shall I draw the curtain?

LEONTES: No, not these twenty years . . .

PAULINA: Either forbear,
Quit presently the chapel, or resolve you
For more amazement. If you can behold it,
I'll make the statue move indeed, descend
And take you by the hand: . . .

LEONTES: What you can make her do
I am content to look on; what to speak
I am content to hear: for 'tis as easy
To make her speak as move.

PAULINA: It is required
You do awake your faith. Then all stand still;
Or those that think it is unlawful business
I am about, let them depart.

LEONTES: Proceed.
No foot shall stir.

PAULINA: Music awake her, strike!

(*Music begins and continues till the end.*)

'Tis time: descend; be stone no more; approach;
Strike all that look upon with marvel. Come,

I'll fill your grave up. Stir; nay come away.
Bequeath to death your numbness, for from him
Dear life redeems you.

(*The statue moves and descends; she weeps.*)

                    You perceive she stirs.
Start not: her actions shall be holy as
You hear my spell is lawful. Do not shun her,
Lest she die again . . .
                    Present your hand.
When she was young you wooed her: now, in age,
Is she become the suitor?
(*Leontes and Hermione touch hands.*)
LEONTES: O, she's warm!
(*They embrace.*)   *The Winter's Tale: V.3.*

CHAPTER NINE

Rehearsing the Text

Orsino and Viola

[The following actors took part in the program that
forms the basis of this chapter: JUDI DENCH, RICHARD PASCO,
NORMAN RODWAY, MICHAEL WILLIAMS.]

*S*o far we've looked at lots of little bits of Shakespeare's text. In this
session we're going to look at a whole scene and we will work on it
as if we were actually rehearsing the play. Lots of the points we've
talked about already will come up again because I want to explore
the way the verse works in dialogue, and in particular the way it
often illuminates the relationship of the characters. Of course if we
were rehearsing the play in full, there would be lots of rehearsals
where the text wasn't talked about except in passing. Much more
time would be spent on the relationships of the characters and on the
staging. But I want to stick here to the basic theme of "Playing
Shakespeare." What hints and help are there in Shakespeare's text,
and particularly in his *verse,* for the actors to use and seize upon?

I'm going to be very selective in what I say. An experiment. I'm
going to try not to say anything about the situation and the characters that cannot be directly deduced from the verse. That's not the
way we would normally rehearse and it may well be that I will load
the actors with too much textual detail. Too much of that is as bad as
too little. But I want to show tonight how many clues there are in the
text. If an actor reads those clues right, he will find that Shakespeare
himself begins to talk to him.

We will take a scene from *Twelfth Night* between Orsino and
Viola. She's disguised as a boy and she's in love with him but he
doesn't know this. She's acting as his servant and messenger. Let's
start the scene off from the top.

ORSINO (*Richard Pasco*): Give me some music! Now, good morrow,
friends!
Now, good Cesario, but that piece of song,
That old and antique song we heard last night.
Methought it did relieve my passion much, . . .
Come, but one verse.
CURIO (*Michael Williams*): He is not here, so please your lordship, that
should sing it.
ORSINO: Who was it?
CURIO: Feste the jester, my lord, a fool that the Lady Olivia's father took
much delight in. He is about the house.
ORSINO: Seek him out, and play the tune the while.

Twelfth Night: II.4.

The beginning is pretty straightforward and we don't need to stop on
it very long. I only want to make one point about the verse. We've
said earlier how Shakespeare gets extra stress by putting a word in
the off-beat position in the verse line, so that the rhythm goes,
"dum-dum" instead of "de-dum." And here Orsino has two or three
such lines to kick the scene off. Dickie, when you say, "Give me
some music," I think you could use it to launch yourself more. You
can do it again with the next line, "Now, good Cesario." And again
with "Come, but one verse." Those three extra stresses at the beginning of the three lines say something about your eagerness and your
energy at the beginning of the scene. You're going to become more
mellow later. But there's one textual hint about the ruminative
nature of Orsino which is worth noting here: "that old and antique
song." You love and indulge in old, antique and ancient songs.

(*They take the passage again.*)

Before we go on to the next bit, let's look at one or two things in the
verse. Look at the clues behind the extra stresses again. In the second
line the phrase "In the sweet pangs" goes "de de dum dum." "Sweet"
is in an offbeat contrapuntal position and has extra stress because of
it. And of course the contrast and clash between "sweet" and
"pangs" needs bringing out because it tells us about Orsino. Love is
sweet to him and he is in pain, but he loves it.

Richard Pasco: *I'm in love with love, right?*

Yes, in love with love. And then at the end of the speech you have a very simple monosyllabic sentence, "How dost thou like this tune?" If you say it as casually as I've just said it, it will go for nothing. But if you give each of the words a stress, as you always should tend to do with a monosyllabic line of Shakespeare's, it will take you into the depth of your love for music, and into your love for melancholy. So in "How dost thou like this tune" each word matters.

> ORSINO: Come hither, boy. If ever thou shalt love,
> In the sweet pangs of it, remember me.
> For such as I am, all true lovers are:
> Unstaid and skittish in all motions else,
> Save in the constant image of the creature
> That is beloved. How dost thou like this tune?
> VIOLA (*Judi Dench*): It gives a very echo to the seat
> Where love is throned.

Maybe we could indulge the love of melancholy even more there. You could have gone even further with the "sweet pangs," and even further with "How dost thou like this tune?" And maybe you should stretch the monosyllables in "For such as I am, all true lovers are." I thought you took that too naturalistically. Just think of those words: "For such as I am, all true lovers are:" "I am the best lover in the world." You are standing outside yourself and summing yourself up. There is self-love there, isn't there? So do it once again and indulge more.

> ORSINO: Come hither, boy. If ever thou shalt love,
> In the sweet pangs of it, remember me.
> For such as I am, all true lovers are:
> Unstaid and skittish in all motions else,
> Save in the constant image of the creature
> That is beloved. How dost thou like this tune?
> VIOLA: It gives a very echo to the seat
> Where love is throned.
> ORSINO: Thou dost speak masterly.
> My life upon't . . .

And spoken masterly, very good. But we've come now to what is probably the most important verse question in the scene. It's a question we've raised before but not for some time. What do you do when a new sentence or a new speech begins halfway through the line? Because you both share the verse-line, you've got to decide whether the cue should be picked up immediately or whether there's a pause. This scene is very rich in choices that way. Sometimes Shakespeare is hinting that you should pick up the cue. But sometimes, because he's written a short verse-line, he is suggesting that there's a pause somewhere. So we've got to look for those as well. There's a number of them coming up in the next few lines. So let's pick it up again from, "It gives a very echo to the seat." I would suggest that Viola's "Where love is throned" and your "Thou dost speak masterly" constitute one such shared verse-line. But why should you pick the cue up at once? Maybe the answer is because you're getting in tune with her. What do you think?

> Richard Pasco: *Well, she is speaking masterly. That's got to register, hasn't it? I mean, he is impressed when he hears something spoken as beautifully as that. And when this boy comes out with this extraordinary remark, it is riveting, isn't it?*

As ever I would stress that these questions about the verse are only questions, so maybe you're right. Or again maybe you do pick up the cue there at once and that the pause comes *after* the line. "'Where love is throned.' 'Thou dost speak masterly.'" Then a pause. At the end of the verse-line.

> ORSINO: How dost thou like this tune?
> VIOLA: It gives a very echo to the seat
> Where love is throned.
> ORSINO: Thou dost speak masterly.
>   (*Pause*)
> My life upon't, young though thou art, thine eye
> Hath stayed upon some favour that it loves.
> Hath it not, boy?
> VIOLA: A little, by your favour.
> ORSINO: What kind of woman is't?

> VIOLA: Of your complexion.
> ORSINO: She is not worth thee, then.

Richard Pasco: *There's another one there, isn't there? "Of your com-plexion."*

Yes, exactly. Judi did pick it up at once.

Judi Dench: *Can you make your own choice about it?*

Yes, you must. But first you've got to be aware that these things are happening in the text. Then you can choose. We've got two or three half-line cues all together here. "'Hath it not, boy?' 'A little, by your favour'" is one verse-line, and you did in fact pick it up, which seemed right. I also thought that pausing after "Thou dost speak masterly" did work better. Then there's another quick cue when Orsino says, "What kind of woman is't?" and Viola answers "Of your complexion."

Maybe you do pause there and maybe you don't, but first it is good to ask the question. Let's do the next bit.

> ORSINO: How dost thou like this tune?
> VIOLA: It gives a very echo to the seat
> Where love is throned.
>   (*Quick cue.*)
> ORSINO: Thou dost speak masterly.
>   (*Pause.*)
> My life upon't, young though thou art, thine eye
> Hath stayed upon some favour that it loves.
> Hath it not, boy?
>   (*Quick cue.*)
> VIOLA: A little, by your favour.
> ORSINO: What kind of woman is't?
>   (*Quick cue.*)
> VIOLA: Of your complexion.
> ORSINO: She is not worth thee, then. What years, i'faith?
>   (*Pause.*)

VIOLA: About your years, my lord.
ORSINO: Too old, by heaven.

When Orsino says, "She is not worth thee then. What years, i'faith?" and you have a *short* verse line, "About your years, my lord," Shakespeare has actually built a pause into the verse there, because it's a short line of six syllables. It's as if there's a pause of four missing beats. What we have to decide is whether that pause comes before or after the line. Which do you think would be best?

> Judi Dench: *I would imagine that it should be before. Orsino has to take in what I've said and it's such a wonderful payoff for him to say, "Too old, by heaven."*

I agree. What I think Shakespeare is doing here is *earning* the pauses for the actors. If you pick up the preceding half-line cues as they're written, then the pause when it comes will be the stronger. But if you make lots of little individual pauses, then the whole scene will go naturalistic and the drive and rhythm of the verse will disappear.

> Richard Pasco: *Can I just be quite sure that I've got the actual lines? "'Hath it not, boy?'/'A little, by your favour,'" end of line./"What kind of woman is't?"*

> Judi Dench: *"Of your complexion."*

End of line.

> Richard Pasco: *"She is not worth thee, then. What years, i'faith?"*

End of line. Pause coming up.

> Judi Dench: *"About your years, my lord."*

There it is. The short verse-line.

> Richard Pasco: *"Too old, by heaven."*

The reason for the pause is pretty clear, isn't it? It's a very important moment for Viola. She doesn't quite know what to say to Orsino. Let's run that section again.

Do you think that worked?

Richard Pasco: *No, not quite. "She is not worth thee, then." I don't think I gave time for that.*

Judi Dench: *I feel I want to pause before "Of your complexion." Because she's caught out there, isn't she?*

There's always a third option about a pause. You can, as it were, pause *within* the words. When you say, "Of your complexion," you could pick up the cue at once but then feel for the rest of the line: "Of . . . (*pause*) . . . your complexion."

Judi Dench: *Ah, lovely, yes. Terrific.*

Then you still follow Shakespeare's rhythm but you have your pause. You need to ask, does the pause come before the line? Does it come after the line? Or can it come in the middle of the line?

Judi Dench: *Or have you earned it?*

Or have you earned it? That's the most important point. But you certainly earned it there. Let's go on to the next bit.

ORSINO: What years, i'faith?
VIOLA: About your years, my lord.
ORSINO: Too old, by heaven. Let still the woman take
An elder than herself; so wears she to him;
So sways she level in her husband's heart.
For, boy, however we do praise ourselves,
Our fancies are more giddy and unfirm,
More longing, wavering, sooner lost and worn,
Than women's are.
VIOLA: I think it well, my lord.

ORSINO: Then let thy love be younger than thyself,
Or thy affection cannot hold the bent.

Richard Pasco: *"Cannot hold the bent" means . . . ?*

Cannot last. Can't endure.

Richard Pasco: *Yes. Now that seemed all perfectly straightforward. Was it?*

Yes, the verse there *is* much more straightforward. Except that there's a little indication that Orsino's thoughts are teeming because he begins a sentence halfway through the verse-line. This is very often a hint by Shakespeare that the thoughts are tumbling out of the speaker. "Too old, by heaven. Let still the woman take." It's good to run that on because Orsino's mind is racing. The one thing you missed was that there's probably a bigger gear-change for Orsino halfway through the speech. After he's said "So sways she level in her husband's heart," you need time before you say, "For, boy, however we do praise ourselves/Our fancies are more giddy and unfirm." You make an important admission about yourself here and you tell the truth about your own self-indulgence as a lover.

Richard Pasco: *It's blokes' talk, isn't it?*

Yes. But if you let the first three lines of that speech pour out of you and then take time with "For, boy, however we do praise ourselves," you'll be able to stand outside yourself and to look at yourself sardonically.

ORSINO: What years, i'faith?
VIOLA: About your years, my lord.
ORSINO: Too old, by heaven. Let still the woman take
An elder than herself; so wears she to him;
So sways she level in her husband's heart.
                    (*Pause.*)
For, boy, however we do praise ourselves,

Our fancies are more giddy and unfirm,
More longing, wavering, sooner lost and worn,
Than women's are.
VIOLA: I think it well, my lord.
ORSINO: Then let thy love be younger than thyself,
Or thy affection cannot hold the bent.
For women are as roses whose fair flower,
Being once displayed, doth fall that very hour.
VIOLA: And so they are. Alas, that they are so,
To die, even when they to perfection grow.

Richard Pasco: *I was a bit self-indulgent there at the expense of the rhythm. Or had I earned it?*

I think you'd earned it. Let me raise a different verbal point here: the importance of verbs. We're good at coloring nouns and adjectives but sometimes the verbs are the active words in a line. For instance you said, "So wears she to him." But surely it's "So *wears* she to him"? And "So *sways* she level in her husband's heart." That's a good example of a sentence where the verbs are perhaps the most important words.

But what about the rhyming couplets at the end of this section? Orsino has one and Viola has one. Now we usually say that if there's a couplet the speaker knows that it's a couplet and consciously makes it one, because he wants or needs it. And here Orsino has to set up his couplet for Viola to answer him with hers. The conscious coining of Orsino's couplet is part of his self-dramatization and self-indulgence and her couplet brings it down to earth again. So Orsino needs to set his up for hers to pay off:

ORSINO: Then let thy love be younger than thyself,
Or thy affection cannot hold the bent.
For women are as roses whose fair flower,
Being once displayed, doth fall that very hour.
VIOLA: And so they are. Alas, that they are so,
To die, even when they to perfection grow.

What do you both think about the couplets? Are they a problem or are they good stuff?

Judi Dench: *It's lovely that this little passage between them ends like that. It doesn't end on a major note, but it just kind of fades away. The two couplets round the scene off before the next bit.*

That's right. I reckon if you give full weight to those couplets, you do round off the scene and earn a pause before Feste and Curio come on.

Judi Dench: *I think I should have made it jokier earlier on.*

Yes. I think that there should be a greater element of humor in both of you in this situation. Viola has a certain wry humor because she is dressed as a boy, and Orsino has the ability, however indulgent he may be, to mock himself as a lover. Especially when he admits to the boy that his fancies are wavering and inconstant.

Richard Pasco: *But it's very sad. This is a very sad reflection.*

Well, let's try taking it from "Too old, by heaven." That's got humor and self-mockery in it, hasn't it? And in "For, boy, however we do praise ourselves," there's surely wry humor there against yourself. Also in "Our fancies are more giddy and unfirm . . . /Than women's are." So admit to her: "I know I'm giddy and unfirm." Of course it's sad when you say "Women are as roses whose fair flower,/Being once displayed, doth fall that very hour." But maybe you shouldn't play the sadness so much. Maybe Orsino is just being callous and sexist about women there. If you go melancholy and mellow on it, then her lines won't break into your couplet. I think that's what Shakespeare's after here. The second couplet is meant to break in on the first. So if you say callously, "Women, they don't last," it's up to Judi to make the melancholy comment and to break into what you say.

ORSINO: What years, i'faith?
VIOLA: About your years, my lord.
ORSINO: Too old, by heaven. Let still the woman take
An elder than herself; so wears she to him;
So sways she level in her husband's heart.
For, boy, however we do praise ourselves,
Our fancies are more giddy and unfirm,

More longing, wavering, sooner lost and worn,
Than women's are.

VIOLA: I think it well, my lord.

ORSINO: Then let thy love be younger than thyself,
Or thy affection cannot hold the bent.
For women are as roses whose fair flower,
Being once displayed, doth fall that very hour.

VIOLA: And so they are. Alas, that they are so,
To die, even when they to perfection grow.

The text was beginning to work on itself. Words qualified words and one sentence qualified another. Viola's speech at the end broke into Orsino's so that the mood was changing all the time. And that's right. You are both talking about the inconstancy and shiftingness of love. So the text itself and the verse has to shift and change. If you play it too evenly you will get a generalized mood which will be boring. But if you play all the contrasts as they come, then there's riches for the audience to latch on to. Let's go on to Feste's arrival.

(Re-enter Curio with Feste.)

ORSINO: O, fellow, come, the song we had last night.
Mark it, Cesario, it is old and plain.
The spinsters, and the knitters in the sun,
And the free maids that weave their thread with bones,
Do use to chant it. It is silly sooth,
And dallies with the innocence of love
Like the old age.

FESTE (*Norman Rodway*): Are you ready, sir?

ORSINO: Ay, prithee sing.

I'd like to make two points about that bit. There's a wonderful example of a rich monosyllabic line here, "And the free maids that weave their thread with bones." If you let that line breathe, if you stretch the words, it will have extraordinary resonance. But if you just throw it off naturalistically and casually, it won't work. It's our old point that if you try and take a monosyllabic line fast you will turn it into a tongue-twister. See if you can find the textual relish and richness of the line by taking your time and envying the maids their innocence and their happiness. Two lines later you admit that you yourself have not got innocence. You say, "I'm sophisticated in love. I, Orsino, I am loveworn. I wish I had that innocence." And then there's another terrific example of a pause built into the text at the end of Orsino's speech. After he's said: "And dallies with the innocence of love,/Like the old age . . ."

> Norman Rodway: *Pause for Feste to decide whether he's finished or not.*

That's right, absolutely.

> Norman Rodway: *"Are you ready, sir?" means "Is it all right to start?"*

Yes, it's quite funny. Perhaps Shakespeare deliberately built in a bit of comedy by writing in a pause there after the short line "Like the old age."

But let me say one thing about the song. Its nature is of course described by Orsino himself: it is "old and plain." Country people sing it and it's about the innocence of love. So that partly tells us too what the song is like, and partly what you, Orsino, think it's like. But what does Feste think it's like? It's quite a long song and it has two verses. I've always felt that they were different from one another. Maybe in the first verse, Feste sings it straight . . . ,

> Norman Rodway: *And then he starts to mock him in the second verse.*

Yes. In the second one he starts to send up Orsino for his love indulgence. Shall we try that way? Mock him in any way you like.

> Richard Pasco: *I thought it might be a good idea if I sat on the floor with my back to him.*

> Norman Rodway: *Yes, if his face is away from me I have a chance to mock him behind his back. And perhaps play some of it off Viola.*

Absolutely. She can see that you're mocking him, but Orsino mustn't.

> ORSINO: O, fellow, come, the song we had last night.
> Mark it, Cesario; it is old and plain.
> The spinsters, and the knitters in the sun,
> And the free maids that weave their threads with bones,
> Do use to chant it. It is silly sooth,
> And dallies with the innocence of love
> Like the old age.

> *(Pause.)*

> FESTE: Are you ready, sir?
> ORSINO: Ay, prithee sing.
> FESTE: *(sings)*: Come away, come away, death
>   And in sad cypress let me be laid.
> Fie away, fie away, breath!
>   I am slain by a fair cruel maid.
> My shroud of white stuck all with yew,
>   O prepare it!
> My part of death, no one so true
>   Did share it.

> *(Mocking Orsino.)*

> Not a flower, not a flower sweet
>   On my black coffin let there be strewn.
> Not a friend, not a friend greet
>   My poor corpse, where my bones shall be thrown.
> A thousand, thousand sighs to save,
>   Lay me, O, where
> Sad true lover never find my grave
>   To weep there.

A word about songs. I always think they're a terrible trap in Shakespeare. It's so easy during an exquisite song for the action of the play to get becalmed and for the story to stop moving. I believe that a Shakespearean song or piece of music must always be treated as part of the action of a scene. I've often seen this scene done with a beautiful song that seemed totally extrinsic. So what does the song *do* here? Presumably, as it's Orsino's favorite song, he uses it to feed his love melancholy. But as it happens the song makes the disease worse.

Richard Pasco: *So it's tear-time for Orsino, isn't it? Almost.*

Well, it's going to lead him to breaking out in a minute. Something is about to snap inside him. He says to Viola quite suddenly, "Go back and see Olivia." It is as important that we should see the song working on Orsino as to hear the song sung by Feste. Because the scene is about Orsino's melancholy. So let's pick it up again from the end of the song.

ORSINO: There's for thy pains.

FESTE: No pains, sir. I take pleasure in singing, sir.

ORSINO: I'll pay thy pleasure, then.

FESTE: Truly, sir, and pleasure will be paid, one time or another.

ORSINO: Give me now leave, to leave thee.

FESTE: Now the melancholy god protect thee, . . . for thy mind is a very opal. I would have men of such constancy put to sea, that their business might be everything and their intent everywhere; for that's it that always makes a good voyage of nothing. Farewell.

There's nothing particularly complex textually there, and you rightly played the professional fool. But I think the text is perhaps a bit more loaded here than you made it. When you said "pleasure will be paid, one time or another" that's something you've learned out of life, so maybe you're trying to teach Orsino a lesson. Within the general flipness there's suddenly, as so often with Shakespeare's fools, a very serious remark. When you say, "the melancholy god protect thee, . . . for thy mind is a very opal," you are talking about the god he worships, the god of melancholy, and you are getting at him. And surely the payoff comes with "that's it that always makes a good voyage of nothing." Orsino's love and self-indulgence is *nothing*.

Richard Pasco: *Which builds the fires in Orsino.*

Norman Rodway: *"Put to sea" means to be as inconstant as the waves and winds, doesn't it?*

That's right. It's quite harsh. But I've often seen it done with Feste frolicsome here. Well, that's his public persona and maybe he is frolicsome on the surface. But underneath his thoughts are much darker. So do it again and try to disturb Orsino more.

> ORSINO: There's for thy pains.
> FESTE: No pains, sir. I take pleasure in singing, sir.
> ORSINO: I'll pay thy pleasure, then.
> FESTE: Truly, sir, and pleasure will be paid, one time or another.
> ORSINO: Give me now leave, to leave thee.
> FESTE: Now the melancholy god protect thee, . . . for thy mind is a very opal. I would have men of such constancy put to sea, that their business might be everything and their intent everywhere; for that's it that always makes a good voyage of nothing. Farewell. (*Exeunt Feste ad Curio*)
> ORSINO: Let all the rest give place. Once more, Cesario,
> Get thee to yond same sovereign cruelty.
> Tell her my love, more noble than the world,
> Prizes not quantity of dirty lands.
> The parts that fortune hath bestowed upon her
> Tell her I hold as giddily as fortune.

We must look now at how the verse helps to put Orsino into orbit for the next section. Orsino has the verse-line, "Let all the rest give place. Once more, Cesario." Now sometimes editors print that as two lines, but I'm sure it's meant to be one verse-line, and that Orsino shouldn't wait for the exit before speaking to Cesario. Feste has built the pressure up, and so Orsino says, "Right, everybody get out, Cesario, come on." From this moment on Orsino's impatience to reach out to Olivia drives him, and so the tempo of the scene changes in the rhythm of the verse. In the speech you've just done, our point about contrapuntal stresses comes up again. The extra stresses are at the beginning of the verse-lines, and this always gives an extra bite to what the speaker is saying. "Get thee," "Tell her,"

"Prizes not," "Tell her I hold as giddily as fortune": four lines beginning with an extra stress. Orsino throws off the reflective mood he has been in throughout the scene and so the rhythm changes totally.

> Norman Rodway: *So in fact Feste's song has had the reverse effect to what Orsino anticipated while he was sitting there.*

That's right.

> FESTE: . . . For that's it that always makes a good voyage of nothing.
> Farewell. (*Exeunt Feste and Curio.*)
> ORSINO: Let all the rest give place. Once more, Cesario,
> Get thee to yond same sovereign cruelty.
> Tell her my love, more noble than the world,
> Prizes not quantity of dirty lands.
> The parts that fortune hath bestowed upon her
> Tell her I hold as giddily as fortune . . .
> VIOLA: But if she cannot love you, sir?
> ORSINO: It cannot be so answered.
> VIOLA: Sooth, but you must.
> Say that some lady, as perhaps there is,
> Hath for your love as great a pang of heart
> As you have for Olivia. You cannot love her.
> You tell her so. Must she not then be answered?
> ORSINO: There is no woman's sides
> Can bide the beating of so strong a passion
> As love doth give my heart; . . . Make no compare
> Between that love a woman can bear me
> And that I owe Olivia.
> VIOLA: Ay, but I know—
> ORSINO: What dost thou know?

I think that the pressure does continue like that between the two of them right up to "What dost thou know?" There's another splendid example there of a quick cue and then a pause being suggested by the way the verse is set out. "'And that I owe Olivia.' 'Ay, but I know'" is set out as one verse-line and obviously Viola interrupts here. But the words which follow, "What dost thou know?" have a verse-line all to themselves, so a pause seems clearly indicated. Once again we have two choices, either to pause before or after the line. If it's a pause before the word it's because Viola herself stops and pulls herself up as soon as she's burst out with, "Ay, but I know." Or else Orsino says the line at once and Viola has to compose herself before answering him. I suspect it's probably the latter.

I think there is only one other possible pause in this section. When Orsino has another short verse line, "There is no woman's sides," what does that suggest to you? Viola says "Must she not then be answered?" and then comes Orsino's line "There is no woman's sides . . ."

> Richard Pasco: *"There is no woman's sides/Can bide the beating of so strong a passion/As love doth give my heart." It's all one sentence, isn't it?*

But what about the short verse-line? Maybe there's a pause *before* "There is no woman's sides," because she's scored. She's said something that's stopped Orsino in his tracks for a moment. Maybe that's the one pause in the section. The short verse-line seems to suggest it.

> Judi Dench: *Can I put a pause before "Say that some lady"? It's as if she takes the decision to open a tiny door there. Is that allowable?*

Yes, you certainly need a pause there, and a pause is always allowable. I'm not against pauses, I love them. All I'm saying is that whereas in our modern work we put in pauses wherever we want them, if we start doing that too much in Shakespeare something will begin to go wrong. You have to earn each one and question each one. If you then feel it's right, go ahead. Pick it up again from "Say that some lady."

> VIOLA: Say that some lady, as perhaps there is,
> Hath for your love as great a pang of heart
> As you have for Olivia. You cannot love her.
> You tell her so. Must she not then be answered?

ORSINO: There is no woman's sides (*Pause.*)
Can bide the beating of so strong a passion
As love doth give my heart; . . . Make no compare
Between that love a woman can bear me
And that I owe Olivia.
VIOLA: Ay, but I know—
ORSINO: What dost thou know? (*Pause.*)
VIOLA: Too well what love women to men may owe.
In faith, they are as true of heart as we.
My father had a daughter loved a man—
As it might be perhaps, were I a woman,
I should your lordship.
ORSINO: And what's her history?
VIOLA: A blank, my lord. She never told her love,
But let concealment, like a worm i'the bud,
Feed on her damask cheek . . .

I want to make one point about what follows. Viola is talking about her love-pain, yet part of her still sees the ridiculous side of it, the funny-sad side. Maybe, Judi, you need to go a bit more for that. Being dressed as a boy and yet having this conversation with the person you love. Maybe the idea of sitting "like Patience on a monument" is a funny idea as well as a touching one. I don't mean you don't have the pain, but very often Shakespeare's heroines do have a rueful humor when they are sad.

ORSINO: And what's her history?
VIOLA: A blank, my lord. She never told her love,
But let concealment, like a worm i'the bud,
Feed on her damask cheek. She pined in thought,
And with a green and yellow melancholy,
She sat like Patience on a monument,
Smiling at grief. Was not this love indeed?
We men say more, swear more, but indeed
Our shows are more than will; for still we prove
Much in our vows, but little in our love.
ORSINO: But died thy sister of her love, my boy?

VIOLA: I am all the daughters of my father's house,
And all the brothers too; and yet I know not.
Sir, shall I to this lady?
ORSINO: Ay, that's the theme.
To her in haste; give her this jewel; say
My love can give no place, bide no denay.

The only thing I want to point out about the verse at the end of the scene is how it breaks the mood again. Viola rightly snapped out of it with "Shall I to this lady?" The verse asks Orsino to pick up the cue: "Ay, that's the theme." No pause for Orsino there: he breaks the mood and rounds the whole thing off with a vigorous couplet. End of scene, couplet, let's go.

Richard Pasco: *Is there the slightest sense from Orsino that the boy is not all he pretends to be?*

I think Orsino realizes there's something very strange about him, although he doesn't recognize he's not a boy. I'm sure it's right to sense something and play it at that moment.

Richard Pasco: *Yes, that's why I paused. Is a pause justified there because of that thought?*

Yes, I think it's justified if you then brush it away and pick up the scene again.

Having done it in little bits we ought to run the whole scene and see what we retain of the points that have come up. Let's go especially for the violent jagged gear-changes in the text. And as a healthy stage of rehearsal let's overdo them and try to go too far.

ORSINO: Give me some music! Now, good morrow, friends!
Now, good Cesario, but that piece of song,
That old and antique song we heard last night.
Methought it did relieve my passion much, ...
Come, but one verse.
CURIO: He is not here, so please your lordship, that should sing it.
ORSINO: Who was it?

CURIO: Feste the jester, my lord, a fool that the Lady Olivia's father took much delight in. He is about the house.

ORSINO: Seek him out, and play the tune the while.

(*Music plays.*)

ORSINO: Come hither, boy. If ever thou shalt love,
In the sweet pangs of it, remember me.
For such as I am, all true lovers are:
Unstaid and skittish in all motions else,
Save in the constant image of the creature
That is beloved. How dost thou like this tune?

VIOLA: It gives a very echo to the seat
Where love is throned.

ORSINO:　　　　　Thou dost speak masterly. } (*Quick cue.*)
My life upon't, young though thou art, thine eye
Hath stayed upon some favour that it loves.
Hath it not, boy?

VIOLA:　　　　A little, by your favour. } (*Quick cue.*)

ORSINO: What kind of woman is't?

VIOLA:　　　　　Of your complexion. } (*Quick cue.*)

ORSINO: She is not worth thee, then. What years, i'faith?

VIOLA: About your years, my lord. (*Pause.*)

ORSINO: Too old, by heaven. Let still the woman take
An elder than herself; so wears she to him;
So sways she level in her husband's heart.
For, boy, however we do praise ourselves,
Our fancies are more giddy and unfirm,
More longing, wavering, sooner lost and worn,
Than women's are.

VIOLA:　　　　I think it well, my lord. } (*Quick cue.*)

ORSINO: Then let thy love be younger than thyself,
Or thy affection cannot hold the bent.
For women are as roses whose fair flower,
Being once displayed, doth fall that very hour.

VIOLA: And so they are. Alas, that they are so,
To die, even when they to perfection grow.

(*Enter Curio and Feste.*)

ORSINO: O, fellow, come, the song we had last night.
Mark it, Cesario; it is old and plain.

The spinsters, and the knitters in the sun,
And the free maids that weave their thread with bones,
Do use to chant it. It is silly sooth,
And dallies with the innocence of love
Like the old age.
FESTE: Are you ready, sir?
ORSINO: Ay, prithee sing.

FESTE (*sings*): Come away, come away, death
    And in sad cypress let me be laid.
Fie away, fie away, breath!
    I am slain by a fair cruel maid.
My shroud of white, stuck all with yew,
    O, prepare it!
My part of death, no one so true
    Did share it.

Not a flower, not a flower sweet
    On my black coffin let there be strewn.
Not a friend, not a friend greet
    My poor corpse, where my bones shall be thrown.
A thousand, thousand sighs to save,
    Lay me, O, where
Sad true lover never find my grave
    To weep there.

ORSINO: There's for thy pains.
                    (*He gives Feste money.*)
FESTE: No pains, sir. I take pleasure in singing, sir.
ORSINO: I'll pay thy pleasure, then.
FESTE: Truly, sir, and pleasure will be paid, one time or another.
ORSINO: Give me now leave, to leave thee.
FESTE: Now the melancholy god protect thee, . . . for thy mind is a very opal. I would have men of such constancy put to sea, that their business might be everything and their intent everywhere; for that's it that always makes a good voyage of nothing. Farewell.
                    (*Exeunt Feste and Curio.*)

ORSINO: Let all the rest give place. Once more, Cesario,
Get thee to yond same sovereign cruelty.
Tell her my love, more noble than the world,
Prizes not quantity of dirty lands.
The parts that fortune hath bestowed upon her
Tell her I hold as giddily as fortune . . . (*Pause*.)
VIOLA: But if she cannot love you, sir?
ORSINO: It cannot be so answered.
VIOLA: Sooth, but you must. }(*Quick cue.*)
Say that some lady, as perhaps there is,
Hath for your love as great a pang of heart
As you have for Olivia. You cannot love her.
You tell her so. Must she not then be answered? (*Pause*.)
ORSINO: There is no woman's sides
Can bide the beating of so strong a passion
As love doth give my heart; . . . Make no compare
Between that love a woman can bear me
And that I owe Olivia.
VIOLA: Ay, but I know— }(*Quick cue.*)
ORSINO: What dost thou know? (*Pause*.)
VIOLA: Too well what love women to men may owe.
In faith, they are as true of heart as we.
My father had a daughter loved a man—
As it might be perhaps, were I a woman,
I should your lordship.
ORSINO: And what's her history? }(*Quick cue.*)
VIOLA: A blank, my lord. She never told her love,
But let concealment, like a worm i'the bud,
Feed on her damask cheek. She pined in thought,
And with a green and yellow melancholy,
She sat like Patience on a monument,
Smiling at grief. Was not this love indeed?
We men say more, swear more, but indeed
Our shows are more than will; for still we prove
Much in our vows, but little in our love.
ORSINO: But died thy sister of her love, my boy?
VIOLA: I am all the daughters of my father's house,

And all the brothers too; and yet, I know not . . .
Sir, shall I to this lady?
ORSINO: Ay, that's the theme. }(*Quick cue.*)
To her in haste; give her this jewel; say
My love can give no place, bide no denay.

Good, I think you took that beautifully. It was a good rehearsal. I know I probably gave you too many textual points to digest all at once. So I must stress that what we've worked on is only one aspect of the business of "Playing Shakespeare." I've been hammering at the verse because I am eager to show how much it is worth our attention. But I don't want to be taken as saying that I am laying down the rules or that an actor should follow the verse slavishly, only that he needs to be aware of what goes on in the verse so that he finds out how it can help him.

Well, we've dug into the material and we've moved the scene on a bit in a particular way, but of course we haven't been trying to find a definitive solution. Just one possibility. With Shakespeare there are always a limitless number of possibilities and different ones come up at each rehearsal. So what have we been trying to prove? Simply that the clues in the text are much richer and more numerous than at first appears. And though the possibilities are infinite, we can only sift the fruitful from the perverse by getting our teeth into the text and the verse itself. If the textual points are ignored, then it's pretty certain that Shakespeare's intentions will be ignored also or at least twisted. Something else will be put in their place, valid in itself but nonetheless a distortion. I'm not trying to knock that kind of work. It can be rich and exciting in its own right. But if it ignores the verse it leads to an alternative to and not a realization of Shakespeare. Shakespeare *is* his text. So if you want to do him justice, you have to look for and follow the clues he offers. If an actor does that then he'll find that Shakespeare himself starts to direct him.

‐‒ ‒‐

CHAPTER TEN

Exploring a Character

Playing Shylock

[The following actors took part in the program which forms the basis of this chapter: DAVID SUCHET, PATRICK STEWART.]

We're now going to try something we've not attempted so far. Because we've been looking at so many fragments we've said relatively little about character in our series. That has been because the way an actor approaches character in Shakespeare is pretty well the same as it is with other playwrights. But to restore the balance we're going to look in detail in this session at one of Shakespeare's most famous parts. *The Merchant of Venice* is perhaps the play that today is most argued about. Many people feel it's deeply anti-Semitic and ought not to be performed. Others react the other way and say that, if you read the text aright, Shylock the Jew is intended by Shakespeare to be a sympathetic and even a heroic character. It's often played that way, so you can take your choice. I have directed the play at different times with Patrick Stewart and with David Suchet. Each of them played Shylock though neither of them saw the other in the part. So we should all declare at the outset what we believe Shakespeare means us to feel about the character. We believe that he shows Shylock as a bad Jew and a bad human being, but that this in itself does not make the play anti-Semitic. If we thought it was so we would not have done it. Anti-Semitism is certainly expressed in the

‐‒ ‐‒ ‐‒ ‐‒ ‐‒ ‐‒ ‐‒ ‐‒ ‐‒ ‐‒ ‐‒ ‐‒ ‐‒ ‐‒ ‐‒ ‐‒ ‐‒

Note: This is the program which probably suffers most from being merely set in print. On television the heart of it lay in the extraordinary contrast between the two Shylocks. I much regret that the printed word cannot capture that but I have still thought the following text worth including here because of the discussions of the character.

play by some of the characters, but of course that doesn't mean that Shakespeare himself approves of what they're saying. There are two other Jews in the play, Shylock's daughter, Jessica, and Tubal; Shakespeare doesn't take an anti-Semitic view of them. But Shylock is a would-be murderer, who refuses to show any mercy to Antonio, the merchant and his intended victim. Those who try to justify Shylock have to work very hard to get round that, though they usually feel that they can do so.

It's interesting that in Israel they don't seem to have many scruples about the supposed anti-Semitism. There have been quite a number of productions of the play there since the war. However, we're not here to talk about anti-Semitism but about character. I only stress it here because I know many people feel very strongly about it. The whole problem really springs from Shakespeare himself because he very rarely expresses his own views explicitly in a play. He shows us a bad Jew and some bad Christians and yet he doesn't directly articulate his view of these characters. He lets them betray themselves by their words and actions. That is Shakespeare's way. He rarely makes his characters all black any more than he makes them all white. Yet different critics or actors are apt to interpret the play accordingly. It's even been said that there are only two ways of playing Shylock, either as a goodie or a baddie. But, as I have urged already, if we are to read Shakespeare truly, we must look for the deliberate ambiguities and inconsistencies that he delights in. These inconsistencies *are* the character: flawed, contradictory, human. If I had to say to an actor one thing only about the part, I think I'd choose to say, Look for the ambiguities and the contradictions and play them. David, have you anything to add on the question of the anti-Semitism?

David Suchet: *Well, being Jewish myself, I'd love to get it out of the way. I remember when I was coming up to perform the role, I got letters from America questioning the very fact that I was doing it at all. You know: how dare I do Shylock? I think that we all have to be very very careful not just to respond to the play in relation to the twentieth-century holocaust. That's unavoidable and there are bound to be people in the audience on every night who were either involved themselves or who knew someone who was, but I think we have to look at what the climate of the time was when Shakespeare actually wrote this play. Marlowe's Barabas in* The Jew of Malta, *for instance, is pretty heavy-going. He dies unrepentant and goes to Hell. Shylock and* The Merchant of Venice *in comparison to the literature around at the time were pretty mild, and Shylock himself is perhaps the first Jew in literature to have the chance of his soul being saved. I think that's important.*

You mean that in Elizabethan terms, Shakespeare was ahead of his day and brought out the Jew's humanity?

David Suchet: *Yes, I think one must forget modern anti-Semitism and concentrate on the play as writ.*

Patrick, what do you think?

Patrick Stewart: *I find myself totally in agreement with David. The anti-Semitism, or rather the alleged anti-Semitism of the play—we agreed it is not an anti-Semitic play—is a distraction. But I also believe that the Jewishness which is so often emphasized in* The Merchant *is equally a distraction. David is right to stress that in the second half of the twentieth century, the anti-Semitic expressions in the play are going to reverberate very powerfully. The director and the actor won't need to emphasize them as the reverberations will be present anyway. But you cannot avoid them and you cannot underplay them. I think however that to concentrate on Jewishness can lead to missing the great potential in the character which is its universality. I think that whenever I've seen a very ethnic, a very Jewish Shylock, I've felt that something's been missing. Shylock is essentially an alien, an outsider. I think if you see him as a Jew, first and foremost, then he's in danger of becoming only a symbol. Shylock is an outsider who happens to be a Jew.*

David Suchet: *I would challenge that. I would say that as Shylock I'm not an outsider who happens to be a Jew but because I'm a Jew. The Jewish element in the play is unavoidable and very important. This is probably where we differ in our interpretations. Shakespeare manages to ring a wonderful change in the way that Shylock, as the Jew, has first a business relationship and then a family relationship, and then is seen responding to his enemies and to his friends, and finally how he demonstrates the laws of the land in which he lives. Shakespeare never lets the audience or the other characters forget the Jewish thing. You only have to look at the trial scene where he's called "Shylock" only six times but "Jew" twenty-two.*

Well, there's an infinite number of possible interpretations, and each actor coming to play the part has to start afresh. So where does he begin? He'll probably begin by reacting against previous interpretations. He will be bound to ask two crucial questions. "What does Shylock look like?" and "How does he talk?"

Patrick Stewart: *I should state here that when the part was originally offered to me, my inclination was to refuse it. It seemed to me that the role was eternally stuck in a kind of tradition or ritual. I feared that if I were to play Shylock, then it would necessarily mean ringlets, a hooked nose, and long, exotic, perhaps semi-oriental gowns, either shabby or decorative to taste. I thought that there was so much traditional appearance and traditional behavior attached to the role that I would never be able to free myself from it, and that I could never find a human being at the heart of that set exterior. But as I began to read the play something else began to unfold. I found that here was a highly complex and very modern creation. I decided therefore that I should avoid the easily recognizable symbolic elements of Jewishness, the ringlets, the gown, the nose and so on. I should add, though, that I had a very large bushy beard and a lot of long, dirty, tangly hair. I wore a shabby, dirty, broken-down frock coat, because I think that the most important thing for Shylock in the play is money, possessions and finance. I thought that if he was obsessed with money he would not waste it on how he appeared. So I made an attempt to make my Shylock very shabby and down-at-heel.*

As for the voice, one thing influenced me. Shylock is living in an alien culture. I think that for an outsider to survive there it's necessary for him to assimilate himself into that culture. I therefore gave him an accent which was more cultured, more refined and more native than the natives. And much more so than the aristocrats in the play. You see, I think that what is truly strange and exotic in Shylock is his foreignness. *And this lies in his language, not in how he appears. No one in* The Merchant of Venice *speaks like Shylock, not even his fellow Jew, Tubal.*

And what about you, David?

David Suchet: *I chose everything in opposition to that. I also discovered, as you did, that there is a certain strange rhythm to the language which I went with to the extent of giving him a very slight accent. But I didn't place this accent in any particular area. I just wanted to make it foreign because his language was somehow foreign. I felt that was important. I also never wanted anybody to forget that I was an outsider. I felt that Shylock would not have tried to alter his accent because he, or rather I, my Shylock, was very proud of his Jewishness. Why should he hide it? Why not exploit it if necessary? Which I think he does in the first scene.*

Patrick Stewart: *Isn't that dangerous? Exploiting it?*

David Suchet: *No, I don't think so, because it's recognizable human behavior. But about his motivation and the money, I agree absolutely. He kept asking "What news on the Rialto?" His thoughts are all on the Stock Exchange and banking and money. As for his dress, I think that he would dress according to the status that he believes he has.*

As we rehearsed I found both those images totally acceptable and, more importantly, totally consistent with the text. Both worked completely in performance. But we should start now to look at the play itself. So what about this famous part that's only got five scenes?

Patrick Stewart: *It's extraordinary, isn't it? It's one of the four or five best-known roles in Shakespeare. Someone who knows nothing about the play whatever will recognize the name Shylock; yet he appears relatively briefly. Five scenes, and one is only a fragment and very short. Although of course for a time there was a tradition of playing a sixth scene, a scene which we never played. Did you?*

David Suchet: *No.*

Patrick Stewart: *I always called it "Shylock's Return." It's the scene after Jessica has absconded from the house with the jewels and with her lover. There was a tradition, particularly in the nineteenth century, of Shylock coming back to his house and finding it deserted.*

Irving had what sounds to me a wonderful return. A large elaborate set: Venice, the Jewish quarter of Venice, partygoers and merrymakers passing over the bridge, sounds of jollity disappearing into the distance, and Irving came slowly over the top of the bridge and walked down to the front of the house and knocked on the door.

Herbert Beerbohm Tree had quite a different approach. He came back, found the door ajar, howled and rushed inside. He had a whole set of his house with different windows and appeared at window after window, throwing them ajar, screaming and shouting for his gold and his ducats, and tearing his clothes. Finally he rushed back out onto the stage, ripped his clothes off and covered himself in ashes.

Yes, I've seen something rather like that done many years ago. But that's the missing scene. What we've got to look at now are the scenes that are actually there.

Patrick Stewart: *They are all different. Did you find that? Each scene has its own characteristic.*

David Suchet: *Yes. Did you have any clear view about what motivated Shylock? I mean, they're all different, those scenes, aren't they?*

Patrick Stewart: *Yes, as I've already said, I found one dominant motivation, one dominant objective for the whole play: money, finance and possessions. Whenever Shylock is given a choice between race and religion on the one hand, and financial security, commerce and business on the other, he always makes the commercial choice. There are scores of examples. "I hate him for he is a Christian;/But more, for that in low simplicity/He lends out money gratis." "He hath disgraced me": yes, he's disgraced his Jewishness, "and hindered me half a million." He always ends his self-explanations by stressing the commercial motive. "Why there, there, there" he says when his daughter has been taken away from him, "A diamond gone." Not a daughter gone, but a diamond. So that was my dominant motivation. But of course it was necessary to isolate the quality and the motivation in each scene.*

David Suchet: *It's a terrifying thing studying such a famous part because of the history of how it's been played. Mostly black, as you say, or white. I was desperate to try to look at that play without preconceptions and to look into each scene for exactly what it was, for what it said to me, and to play that. Also to play the inconsistencies throughout the role, and to see what happened if I just went with each scene without overlaying them with something that I had worked out before.*

Patrick Stewart: *Terrific. With the belief that, if you played all the inconsistencies, when the final inconsistency slotted into place like a piece of a jigsaw puzzle, then you would no longer have an inconsistency but a complete and wonderfully colorful and complex whole.*

David Suchet: *Yes, it was as though little doors began to open throughout.*

Patrick Stewart: *Instead of getting all the consistencies, putting them in a pot, stirring them up, making a blend of them and playing the blend, from the beginning to the end . . .*

David Suchet: *That gives you nowhere to go.*

Well, let's get on our feet now and look at some of the key moments. Scene One, the Rialto. Shylock meets the merchant Antonio. Let's have a go at it both ways. One of you do your Shylock and the other do Antonio, and then we'll reverse it and see how the differences work out.

(*Patrick Stewart takes the text, followed by David Suchet.*)

SHYLOCK: Signor Antonio, many a time and oft
In the Rialto you have rated me
About my moneys and my usances.
Still have I borne it with a patient shrug,
For sufferance is the badge of all our tribe.
You call me misbeliever, cut-throat dog,
And spit upon my Jewish gaberdine,
And all for use of that which is mine own.
Well then, it now appears you need my help.
Go to then. You come to me and you say,
'Shylock, we would have moneys,' you say so,
You, that did void your rheum upon my beard
And foot me as you spurn a stranger cur
Over your threshold, moneys is your suit
What should I say to you? Should I not say,
'Hath a dog money? Is it possible
A cur can lend three thousand ducats?' Or
Shall I bend low, and in a bondman's key,
With bated breath and whispering humbleness,
Say this:
'Fair sir, you spat on me on Wednesday last,
You spurned me such a day, another time
You called me dog, and for these courtesies
I'll lend you thus much moneys'?   *The Merchant of Venice: I.3.*

Good. That revealed the differences between Patrick and David very clearly. Patrick was ingratiating and cringing, while David stood on his dignity. Both however had one thing in common: a great deal of humor. I think that is an essential quality in the part which we would all agree on. Let's move on now and talk a bit about the next scene in Shylock's house: Shylock with his daughter Jessica.

Patrick Stewart: *I have to confess that whenever this scene ended, I always felt that the substance of the play was over for me. It was the scene that consistently gave me the greatest satisfaction. It differs in one important way from every other scene in the play. It is Shylock's only private scene. He is not on show. For me the fact that in the other four scenes he was in the public eye meant that he was always under pressure to perform. To appear as some kind of personality. He's an actor, isn't he? But in this scene it is not necessary. He is at home, the one place where acting and performance are unnecessary and cannot be accepted. So it was the scene in which I wanted to show the real man, the true man that lay underneath those wonderful multicolored disguises. A man deeply unhappy and embittered, a man from whose life love had been removed. And therefore Jessica was a creature who could give him no love, nor could he return it. I found it a harsh, bitter, unhappy scene, and it lay at the very heart of the part for me. It was always a sad moment when we left it.*

David Suchet: *I was always so relieved when I left it. Every time when I got to this scene, both in rehearsal and performance, oh dear, I never found it. I never found the right way for me to play it. Patrick's absolutely right, Shylock is on his own. And he's also right that in the text—I remember you pointing it out to me, John— there's hardly any word of endearment to his daughter. My main concern was that, since it's such a short scene and the only scene that he has with his daughter, I was desperate to give Jessica the necessary reasons for running away with Lorenzo and stealing an enormous amount of money. My aim was to make her feel smothered and claustrophobic because of her father's overpossessiveness. But in doing that, I found I had problems, because very often I had to bend the lines to let me do it. If I ever do Shylock again it'll be to get that scene right. I know I didn't solve it.*

What about your daughter? What did you feel about Jessica? How much did you care?

Patrick Stewart: *How much does Shylock care about her? The caring is enormous but because of his concentration on survival, so much*

has been killed in him. The real, natural, warm, human, affection-
ate, loving responses have been cauterized in the man and she is a
victim of it. So it is impossible for him to show the undoubted love
that lies there underneath. It's so far down it can never be tapped.
In our production—do you remember?—we had a controversial
moment when I struck her very hard. After the blow I made some
attempt at a reconciliation: "Perhaps I will return immediately." But
by then the damage had been done and she was bound to reject him.

Your point about the commercial-mindedness of Shylock comes up
here, doesn't it? In the end the money matters to him more than his
daughter, as we shall see when we go on to the second scene on the
Rialto. His parental love is not as deep as his money love.

Third scene: a café on the Rialto. Let's look at the long speech to
the Salads, Salerio and Solanio, because it's a different area of interpretation and it's one of the most famous bits in the text.

(*Patrick Stewart reads Salerio, and David Suchet Shylock. Then vice
versa.*)

SALERIO: Why, I am sure if he forfeit thou wilt not take his flesh. What's
that good for?
SHYLOCK: To bait fish withal. If it will feed nothing else, it will feed my
revenge. He hath disgraced me and hindered me half a million, laughed
at my losses, mocked at my gains, scorned my nation, thwarted my bar-
gains, cooled my friends, heated mine enemies, and what's his reason? I
am a Jew. Hath not a Jew eyes? Hath not a Jew hands, organs, dimen-
sions, senses, affections, passions? Fed with the same food, hurt with
the same weapons, subject to the same diseases, healed by the same
means, warmed and cooled by the same winter and summer as a Christian is? If you prick us, do we not bleed? If you tickle us, do we not
laugh? If you poison us, do we not die? And if you wrong us, shall we
not revenge? If we are like you in the rest, we will resemble you in that.
If a Jew wrong a Christian, what is his humility? Revenge. If a Christian
wrong a Jew, what should his sufferance be by Christian example?
Why, revenge! The villainy you teach me I will execute, and it shall go
hard but I will better the instruction. *The Merchant of Venice: III.1.*

I think the interesting thing there was that at bottom, underneath the surface difference, both of you played the scene alike. You both did something that we worked on together which is not usually how that speech is taken. It is usually played as an appeal for pathos. "Hath not a Jew eyes?" and so on. Most Shylocks try to say "I am a poor wronged fellow, and this is strangely moving." But if he does it that way, the balance of the play is tipped in terms of its sympathies. If you do go for pathos in that speech and sentimentalize it, then the seeds of playing the martyred, sympathetic Shylock are sown.

> Patrick Stewart: *For weeks in rehearsal it was a black hole for me. I stumbled a lot because I was still seeing it in the traditional way. In acting Shakespeare, past tradition is constantly present. We are bombarded by received impressions: performances we have seen, reviews that we have read. It's very difficult to rid yourself of those impressions and go for something which is original. So I believed that this was a great speech about humanity and a plea for compassion, understanding, and racial tolerance. Then I was lucky to make the discovery that the speech in fact is none of those things but is a calculating, cold-blooded justification of revenge. The complete opposite of its conventional interpretation.*

> David Suchet: *I agree. The big trap is the temptation to play for sympathy. I too was terrified by this purple passage. Such speeches are terrifying. My way into it was to take as a clue what Salerio and Solanio say of him in an earlier scene. They describe his behavior when he hears about his daughter's flight, which we never actually see. They tell how he's been ranting and raving and knocking at doors and saying, "Get out of bed, find my daughter, find my daughter." But having blown his top like that, what is the man's state now? He's had enough. So when these two men here taunt him and mock him, his deep anger suddenly vents itself again. That was my way into it.*

> Patrick Stewart: *What was your physical state? Did you feel a sense of exhaustion at the beginning of the scene? As you say, Shakespeare describes Shylock at the height of his passion offstage. We never see*

it. It's all reported by someone else. So the man that we see is some-one who, as you say, has been over that hill and is now down on the other side.

David Suchet: *Yes: I'm on my way home, I'm finished. If Salerio and Solanio didn't speak, I'd go straight off the other side of the stage.*

Let's look at the end of the scene now and ask the question, "When does Shylock decide that he's going to claim his pound of flesh? When does he decide that he's going to get Antonio?" Usually his decision is made quite early on, probably in the speech you've just heard. But we worked for keeping it later and later and later in the scene. Let's look now at how Patrick and David each came to that decision. It comes in the dialogue with Shylock's fellow Jew, Tubal. We played him as a rich, even more successful Jew than Shylock. He watched quizzically as Shylock let off steam.

(Patrick Stewart plays Shylock and David Suchet Tubal. Then vice versa.)

SHYLOCK: How now, Tubal! What news from Genoa? Hast thou found my daughter?
TUBAL: I often came where I did hear of her, but cannot find her.
SHYLOCK: Why there, there, there, there! A diamond gone cost me two thousand ducats in Frankfurt! The curse never fell upon our nation till now; I never felt it till now. Two thousand ducats in that, and other pre-cious, precious jewels. I would my daughter were dead at my foot, and the jewels in her ear! Would she were hearsed at my foot, and the ducats in her coffin! No news of them, why so?—And I know not what's spent in the search.
    (Tubal gives him a bill.)
Why thou loss upon loss! The thief gone with so much, and so much to find the thief! And no satisfaction, no revenge! Nor no ill luck stirring but what lights o' my shoulders, no sighs but o' my breathing, no tears but o' my shedding.
TUBAL: Yes, other men have ill luck too. Antonio, as I heard in Genoa—
SHYLOCK: What, what, what? Ill luck, ill luck?
TUBAL: —hath an argosy cast away coming from Tripolis.

SHYLOCK: I thank God, I thank God! . . . Good news, good news! Ha, ha! Heard in Genoa?

TUBAL: Your daughter spent in Genoa, as I heard, one night, fourscore ducats.

SHYLOCK: Thou stick'st a dagger in me. I shall never see my gold again. Fourscore ducats at a sitting, fourscore ducats!

TUBAL: There came divers of Antonio's creditors in my company to Venice that swear he cannot choose but break.

SHYLOCK: I am very glad of it; I'll plague him; I'll torture him. I am glad of it.

TUBAL: One of them showed me a ring that he had of your daughter for a monkey.

SHYLOCK: Out upon her! Thou torturest me, Tubal. It was my turquoise, I had it of Leah when I was a bachelor. I would not have given it for a wilderness of monkeys.

TUBAL: But Antonio is certainly undone.

SHYLOCK: Nay, that's true, that's very true.

(*Shylock very slowly finds the decision to take revenge on Antonio.*) Go, Tubal, fee me an officer; bespeak him a fortnight before. I will have the heart of him if he forfeit, for were he out of Venice I can make what merchandise I will . . . go, good Tubal, at our synagogue, Tubal.

The Merchant of Venice: III.1.

There was a great diversity there but again at bottom you both interpreted the scene alike. You both reached the decision about what you were going to do about Antonio at the same time. I think my only comment would be to stress how much the way the scene is played depends on Tubal. It's what he thinks of Shylock that perhaps tells an audience how the Jewish community looks at Shylock. It seems that this scene often goes wrong because Tubal is played as a sniveling, sympathetic sidekick to Shylock. What both of you did as Tubal was to be dispassionate, detached and in the end disapproving. And that's terribly important to maintain the right balance of sympathy in the play.

We'll jump quite a bit now, leave the little short scene when Shylock meets Antonio, and go on to the trial scene. We won't look at the main part of the scene, the encounter between Shylock and Portia, partly because we haven't got Portia, but mainly because it's the most straightforward bit of the part as far as interpretation is concerned. Let's just look at the end of the scene. What everybody remembers a Shylock by is how he makes his final exit. Shakespeare leaves the question open-ended because he here gives Shylock, the man of teeming words, virtually nothing to say. So what do you do on that exit? What is your final statement to the audience?

Patrick Stewart: *Yes, that's always the great question for any actor playing Shylock, again because of tradition. There are a whole series of stories about how actors have got off. I remember you saying to me quite early on in rehearsal, "How are you going to get off?" You said that I had to find a way, because every actor must have a final exit and history has told us of some extraordinary ones. Kean apparently went through a startling physical transformation at that moment. Edwin Booth invented a detailed and elaborate mime which went on for minutes. And Irving was still and silent as he moved to the door, and then let out a long sigh as he left. And of course we have a great modern version of it too: Olivier's howl from somewhere way off in the corridors of the Old Vic.*

It is extraordinary that Shakespeare provides nothing at the end, isn't it?

Patrick Stewart: *At the beginning of the trial scene, when Shylock is on top, he gets hysterically high when he feels that for once there is someone on his side. Portia says, "Oh yes, you're right. You shall have your pound of flesh. I think you shouldn't do it, but nevertheless you are in the right." When the tables are finally turned on him by the Christians, he realizes he is in danger of losing everything. It seemed to me that if money and possession had been his dominant interest, that the only thing to do then was to get away with as much as he could. And therefore for me that meant humiliating myself and crawling.*

O.K. David first as Shylock this time. Portia has pointed out to Shylock that he has brought his ruin upon himself because he has insisted on justice at the expense of mercy. Just the last bit of the scene.

(David Suchet plays Shylock and Patrick Stewart the other parts. Then vice versa.)

DUKE: That thou shalt see the difference of our spirit,
I pardon thee thy life before thou ask it.
For half thy wealth, it is Antonio's,
The other half comes to the general state,
Which humbleness may drive into a fine.

PORTIA: Ay, for the state, not for Antonio.

SHYLOCK: Nay, take my life and all! Pardon not that!
You take my house when you do take the prop
That doth sustain my house. You take my life
When you do take the means whereby I live.

PORTIA: What mercy can you render him, Antonio? . . .

ANTONIO: So please my lord the Duke and all the court,
To quit the fine for one half of his goods,
I am content, so he will let me have
The other half in use, to render it,
Upon his death unto the gentleman
That lately stole his daughter.
Two things provided more: that for this favour
He presently become a Christian;
The other, that he do record a gift
Here in the court of all he dies possessed
Unto his son Lorenzo and his daughter . . .

PORTIA: Art thou contented, Jew? What dost thou say?

SHYLOCK: I am content.

PORTIA: Clerk, draw a deed of gift.

SHYLOCK: I pray you give me leave to go from hence,
I am not well; send the deed after me,
And I will sign it.

DUKE: Get thee gone, but do it.

The Merchant of Venice: IV.1.

So, apart from the obvious moral that there's an infinite diversity in the way different actors can play the same part, I would like to add a personal footnote to what we've just seen. What was my part as director in shaping these remarkable performances? Basically I gave

Patrick and David the same directions and made the same points, both in detail and in general. Yet, as you've seen, the result was utterly different and individual. That was partly because they each selected what they agreed with and found useful, and partly because the same point made to two different actors will always be transformed by their individual imaginations and personalities. I've often worked with two or more actors on the same part, and that always happens. I say this to put into proportion the director's contribution to a performance. However much he may lead and prod in rehearsal, the end result will always belong rightly to the actors. Both in terms of what they consciously interpret and what their stage personae themselves communicate. That's why I always feel that though the conception of a production may be mine, the actual performance is something that in a deep sense no longer really belongs to me. So though I may have strong views about how Shakespeare saw Shylock, these views were rightly transformed by Patrick and David. Their rich performances are therefore theirs more than mine. And that, I think, is how it should be.

CHAPTER ELEVEN

Contemporary Shakespeare

A Discussion

[Taking part in the program which forms the basis of this chapter
were JOHN BARTON and IAN MCKELLEN.]

Ian McKellen: *John, taking part in some of these programs, I've
been reminded that it is actually over twenty years since I first heard
you expound some of the matter which you've been going into in
"Playing Shakespeare." Like the rest of us, in the intervening two
decades, I've not only worked with you, but I've been very grateful
to you for the productions of Shakespeare of yours which I've seen.
I've been able to measure what you've been saying in these sessions
of an academic and detailed nature, against your achievements as a
director in the theater. I wonder if some people are thinking "Why
did John Barton ever come into the theater at all? Why didn't he
stay at Cambridge and be a brilliant academic and write books on
this subject? Why didn't he start a drama school? Why didn't he
become a critic and chastize everybody who wasn't doing it like he
was?" I know you're devoted to the theater, but tell us what it is
about the theater which keeps your adrenaline running?*

You're asking me about things for which I never had any urge or
capacity. The most important thing I learned painfully at Cambridge
was that I had no aptitude for academic life. I tried to write as a critic
but found I couldn't do it. I never wanted to be a teacher except
insofar as it helped towards a particular piece of work I was doing in
the theater at the time. And I never wanted to write a book about
Shakespeare because I could only express my views and feelings in
the form of individual productions.

But I am answering you in negative terms, not positively. I suppose I should rather say that though the text and the characters and the stories in Shakespeare have always stirred me deeply, I could only articulate what I felt about his plays by working with living actors. My thoughts and feelings usually remain inchoate as long as I'm alone with the text in the study. But once actors get on their feet in the rehearsal room and start to speak that text, then my thoughts begin to take shape. However fired I may be when I read Shakespeare, it is what happens to him in performance that matters to me most, provided of course that it's done well enough. And it often isn't. I suppose I believe that in the theater, the actors are, for that moment, more important than the text. But of course we also know in the theater that in another sense we are very unimportant. Our work is ephemeral and only exists for the few hours we perform it. We are of today but the text endures.

That's why I want to talk now about "Contemporary Shakespeare." However much we dig into the text as we've been doing, it is what we are and how we think today that really defines how we do the plays and how audiences respond to them. So let's look at what's good and bad in our contemporary thinking. For instance, there are problems that exist today in presenting a play like *The Merchant of Venice*. Directors, designers and audiences all have their share in trying to solve those problems, but as ever I think the actor should be our starting point. So, Ian, what are the most important things in your mind when you come to play Shakespeare today?

> Ian McKellen: *I think it's the humanity of the characters. That's what all actors will want most to concentrate on. We view Shakespeare through the teaching of Freud and the method of Stanislavsky. Yet at the same time we try to understand, as academics, why Shakespeare wrote as he did—long before our modern approaches to human nature.*

I would, in passing, challenge you for saying that what we have been looking at in "Playing Shakespeare" is of academic nature. All that we've been looking at is of the theater.

> Ian McKellen: *Yes, but you are a director and what really makes our theater and "Contemporary Shakespeare" different in Britain is the*

predominance of the director—though I notice that you have con-
tinually played that down in the course of these programs. Shake-
speare's plays, like all plays, of course, have to be organized and it's
as well to put one person in charge. In the past in Britain I think that
person was the star actor or maybe the playwright himself. David
Garrick, of course, wrote plays that he was in, and indeed amended
Shakespeare's plays for his own purposes; and Henry Irving was
very firmly in charge of his own company and Herbert Beerbohm
Tree and so on. But in the twentieth century this new kind of person
arose, I think probably out of the ranks of the stage management.
People who perhaps had been actors, but had an eye over the general
scheme of things, and now they are the men who are running the
Royal Shakespeare Company and the National Theatre and all the
repertory companies up and down the country. And it's true abroad
as well, that directors are the people who decide which plays are
going to be done and how they are going to be cast. They are the
people who organize, who influence, who make the decisions.

I am not against that system as long as the actor finds that he is not
in a cage, but is perhaps released from the cage of his own personality
by the director who can turn the key for him. But there are some
directors, who limit the process and don't give the actor enough free-
dom. I don't think you are one of them, but I think that Shakespeare
or other plays can go wrong if a director takes too much power on
himself.

In just the same way, if a star actor is in charge and takes too much
power upon himself, it will lead to distortions. But on the good side it
also explains why we are so interested in the detail in Shakespeare.
The director has no axe to grind and will not be there on the night
and will not be performing. Therefore he has a benevolent interest
in every section of the play, and that of course is a modern attitude to
Shakespeare. In the past I think star actors have been interested in
the main part only. A director today, particularly if, like you, he has
studied at university, is interested in every little corner of the text
and so we, the actors, get interested in every little corner also.

Though directors have great power and great responsibility I am
most aware of how we are in a sense powerless and unimportant

once a production goes into performance. I always feel when we've opened that the production doesn't belong to me anymore; it's yours, it belongs to the actors.

> Ian McKellen: *However, I do remember on the last performance of a play, you came round to the dressing room and I'd finished the part forever, and you gave me some notes on that evening's performance.*
>
> *I do wish there was more room within our scheme of things for different sorts of discipline to come to the fore. I would like to see companies run by communes of actors, let us say, experimenting without a director.*

In a way that's how Shakespeare's original actors worked. They didn't have a director in our sense at all.

> Ian McKellen: *Perhaps it's because Shakespeare himself was an actor that he uses the metaphor of the actor and of the theater so often in his plays. Often when a character is at the peak of his emotional problems he compares himself with an actor: "struts and frets his hour upon the stage." This has a wonderful resonance for an audience, reminding them that they are in a theater and that the man who is speaking the lines is not only the character he is exploring. Both are inside me as I'm speaking on the stage and sympathizing with the character's predicament. And if I can do that the audience can do it as well and are brought faceup against it. When you are in a theater— and this is why television will never supersede the theater as far as Shakespeare is concerned—you are not only there listening to and watching the actors but you are aware that the person next door to you is doing so also. And the person along the row behind you and in front of you. And when those words Time, Death, Grave, Man, Woman, Child, Father, Son reverberate round the theater you are reminded of your own humanity and your relationship with other people's humanity.*

Yes, Shakespeare constantly reminds us that the characters' predicament and humanity is very like our own. And that's the heart of what the actor must always go for, today and always.

Ian McKellen: *Another aspect of contemporary Shakespeare which I tap when I'm rehearsing is that I always look for a modern parallel for the character I'm playing.*

For yourself, not for the audience?

Ian McKellen: *No, no, for myself. Because I must believe in what I'm doing. So I had a problem when I was playing Macbeth. I don't believe in witches and I don't believe in God, and Macbeth clearly believes in both those concepts. I've never killed a man and he is a professional soldier. I've never murdered a man and he does. I've never been married, and so I have to imagine my way into all those aspects of his life by thinking of people I know, or it may be by thinking of a modern man, a contemporary whom I don't know personally but who's vaguely in Macbeth's position.*

When I was rehearsing I tried to think of generals who had gone into politics in the way that Macbeth seems to be wanting to go into politics. Then I thought, wait a minute, it's something more than that because Macbeth is the glory of the world, he's the golden boy. So who would be a modern parallel? At the time in the late seventies, Mohammed Ali was the greatest athlete in the world, so I asked myself what it would be like if he were to decide that he wanted to be president of the USA. I thought about it and then forgot about it, but about six months later Mohammed Ali announced that his only ambition was to be president of the USA. I knew he wasn't going to commit murder to get it, so I had to go on imagining! But it's useful to think like that and to base things on modern life.

That kind of thinking is a good aspect of "Contemporary Shakespeare": tapping the life we live so that it feeds into what we're doing. What isn't so good is saying, "This is what the play is actually about." I think it's important to make it clear that you are not saying that Macbeth is like Mohammed Ali and that the play should be performed accordingly, only that such a comparison can feed your imagination. This is an important distinction and bears on what is good and what is not so good in our contemporary approach to Shakespeare.

Ian McKellen: *Yes. And another important ingredient is the spaces we work in. Have you been struck, watching your actors work at a conversational level in this studio with the cameras very close, how speeches have taken on a life that you haven't heard before? You may recognize it because you sit in the rehearsal room close to the actors and you are used to that conversational level. But it's so rare in the theater—even in the small theaters where we sometimes work—to get that intimacy in which the audience can catch the breath being inhaled before it is exhaled on a line, and feel the excitement and certainty that what is happening is for real. The voice is wonderfully communicated but it isn't projected. The force behind it isn't exaggerated; there's nothing getting in the way. That's a level at which I like to work, and of course it's quite contrary to the level at which Shakespeare's own actors worked in their open-air theater or actors in the eighteenth century and nineteenth century experienced in their large theaters.*

We are so often controlled by the building we perform in. When a theater is big it takes over and transforms us and becomes our lord rather than our servant.

Ian McKellen: *And it's surprising how doing a play in a small theater can release it in some way. When I played Henry V I worked in a very small theater and we had no army. So I imagined that the army was in the audience and I knelt down at the front of the stage and whispered "Once more unto the breach, dear friends, once more,/Or close the wall up with our English dead." I was able to get just as much passion into that and bravado and patriotism by whispering as I could by shouting. In fact I think I got more because it was more real.*

That kind of intimacy is one of the best things we sometimes get with "Contemporary Shakespeare." But most of the time we have to work in the bigger theaters and be real there too. I think we ought to talk a bit about design now, because, whatever the size of theater we're in, the costumes and sets are one of the things that give a production its contemporary flavor. I don't necessarily mean modern dress. I am thinking of a fashion we have just now, which I approve of, of designing shows so that their period can't be pinned down precisely. We go for a mixture of modern elements and Renaissance, Elizabethan or Jacobean elements. The word we use to describe it is "timeless." It springs from the belief that to put actors into, say, Renaissance costumes is to put them into fancy dress and to diminish their humanity. They don't seem real and their social background is often left obscure. But we also believe that to put them in modern dress can all too easily distort Shakespeare. This "timeless" style is of course a healthy reaction against finicky historical exactness. And Shakespeare's actors themselves performed in what, in their terms, was modern dress; this went on right through the seventeenth and eighteenth centuries. It was the nineteenth century that invented the idea of meticulous historical accuracy; and films and television have perpetuated the fashion. It is not what Shakespeare himself had in mind and it is useful to remember the Elizabethan way. And particularly to root a play in recognizable social detail.

> Ian McKellen: *But what about the other fashion of changing the period that a Shakespeare play is set in? What about moving it forward or backwards in time?*

I think there's sometimes a case for it if it really helps to define the social background. But it can be a glib solution if a director and designer seize on it without really and honestly working out the implications. I'm always nervous of it myself and have only done it once or twice in twenty years. What do you think?

> Ian McKellen: *Well, I remember your* Much Ado about Nothing, *which was set in the dying days of the Empire in India, was it not? I thought that released my view of the play enormously. It did what you always have to do with that play, which is to provide a strict social setup to explain why Beatrice is the woman she is and why Benedick is the man he is, and why they are somehow, despite themselves, trapped in a set of conventions. Whether those conventions are the Empire in India or a border town in Mexico or in Italy or France or England or America doesn't really matter to me. But I agree that the design must be chosen with honesty.*

I think the great question about changing the period of a play is "Does it help unlock something that is truly in the text, or does it distort the play?" Too often a change of period gives easy dividends. You put up your Veronese image or your Jacobean image or your eighteenth-century image, and everyone thinks they know where they are. The audience think, "So that's what it's about." And so the design style becomes an interpretation. But it's not really an interpretation, it's more likely to be an imposition. I still don't know if I was right or wrong but I tried once setting *Othello* in the nineteenth century. I did it for the reasons you've just described; I wanted to define the social background. I tried to set Venice as a city in the Austrian Empire and Cyprus as an outpost of that empire. I particularly wanted to clarify the different rank of the soldiers, with Othello as general, Cassio as a lieutenant colonel and Iago as a warrant officer. I hoped thereby to make Othello himself a mythical, heightened figure who stood out from this real world of soldiers. So I was quite pleased with myself at first, but in the end I felt that, with the best intentions, I had somewhat diminished him by putting him into a world too small for him. And that seems to me the great danger in modern-dress Shakespeare. It can reduce rather than resonate.

Ian McKellen: *But the intention with which you started is the one which I admire. The only reason we get together and talk in this way, and the only reason we work hard in the privacy of the rehearsal room, is to be of service to the play. Not for the benefit of ourselves, although that's a wonderful bonus, but for the benefit of the audience. So if your intention is to reveal the play or what you can see in it to the audience, then your heart's in the right place and I forgive you time and time again. Every so often it works spectacularly well.*

Maybe, but I am still nervous. An even more important ingredient of design today is the way we take great care to create the right scale for a production. We ask, for instance, whether a particular play requires an epic stage or what we call a chamber stage.

Ian McKellen: *I think the most interesting designs during my theater-going lifetime as far as Shakespeare is concerned are those which have provided a proper place or space in which the play should be performed. I'm thinking of the space that Peter Brook provided for his* Midsummer Night's Dream, *for example, which was simply a white box. The space which was provided for a whole season of different plays at Stratford-upon-Avon in 1976 was a formal, fixed set which carried the audience round from the huge auditorium to sit at the back of the stage, so that the actors for the first time in that theater were having to perform in the round. It was a wooden structure with balconies and archways, and you used it for* Much Ado *and I used it for* Romeo and Juliet. *And again there was the space that Trevor Nunn and John Napier provided for the* Macbeth *that Judi Dench and I were in. There were just bare boards with a circle painted on them, a magic circle, in which the magic happened and the play was performed. And those were remarkable productions, and I think they were remarkable because the relationship between the audience and the actors was helpfully defined by the designer. When the curtain or the lights go up on a very fussy set, full of atmosphere, telling me that we're in Verona or Venice or on an island in the middle of space, my heart sinks because I think I'm going to get very distracted by all that and I won't listen properly.*

We still haven't entirely escaped from the tradition that a set should be gorgeous and luscious to look at for its own sake. That doesn't help the actor, who needs to work in design which humanizes and which gives useful information. If we go back to costume, for instance, it's vital that the design details should build up the character's reality and not overlay it with some dehumanizing concept. All the elements in a costume and all the props that an actor uses must be relevant to the character he is playing.

Ian McKellen: *May I give an example of a good bit of relevance and a bad bit? In Peter Hall's production of* Hamlet *some years back, Claudius always had a glass with a drink in it, and because it was tumbler-shaped I knew that the liquid in it was whisky. That told me something precise about Claudius: he drinks whisky. It wasn't your all-purpose goblet with nothing in it but watered-down blackcurrant juice. If however the relevance had been that Claudius had been dressed in Nazi uniform there would have been all sorts of*

*reverberations which are nothing to do with the play at all. In the
same production, Polonius carried a briefcase and that was also relevant in a good way. You know what's in a briefcase; there are
papers—to do with law and politics. It wasn't some sort of mocked-
up Elizabethan satchel or a scroll which you can't believe has anything written on it. This sort of reality in design can be very helpful
and very modern and very specific, in the right way.*

Yes, in the right way. You mention the Nazis and I'd like to follow
that up. There's a vital distinction here between two contradictory
meanings that lie behind the phrase "Contemporary Shakespeare."
On the one hand it can mean drawing upon modern parallels to feel
one's way into a character or situation or to make a character point
vivid to the audience, like the whisky. This I believe in. On the other
hand it can apply to the overt bringing out of specific modern parallels in the production itself. This I do not believe in, or only rarely. It
derives of course from directors and designers rather than actors,
and we've already talked about how design can distort a play in this
respect. But of course it can only happen if a director conceives a
whole production in such terms, and some directors believe passion-
ately in this approach. They argue for relevance and particularly for
political relevance.

I've recently heard it argued, for instance, that the first duty of a
director tackling *Hamlet* should be to place the play in its political
and social context, and that Shakespeare was boring if not explored
in that way. But boring to whom? I suppose the answer would be "to
the audience," but I think that what people who talk that way really
mean is that Shakespeare is boring to *them* unless it is made overtly
"relevant." So they make *Hamlet* be about the Lebanon, the Falk-
lands or Vietnam, or whatever war happens to be in the news at the
moment.

I do not believe in that. I believe that "Contemporary Shakespeare" in that sense is rarely justified, except as a useful shorthand
in the rehearsal process. In performance it distorts Shakespeare more
often than it illuminates him. It is usually a way of avoiding grappling with a problem or getting into touch with the play itself. It's
not just a con on the audience, it's very often a form of self-deception

by a director or an actor. Yet I must confess that it is a seductive viewpoint and that I have sometimes been seduced by it.

Of course we must take note of political and social ingredients. They are very important, but they must be kept in proportion. It depends on how much Shakespeare himself asserts them in a particular play. Proportion and balance again. The name most often quoted as a sanction of this approach is the Polish critic Jan Kott, whose book *Shakespeare Our Contemporary* has had a lot of influence in the theater over the last twenty years. Kott himself, however, has not only changed his views somewhat during that time but he has been much misunderstood from the outset. Let me quote him briefly as he specifically rejects the idea of updating Shakespeare.

> What I have in mind is not a forced topicality . . . Shakespeare does not have to be modernised or brought up to date . . . What matters is that through Shakespeare's text we ought to get at our own modern experience, anxiety and sensibility.   *Shakespeare Our Contemporary*

That is very accurate. The priorities are right. We should get at our own experience through Shakespeare's text. *Not:* we should get at Shakespeare's text through our own experience. Yet it's easy to see how this kind of "Contemporary Shakespeare" comes about. It is partly because of a director's political preconceptions but also because Shakespeare very often *is* a political writer. But the degree of his political interests varies enormously from play to play. His English history plays and his Roman plays are immensely political, but there are also many plays with no political element. There are also the plays where the political element is important but not dominant, like his great tragedies, *Lear, Othello, Macbeth* and particularly *Hamlet.* I suppose it is with these that it's most easy to go wrong.

Maybe we can clear our heads a little by asking what Shakespeare's own political opinions are. I think there is a split in Shakespeare himself. It is sometimes said that he is temperamentally a right-wing writer. And it is true that he has an intense vision of order, or perhaps one should say an intense fear of disorder. Again and again he shows us the consequences of order breaking down and destruction and violence taking over. But when Shakespeare shows this, I do not think it derives from a political philosophy but from his sense of human nature. I also sometimes feel that when chaos breaks out Shakespeare himself is in some way liberated. When Antony talks of letting slip the dogs of war, or when Timon rejects men and the social order, Shakespeare seems in some way released. In *Troilus and Cressida* he seems almost to exult in the character of Thersites, who relishes the violence and lechery in the play.

But of course this begs the question of whether Shakespeare identifies with his characters. That is always hard to judge, so it is perhaps safer to say that Shakespeare identifies with *all* his characters, just as his actors have to do. Unlike many political playwrights he usually articulates impartially the arguments on either side of a question. He shows what is just and noble and what is flawed and vicious in each character. This is hugely apparent in the four main characters in *Julius Caesar:* Brutus, Cassius, Antony and Caesar himself. We are once again up against Shakespeare's love of ambiguity. The best productions of *Caesar* bring that ambiguity out, but different directors and companies have seen the play as clearly right-wing or clearly left-wing in its viewpoint. Another political play, *Coriolanus,* got a very fascist production in France in the thirties and a very left-wing production from the Berliner Ensemble in the fifties. I always wonder what a "politically committed" production is trying to prove and to whom. They either preach to the converted, or they wash over the heads of those with contrary political opinions, who either dismiss them or ignore them.

I'm sometimes asked about my own political views. I usually answer that they are Shakespearean in the sense that I am always acutely aware of the appalling mixture of right and wrong on both sides in most political situations. I hope this is not an evasion but a reasonably honest answer. But I realize that in saying it I am probably like everyone else, reading my own viewpoint into Shakespeare as much as I am responding to what he has written. It cannot be otherwise.

Yet what you said about an actor searching first and foremost for the humanity of a character surely suggests the right habit of mind for a director as well. If he goes for that he will find that Shakespeare is neither right-wing nor left-wing in his philosophy or temperament. In political terms he is *wingless*. If we must have a definition it's perhaps more useful to think of Shakespeare not of the right or the left but of up and down. Up into men's aspirations and down into their brute reality. Ariel and Caliban, Claudius and Hamlet.

Perhaps "Shakespeare Our Contemporary" is the wrong label. Many people prefer to say "Shakespeare must be relevant." I dislike that also. In practice it's a glib phrase used to sanction whatever one happens to be doing. If we must have a label, I prefer a third word we've used already: "timeless." Shakespeare is timeless in the sense that he anatomizes and understands what is in men and women in any age, and what he has to say is always true and real. It is this element that is truly contemporary and which the wise actor or director will try to bring out.

Let me come to a point. I am not going on about Shakespeare and politics for its own sake but because it leads to something else that is more important. I've touched on it already. It's the idea of *opening up* and *narrowing down*. In rehearsal we open ourselves to as many possibilities as we can but in performance we have to define and be specific. Whatever we put in must lead to something else being left out. But of course what really defines a production is our own nature and consciousness. A director is bound to tap his political and social preconceptions, maybe unconsciously. He and the actors are bound and limited by their imagination and knowledge of human nature, so some sort of narrowing down is inevitable. It is salutary to quote Kott again here. "Shakespeare is like the world, or life itself. Every historical period finds in him *what it is looking for.*" It is good to remember that and beware of leaping to easy conclusions. We must try to open up to all possibilities before we narrow our sights and make definitions.

But I am afraid I am generalizing. So what do you think?

Ian McKellen: *As you have been saying that, I've been nodding in agreement and then sighing and shaking my head in disagreement. I tend to agree with you that there are no simple answers and that Shakespeare, like life, should be open to as wide an interpretation as possible. But that leads to one disagreement that I would have with you. It doesn't worry me if someone comes along and does a right-*

wing or a left-wing production of Coriolanus, *which in your view limits the play, because I know or hope that I am always going to be able to see a contrary view of the play presented in the next year or so.*

And of course you're right. When people rebuke us for doing a play in a particular way, they seem to think that we've damaged the play forever. But it's open for grabs, thank God, for anyone who wants to have a go at it.

Ian McKellen: *Let me tell you a story. In 1969 I played Richard II in a production which we took round England and then briefly to Europe and we went to Czechoslovakia. The costumes were of the actual period of Richard II but the scenery was minimal because it was a touring production. On the whole we concentrated on the humanity of the characters rather than their political nature. We thought of the political factions as a family, Richard II as a man with cousins and uncles and other relatives, and I think it was in that sense that we looked at the politics in it.*

However, we landed in Czechoslovakia only six months after the prime minister, Dubcek, had been removed by his neighboring allies, the Russians. One result of this political change was that they didn't want visiting foreigners with their plays. They tried to stop our visit, but it was too late. It was arranged, and we arrived. We only played two nights and the houses were full, although all our posters had been pulled down. So perhaps the audiences were ready to see this visit as a special occasion and indeed a political occasion, in that we were from the West.

When I came to the speech where Richard II returns from Ireland to discover that his nation has been overrun by his cousin Boling-broke, and he kneels down on the earth and asks the stones and the nettles and the insects to help him in his helpless state against the armies who had invaded his land, I could hear something I had never heard before, nor since, which was a whole audience apparently weeping. It shakes me now to think about it, because in that instant I realized that the audience were crying for themselves. They recognized in Richard II their own predicament of only six months previously when their neighbors and as it were their cousins had invaded their land, and all they had were sticks and stones to throw at the tanks.

I would never have talked about the play in those terms. We hadn't seen it as directly relevant to any modern political situation. Shakespeare couldn't have known about communism, about the East or the West. Afterwards I said to one of the new men, the anti-Dubcek faction, to one of their leaders who was in the audience, "Who did you side with in the play, Richard II or Bolingbroke? The man on the ground or the invader?" And he said, "Both right, both wrong."

A very Shakespearean answer: Shakespeare's view of politics and of men in a nutshell. But I think your story tells us something else. We are apt to overlook the difference between what we think we are doing and what an audience thinks we are doing. In the end of course we are in their hands. We can interpret as much as we like and try to control how that interpretation works in the theater, but finally it is the audience who decide what we mean by "Contemporary Shakespeare." So in the end we leap in the dark and have to hope for the best.

Ian McKellen: *Or we have to make some leaps forward. I don't quite see, and I don't know if you do, where the next leap is going to be. There was a big leap forward of course when we began to examine the text for the first time in the history of Shakespeare productions. That's still quite recent and has happened in the last thirty or forty years. But where it's going to lead I can't quite see, unless it's into places like this, into studios and away from theaters.*

I don't know where that leap will be either. I've been asking myself as we worked on this series whether in some way we are not expounding an already old tradition. Part of me is uneasy, because I sometimes suspect that like everyone else, we are stuck in a rut of some sort, and we're so deep inside it that we don't even know it's there. If I had to hazard a guess about the future, and it would only be a guess, I might make a different prophecy that we may move somewhat away from "contemporary relevance" to something much harder to talk about, poetry and myth. This is the way that Shakespeare himself went in his last plays. You are quite right that there has been a big leap forward in scrutinizing the text in the last few decades, and that is reflected in the kind of work we've been doing in this series. But you notice how I have throughout tended to steer clear of talking specifically about Shakespeare's poetry. That's not because I'm indifferent to it—far from it—but because I think it still comes near the back of the queue in our acting tradition today. It is still a low priority in most actors' minds. For even if an actor responds to the sort of textual challenges we've been talking about, it doesn't mean that he will necessarily bring Shakespeare's poetry alive. I have therefore put off talking about it till our last session.

But let me end my prophecy here. I believe that if the way we do Shakespeare does become more poetic, whatever that means, it won't be because directors hammer at it, but because something changes in our contemporary tradition and way of thinking and feeling, and this in turn changes something inside the actor. Poetry cannot be taught, though perhaps it can be released. So once again I'm saying that it all comes back to the actor.

CHAPTER TWELVE

→→ ←←

Poetry and Hidden Poetry

Three Kinds of Failure

[The following actors took part in the program which forms the
basis of this chapter: PEGGY ASHCROFT, LISA HARROW,
ALAN HOWARD, BEN KINGSLEY, IAN MCKELLEN,
DONALD SINDEN, DAVID SUCHET.]

*T*hroughout our work on "Playing Shakespeare" I have had a private specter which has haunted me. I have been aware that I have
been irresistibly led into laying down the law about Shakespeare. It
is partly because I've been trying to cram a lot into the space available and partly because I have had to put in summary form many
points which in rehearsal I would put much more tentatively and
discuss with the actors more fully over a length of time. I feel that
circumstances have led me against my will and instincts into playing
the high priest. Though I have often stressed that playing Shakespeare is an open-ended business with few absolute rules, I realize I
have been continually formulating rules and giving answers.

So to put things a little into proportion I want to end our series by
talking about failure. There are three ways in which I believe that the
sort of work I'm talking about always falls shorts of our hopes and is
always bound to do so. In rehearsal we work, we dig, we analyze, we
argue and we rootle, and so we learn a lot about what goes on in that
text. But of course in performance we can't put into the work more
than a fraction of what we've talked about. I wonder how many
times I've been at a marvelous rehearsal where a passage has been
thoroughly explored and where the actor suddenly takes off because
it seems he has found the truth of it. And yet when he comes to do it
in performance he never quite recaptures what he found in that

rehearsal. One can't quite put one's finger on what is wrong but there is a kind of textual, emotional and poetic thinning-out.

That's the first sort of failure. Everyone in the theater knows about it, and it's not something that happens only with Shakespeare. But there's a second kind of failure that I want to concentrate on in our last session: our frequent failure to do justice to Shakespeare's poetry. It's a problem that's haunted me over the years and which I've never really solved. When I read a Shakespeare text I'm moved and stirred by the power and the resonance of individual lines. I have a dim, ancient memory that it was this which first drew me to him and how bits of text began to move and haunt me when I was at school. The poet Houseman once described the actual physical effect upon him of recalling a line of poetry when he was shaving.

> Experience has taught me . . . to keep watch over my thoughts, because, if a line of poetry strays into my memory, my skin bristles so that the razor ceases to act.

Fortunately audiences don't shave in the theater, but shouldn't they be thrilled by poetry just as Houseman was? Shouldn't our senses be stirred by the language? Yet though we've said much about Shakespeare's verse and prose and heightened language, and though I've talked about marrying our two traditions, Elizabethan and modern, it isn't enough. It doesn't necessarily help to bring onto the stage what I can both hear and feel in the lines as I read them. I can talk about "intentions" and "character" and "verse" and "key words" and "situation" and all that. And yet I know I'm missing something, and in rehearsal I often don't know what to say or how to help the actor.

> Ian McKellen: *What about just saying to them as somebody said in* Alice in Wonderland: *"Look after the sense and the sounds will look after themselves"?*

Those are comforting words to an actor. But are we sure that they are true? I think that they are good counsel for starting work but I'm not sure that they take you all the way. What do you all think?

Alan Howard: *I think that what Ian has just said is fair enough as far as the question of intellectual comprehension is concerned. Obviously you need to comprehend as well as you can what the lines mean. But I think that the other aspect of the actual sounds, the textures and the rhythms, invoke a word which perhaps we don't understand so well today. The word is "apprehension" as opposed to "comprehension." Something we sense. I think that "apprehension" to the Elizabethans was a very palpable thing. They were sensually highly aware of how rhythms, sound and texture could combine with comprehension to bring about something which goes beyond just the sense.*

That's very good. You're talking about an acting sixth sense which isn't to do with analyzing or with the mind. It's something that we have to feel and smell and taste.

Alan Howard: *And it lasts only during the time in which it takes place. It lives as it dies, or it dies as it lives.*

But how can we work on it? How can we find our way with it? I don't think it's all that hard with purple passages. Where the poetry is *obvious* poetry, most actors respond to it and the text at least in part does its own work on an audience. I'm thinking rather of text which is poetic and yet not obviously heightened. Now that's saying something I haven't raised so far. Of course I said at the beginning that neither verse nor heightened language were in themselves necessarily poetic, but now I want to stress the opposite.

The simplest language can often contain the most powerful poetry, the most thrilling and the most resonant: that is what I mean by "hidden poetry." It is easy to overlook and quite different from the overt poetry which we find in rich and heightened language.

This is particularly true of Shakespeare's monosyllabic lines. That's a point we have covered already but we didn't spend much time on it. I want to go further with it here because I believe it's one of the most important ingredients in Shakespeare's poetry, and yet it's terribly easy to overlook it. Listen first to one of the first lines we considered at the beginning.

ANTONIO (*Ian McKellen*): In sooth I know not why I am so sad.

The Merchant of Venice: I.1.

Good. Ian caught something then which I didn't point to earlier because we were looking at other things. Although the line is quite naturalistic on the surface, it also has a poetic ring, uneasy, haunting and resonant, though it's hard to define it in words. We may not understand it but perhaps we can apprehend it. What word to describe it? It reverberates, it haunts, it rings a bell. Bear with me and listen to some other lines. Here is a prose example we've also heard already. Once again, all but one word are monosyllables.

MERCUTIO (*David Suchet*): Ask for me tomorrow, and you shall find me a grave man.   *Romeo and Juliet: III.1.*

Now listen to Lear when he awakes from his madness.

LEAR (*Donald Sinden*): You do me wrong to take me out o'the grave.
Thou art a soul in bliss; but I am bound
Upon a wheel of fire, that mine own tears
Do scald like molten lead.   *King Lear: IV.7.*

Thirty-four words, and all but two are monosyllables. And one more example. In *All's Well That Ends Well* the Countess talks about what it's like to be in love.

COUNTESS (*Peggy Ashcroft*): Even so was it with me when I was young.
If ever we are nature's, these are ours; this thorn
Doth to our rose of youth rightly belong;
Our blood to us, this to our blood is born.
It is the show and seal of nature's truth,
Where love's strong passion is impressed in youth.
By our remembrances of days foregone,
Such were our faults, or then we thought them none.

All's Well That Ends Well: I.3.

Seventy-one words and again all but ten are monosyllables. Shakespeare loves to use monosyllabic lines for particularly charged or heightened moments. They need air, they need to go more slowly than other lines, and they tend to do so naturally. Polysyllables trip easily off the tongue: "characterization," "repudiation," "apprehension" and so on. Monosyllabic lines and words are packed with thoughts and feelings. You can't rush them. Let's try taking one or two monosyllabic lines very fast and then see what happens with them.

Ian McKellen: *"In sooth I know not why I am so sad."*

David Suchet: *"You do me wrong to take me out o'the grave."*

Ben Kingsley: *"That struts and frets his hour upon the stage."*

Lisa Harrow: *"Even so it was with me when I was young."*

There, you can't do it, can you? And you wouldn't dream of doing it. So let's go back to Antonio again, slowly.

Ian McKellen: *"In sooth I know not why I am so sad."*

One of the problems with this line is that it's a difficult moment for Antonio. He doesn't know why he's so sad. So he's feeling for something but he himself doesn't quite know what it is. So though he uses words, he can't quite word it. Perhaps that's what makes it a poetic line. There's a resonance which can't be defined or pinned down. So each of you take the Antonio line one after another and see if you can search it, feel for it or disturb me poetically with it in some way.

(*The actors each fill out the line* "In sooth I know not why I am so sad" *in different ways.*)

Well, I think something was captured and caught there. Because you took it as an exercise you actually did something that you don't often do in the theater and yet perhaps it's valuable.

Lisa Harrow: *Don't you think that behind what you're after is the old idea about reading Shakespeare being better than seeing it on the stage? Do you really believe that old ghost?*

Well, I think it's a ghost that's got some blood in it. Perhaps we should read Shakespeare to ourselves more often when we're rehearsing him. Perhaps there's a moral in that. It touches on something that we don't think about when we're worrying about character and moves and situation and plotting. Here's a literary man, writing just fifty years ago of Constance's love and grief for her dead son Arthur in King John.

> Ian McKellen: "'Of nature's gifts thou mayst with lilies boast
> And with the half-blown rose . . .' Bother that half-blown rose! It's beauty blurs my eyes, and I can hardly go on quoting.
> 'Grief fills the room up of my absent child,
> Lies in his bed, walks up and down with me,
> Puts on his pretty looks . . .' Where's my handkerchief? I can't quote any more." Logan Pearsall Smith: *On Reading Shakespeare*

We can laugh at him, and indeed I suppose he's half laughing at himself. But isn't he at bottom right? Don't the lines move you a little when you just listen to them, even out of context? And if the feeling is there in reading, shouldn't we try to recapture it in the theater? And don't we sometimes give short shrift with the poetry? The answer is surely "yes," but the question is "how?"

> Lisa Harrow: *In the old days directors used to tell the actor how to do the line and what the tune was. And it still happens sometimes. I remember when I first started you used to do it to me all the time. You told me how to say a line because I'd got the inflection or things like that wrong. Do you believe in that?*

I'm very torn about it. Sometimes I think it's a good thing and sometimes I think it's a terrible thing. Let me confess why I am drawn to it. When I read a line, I can often half hear it being spoken in my head. What I hear is at once poetic and very real and human. I have long realized that this is a dangerous quirk in a director, because it makes me long to get an actor to capture the sound or sounds which I can hear. I therefore deeply suspect my instincts here. I think the prejudice in the modern theater against telling an actor how to say lines is healthy because to do so would make the actor a mimic. He'd be playing a set tune rather than spontaneous intentions and would either not be or not feel real. Anyway, why should I think that I could do it better? So, you see I'm torn and doubtful and I've never quite made up my mind about it. What do you think?

> Alan Howard: *It takes us back to Hamlet's instructions to the Players. Perhaps they tell us more about Hamlet than about Shakespeare himself. I wonder whether he would have given the same instructions at the end of the play that he gives so certainly at the beginning. A director should indeed be able to explain as well as possible, but he must always allow actors to feel in a secure enough atmosphere that they can experiment. And of course the director will want to do that as well.*
>
> *From that process something new can be found. But if everybody followed Hamlet's instructions absolutely all the time and never did more than what he talks of, half his plays would have fallen by the wayside by now. I don't think his advice applies absolutely all the way through the work. And anyway the words are open to every kind of interpretation. The most important thing is to find a balance.*

Let's go back to our theme of hidden poetry. Obviously before an actor can tackle it he has to know it's there. He has to sense it, or in Alan's words, to "apprehend" it.

We're going to take seven bits of text now which are in different ways poetic. Some are clearly so but some not so clearly. I'm not going to work on them much. I just want to invite you all, audience and actors, to listen and to *sense* what I'm after. All these passages have to do in some way with the two great Shakespeare themes of Death and Time. The first one is a prose dialogue which we've heard before between Falstaff and Doll Tearsheet from *Henry IV, Part II*. On the surface it is naturalistic but the poetic resonance is also very strong.

> DOLL (*Peggy Ashcroft*): Thou whoreson little tidy Bartholomew boar-pig, when wilt thou leave fighting a-days, and foining a-nights, and begin to patch up thine old body for heaven?

FALSTAFF (*Donald Sinden*): Peace, good Doll, do not speak like a death's head; do not bid me remember mine end.

DOLL: Sirrah, what humour's the Prince of?

FALSTAFF: A good shallow young fellow. 'A would have made a good pantler; 'a would ha' chipped bread well.

DOLL: They say Poins has a good wit.

FALSTAFF: He a good wit? Hang him, baboon! His wit's as thick as Tewkesbury mustard . . .

DOLL: Why does the Prince love him so, then?

FALSTAFF: Because their legs are both of a bigness, and 'a plays at quoits well, and eats conger and fennel, and drinks off candles' ends for flap-dragons, and rides the wild mare with the boys, and jumps upon joint stools, and swears with a good grace, and wears his boots very smooth like unto the sign of the leg, . . . and such other gambol faculties 'a has that show a weak mind and an able body, for the which the Prince admits him. For the Prince himself is such another . . . Kiss me, Doll . . .

  (*They kiss.*)

Thou dost give me flattering busses.

DOLL: By my troth, I kiss thee with a most constant heart.

FALSTAFF: I am old, I am old.

DOLL: I love thee better than I love e'er a scurvy young boy of them all.

FALSTAFF: What stuff wilt have a kirtle of? I shall receive money a-Thursday; shalt have a cap tomorrow. A merry song! Come, it grows late; we'll to bed. Thou'lt forget me when I am gone.

DOLL: By my troth, thou'lt set me a weeping an thou sayst so. Prove that ever I dress myself handsome till thy return. Well, hearken a'th'end. *Henry IV Part 2: II.4.*

The poetry there is not so hidden, is it? The scene is about Falstaff's fear of death and the language Shakespeare uses gives us that sense, both in character terms and poetic terms. The two are fused. Listen again to three lines about the old man's envy of youth: "'A plays at quoits well, and eats conger and fennel, and drinks off candles' ends for flap-dragons, and rides the wild mare with the boys." Drinking off candles' ends for flap-dragons means trying to drink out of a tankard with a lit candle in it, and trying to drink it without putting the candle out. Are not these phrases poetic? Don't they say more than the things they actually describe? It's hard to pin down and define, but you can surely apprehend it.

Now let's look at a passage where the poetic ingredient is not so obvious. It all seems pretty naturalistic, except for one line which can easily pass by unnoticed, but which also sends a shiver through me in the way that Houseman describes. It's at the end of *Othello*. Othello has killed his wife, Desdemona, and Iago's treachery has been found out. Emilia, Iago's wife, has discovered that he's been saying Desdemona went to bed with Cassio, and the pressure is on.

> EMILIA (*Peggy Ashcroft*): She false with Cassio! Did you say with Cassio?
> IAGO: (*David Suchet*): With Cassio, mistress! Go to, charm your tongue.
> EMILIA: I will not charm my tongue; I am bound to speak:
> My mistress here lies murdered in her bed.
> ALL: O heavens forfend!
> EMILIA: And your reports have set the murder on.
> OTHELLO (*Donald Sinden*): Nay, stare not masters: it is true indeed . . .
> EMILIA: Villainy, villainy, villainy!
> I think upon't, I think—I smell't—O villainy!
> I thought so then; I'll kill myself with grief.
> O villainy, villainy!
> IAGO: What, are you mad? I charge you get you home.
> EMILIA: Good gentlemen, let me have leave to speak.
> 'Tis proper I obey him, but not now.
> Perchance, Iago, I will ne'er go home.   *Othello: V.2.*

You can probably guess that the line that always moves me is the last line, "Perchance, Iago, I will ne'er go home." It's a perfect example of a seemingly simple naturalistic line which has a much greater resonance than at first appears. How can I explain it? In the general turmoil it comes suddenly as a still line where Emilia's emotion is channeled into a single thought and she stands outside herself. Partly because she is standing up to her husband Iago for the first time in her life, and partly because she subconsciously senses that he is about to kill her. So the line is ambiguous: it means, "I won't go home with you" and it means, "I'm going to die."

The next three passages I'd like you to hear are much more obviously poetic. I include them because I think it would be perverse to restrict a program on poetry entirely to hidden and seemingly naturalistic poetry. Each is in its different way about Time, a subject which, again and again, Shakespeare handles poetically. The first of them is the poetry of rhetoric. The problem is different here. The poetry declares itself and therefore the actors need to go most for humanity and character. It's a bit from *Richard III* which we've used already. Queen Margaret is talking to the widow of the dead king Edward IV. The speech is also about Time.

> ELIZABETH (*Lisa Harrow*): O, thou didst prophesy the time would come
> That I should wish for thee to help me curse
> That bottled spider, that foul bunch-backed toad!
> MARGARET (*Peggy Ashcroft*): I called thee then vain flourish of my
> fortune;
> I called thee then poor shadow, painted queen,
> The presentation of but what I was ...
> A sign of dignity, a breath, a bubble,
> A queen in jest, only to fill the scene.
> Where is thy husband now? Where be thy brothers?
> Where are thy two sons? Wherein dost thou joy?
> Who sues and kneels and says, 'God Save the Queen'?
> Where be the bending peers that flattered thee?
> Where be the thronging troops that followed thee?
> Decline all this, and see what now thou art:
> For happy wife, a most distressèd widow;
> For joyful mother, one that wails the name,
> For one being sued to, one that humbly sues;
> For queen, a very caitiff crowned with care; ...
> Thus hath the course of justice whirled about
> And left thee but a very prey to time.   *Richard III: IV.4.*

What does Shakespeare himself think about Time? He is haunted by the word and looks at it very ambiguously. It's an enemy and yet a friend.

Here's another nondramatic piece which shows his attitude very clearly. It is amazingly Shakespearean, yet few people know it. It's from *The Rape of Lucrece*. Alan. Imagine you are Shakespeare and share the lines with us all and tell us what you really think about your old friend. You know him, you love him, you fear him and above all you accept him. It's not just text, it's your own experience.

> *Alan Howard:* "Time's glory is to calm contending kings,
> To unmask falsehood and bring truth to light,
> To stamp the seal of time in agèd things,
> To wake the morn and sentinel the night,
> To wrong the wronger till he render right,
>   To ruinate proud buildings with thy hours,
>   And smear with dust their glittering golden towers;
>
> To fill with worm-holes stately monuments,
> To feed oblivion with decay of things,
> To blot old books and alter their contents,
> To pluck the quills from ancient ravens' wings,
> To dry the old oak's sap and cherish springs,
>   To spoil antiquities of hammered steel,
>   And turn the giddy round of Fortune's wheel;
>
> To show the beldame daughters of her daughter,
> To make the child a man, the man a child,
> To slay the tiger that doth live by slaughter,
> To tame the unicorn and lion wild,
> To mock the subtle in themselves beguiled
>   To cheer the ploughman with increaseful crops,
>   And waste huge stones with little water-drops."
>
> *The Rape of Lucrece, ll. 939–59*

I only want to point out one thing about that extraordinary piece of writing. Monosyllables again: in cold statistics, there are 160 words here and 123 are monosyllables. The text is simple and almost naive on the surface, yet at the same time rich and packed and dense. And Alan rightly took time here to tell us about Time, so the monosyllables worked on us. Sometimes Shakespeare addresses Time as if it's almost a character, not something impersonal, but somebody he knows. His feelings about it are constantly shifting. Sometimes he accepts Time, as in *The Rape of Lucrece,* but sometimes he is defiant. Here is a sonnet where the verse is not reflective but explosive and vigorous.

> *Peggy Ashcroft:* "Devouring Time, blunt thou the lion's paws,
> And make the earth devour her own sweet brood;
> Pluck the keen teeth from the fierce tiger's jaws,
> And burn the long-liv'd phoenix in her blood;
> Make glad and sorry seasons as thou fleets,
> And do what'er thou wilt, swift-footed Time,
> To the wide world and all her fading sweets:
> But I forbid thee one more heinous crime:—
> Oh carve not with thy hours my love's fair brow,
> Nor draw no lines there with thine antique pen;
> Him in thy course untainted do allow
> For beauty's pattern to succeeding men.
>   Yet do thy worst, old Time: despite thy wrong
>   My love shall in my verse ever live young."   *Sonnet 19*

Perhaps we're cheating by taking two nondramatic bits. So we'll go back to the plays now and to one or two more examples of hidden poetry. Here is another prose passage. It's a lively jolly bit with the poetic sadness underneath and not on the surface. It is built on another key word which in Shakespeare is usually linked with the word "Time." The whole passage is built on the resonance of the single word "Death." Old Justice Shallow in *Henry IV Part Two* talking to his even older friend Silence.

(Ian McKellen as Shallow and David Suchet as Silence play the passage very slowly.)

> SHALLOW: Jesu, Jesu, the mad days that I have spent! And to see how many of my old acquaintance are dead!
> SILENCE: We shall all follow, cousin.
> SHALLOW: Certain, 'tis certain, very sure, very sure. Death, as the

Psalmist says, is certain to all; all shall die. How a good yoke of bullocks at Stamford fair?

SILENCE: By my troth, I was not there.

SHALLOW: Death is certain. Is old Double of your town living yet?

SILENCE: Dead, sir.

SHALLOW: Jesu, Jesu, dead! 'A drew a good bow, and dead! 'A shot a fine shoot. John o'Gaunt loved him well, and betted much money on his head. Dead! 'A would have clapped i' th' clout of twelve score, and carried you a forehand shaft a fourteen and fourteen and a half, that it would have done a man's heart good to see. How a score of ewes now?

SILENCE: Thereafter as they be; a score of good ewes may be worth ten pounds.

SHALLOW: And is old Double dead?   *Henry IV Part II: III.2.*

I want you to do it again because you were both so old and so slow that you were already in your graves. Although Shallow is very ancient and senile, he doesn't know he is. The paradox and the fun of the scene lies in the fact that he's full of life and he's surely got a terrific manic energy and zest. And he is set against old Silence, who is a slowcoach and ponderous and bovine. So try it again.

Ian McKellen: *One of the troubles with parts which are quite short is that you try and make them rather longer by putting in a lot of pauses.*

But you've both got to *earn* the pauses and the golden moments, haven't you? The scene has got to have a basic drive and energy. So that you can break through the rhythm with the really important lines and the realization of death when it comes.

Ian McKellen: *But do you think that Shallow by the end is relating the fact that Double has died to the fact that he is going to die? Or is he actually absolutely thrilled that he's outlived old Double?*

I think that he's thrilled at his own living, but he doesn't realize till the very last "Is old Double dead?" that he is going to die. Not till then.

(*They play the scene again.*)

That was great. It reminded me of a point we made right at the outset about how Shakespeare loves to make sudden changes. He keeps switching from little details of daily living to the sudden reality of death. It's these sudden jagged gear-changes which we have to relish. They enrich both the poetry and the character.

> Ian McKellen: *And of course for the Elizabethans death was an ever-present fact of life. With our modern medicine, death is at the end of something rather long that has preceded it. But death was more of a presence then. You could see it in the streets.*

Yes, no wonder Shakespeare had such an acute sense of Time. Here's one further passage about it which is perhaps the most loaded example of all. Once again, the text is largely monosyllabic. In *Julius Caesar* Brutus is talking to the dead body of Cassius, his friend.

> BRUTUS (*Ben Kingsley*): The last of all the Romans, fare thee well!
> It is impossible that ever Rome
> Should breed thy fellow. Friends, I owe more tears
> To this dead man than you shall see me pay.
> I shall find time, Cassius, I shall find time.   *Julius Caesar: V.3.*

What do you feel and think about Time at the moment that you say it there?

> Ben Kingsley: *Well, it's hard to divorce what one feels and thinks about Time at that moment from the information that has accumulated throughout playing the role. But I do get one or two clues off the page. Yes, it's monosyllabic. "Impossible" is one of the longest words in the whole section. There's a relentless driving force in this speech. Brutus doesn't give himself time for grief. The writing doesn't allow it. But I think that in the last line Shakespeare allows the character, by repetition, to take himself by surprise. I think that when he first says, "I shall find time" it is quite genuine, and then when it's said again it is of course totally ironic, because it's too late now to find time. And the second time he says it, the thought of his own death is resonating in it also.*

Yes, it's the problem of ambiguity again. You're trying to reach out to Cassius with your love, but also, like Emilia, you're thinking of your own death. And among other things, you're mocking yourself for all your high aspirations in the play which have come to nothing.

Ben Kingsley: *I think that there is a danger here. If you try to compress too many objectives into those four or five lines, they'll start to neutralize one another. It's very hard to hold abstract information in your head, especially if you haven't got the accumulated information of the rest of the play to feed on. In other words, if the rest of Brutus has been a washout, you're not going to find your way out of it in these lines.*

It's always dangerous to try to think of too many things at once. And yet those lines have many meanings, and Shakespeare is asking us to get all those meanings out of them.

Ben Kingsley: *With spare short words as well.*

That's right. Probably you have just to trust the poetry and let it carry you. You can't worry about it while you're doing the line. Or can you?

Ben Kingsley: *I think you've got to let go and trust it. It's rather like pouring molten metal into a mold that Shakespeare has made for you. Providing your metal is hot enough the mold will shape it, but if it's not it won't.*

I thought you did the speech marvelously, and yet one bit of me was wanting to say, "Get more out of it, get more of the resonance out of it." But maybe I shouldn't say so because you can only take in so much or put so much into it at a time.

Ben Kingsley: *Well, let me hear it. I find often that the objective side of a speech is unlocked when I hear somebody else say it. It remains subjective if I myself say it and I mustn't listen to myself anyway. That's a false exercise. So there's Cassius's body, John. So let me hear you. It would help me.*

(John Barton overloads the speech and does it less well than Ben Kingsley.)

I fell into a trap there. I tried too hard to catch the poetry, and that's as bad as ignoring it.

While we've been going through these seven passages I've been cheating, haven't I? I have been pointing to what is poetic in them but I've said very little about how actually to play it and bring it out. If I am honest I must confess I've dodged it. Because after thirty years I still don't know clearly how to do it. It is relatively easy to give a rule in rehearsal about intentions or character or the verse. Most actors pick them up pretty quickly because we share a rehearsal language. But poetry is at best a slow business and a slog. Sometimes to talk about it in detail inhibits and confuses, and sometimes a crude single word serves best. "Quicker," "slower," "quieter," "angrier" and so on. As I try to articulate my thoughts now I can only say something tantalizingly general. Although, here as elsewhere, we must still take as our starting point that the intentions and the character must first be found, we are in an area where they alone are not enough. There's a kind of leap in the dark to be made here. It's a leap in the dark because we probably can't—and I certainly can't—quite articulate how that leap should be made. I can't do better than repeat lamely what Alan said: it must be apprehended rather than comprehended. Occasionally we get it but it comes obliquely: some little nudge in rehearsal, a few lucky words at the right moment, some sudden flash of light.

I'm tempted to say that it's not something that can be directed. The best Shakespearean actors know instinctively everything that I've been saying in this series, and so they do not need instructions. Maybe it's simpler and more honest to say that some actors have a feel for poetry and some don't, and if they don't have that feel nothing I say can release it. If, for instance, they have no instinct for inflecting the words and their speech is flat, it usually has to be accepted, just as one has to accept that someone is musically tone-deaf. Yet often an actor who does have a strong apprehension of the poetic can't manage to tap it in an individual line or passage. Very likely because he has a hang-up about the character at that point rather than because he lacks poetic sensitivity.

We've talked about two kinds of failure so far this session but there is also a third sort. Sometimes after doing a good bit of work, we like to think we've solved the way of approaching Shakespeare, and that we do him more justice nowadays than used to be the case. There's supposed to be a modern way of playing Shakespeare which is sometimes coupled with the name of the Royal Shakespeare Company. But I suspect it's not so new as we sometimes like to think. I wonder what playing Shakespeare was like fifty years ago, and what it'll be like fifty years hence. I'm sure that what we do now will be mocked as we sometimes mock what we hear of the old actors. Listen to an old sound recording of Henry Ainley, playing Othello in 1938, and going over the top:

OTHELLO: Cold, cold, my girl!
Even like thy chastity. O cursèd slave!
Whip me, ye devils,
From the possession of this heavenly sight!
Blow me about in winds! Roast me in sulphur!
Wash me in steep-down gulfs of liquid fire!
O Desdemona! Desdemona! dead!
Oh! Oh! Oh!   *Othello: V.2.*

We can laugh and give ourselves a pat on the back. But it's sad too. He feels he's doing it so well. Yet the past is full of contradictions. Listen to a recording of Peggy Ashcroft as Viola in the 1940s:

VIOLA: I left no ring with her; what means this lady?
Fortune forbid my outside have not charmed her!
She made good view of me, indeed so much
That—methought—her eyes had lost her tongue,
For she did speak in starts, distractedly.
She loves me, sure, the cunning of her passion
Invites me in this churlish messenger.
None of my lord's ring? Why, he sent her none.
I am the man!   *Twelfth Night: II.2.*

That doesn't sound dated, does it? It could have been recorded yesterday. Peggy, you recorded that thirty-five years ago and your experience of Shakespeare is much greater and richer than mine. Does the way that we play him now seem very different from the way you first knew it?

Peggy Ashcroft: *Oh, John, what a question. It's simply huge. First of all I must make a little comment about the Henry Ainley excerpt, because it's said to have been made in 1938. But in 1932 I recorded the whole of* Othello *with him, and he didn't do it like that at all. He did belong to another era, but I don't think there is such a great difference between that era and what we do today.*

But if I might take you up on your favorite theme, Time. I could use it in two senses. First, how lucky we are today that we have time: we have seven weeks' rehearsal. In those days we had three, or four if we were very, very lucky. Now I think that time, in that sense, makes an enormous difference. But it's very difficult to try and divide the approach to acting into eras. I maintain that the approach is always the same with actors who are really true actors. You can't put it into decades. I remember back in 1920 seeing the most miraculous production, the first modern-dress Hamlet, *done by the Birmingham Repertory Theatre. And at very much the same time I saw John Barrymore playing Hamlet at the Haymarket, which I thought even then was a disaster. No, I don't think time makes all that difference. I think of John Gielgud's production of* Romeo and Juliet, *where our approach was very much as it is now, although we had fewer weeks.*

That is the one you did in the thirties?

Peggy Ashcroft: *In the thirties. We had Edith Evans, who had the most wonderful delivery of Shakespearean verse which she learned from that master, William Poel. There was John Gielgud, with his older tradition of perfect speaking of verse, with that marvelous sense of phrasing that's almost unequaled. And there was Larry Olivier, who was, in a sense, the most of an innovator. He above all went for character, and that's where I think we all as actors merge.*

Donald Sinden: *But if you take some of John Gielgud's recordings of the thirties, they seem dated today. But he's grown over the years.*

It's a question of style and of period, isn't it? I mean, I can't believe that one of Ainley was done in 1938. I'm sure it's older than that.

Peggy Ashcroft: *Well, he might have been lured into a studio, mightn't he? And done a rather ham version of that speech.*

Donald Sinden: *I remember hearing him during the war on the radio, doing* Les Misérables. *It was really over the top. With so many of those older actors it's unfortunate in a way that they're recorded.*

Peggy Ashcroft: *I think it's very unfortunate that any of us are recorded. Look what you're responsible for here, John.*

Donald Sinden: *Ainley didn't have the experience of being in the studio like this ever in his life.*

Yes, and I keep being filled with the melancholy thought that when we're looked at in years to come, we'll seem quite as strange as Ainley does to us now.

Donald Sinden: *But on the other hand if you look at old films of actors there's such a variety. There's the film of Forbes Robertson's 1911* Hamlet. *There are some performances in it that are so awful, it just isn't true, but he himself is marvelous, absolutely marvelous. And the film of Eleonora Duse is wonderful, it could have been shot yesterday.*

But what you're really saying to us, Peggy, is that the assumption that's sometimes made today that our Company found and founded a new style with Shakespeare just isn't true. We've picked up an existing tradition and perhaps moved it on a little.

Peggy Ashcroft: *And built on it. I think all theater is continuity, don't you?*

Donald Sinden: *It moves forward the whole time.*

We do have a long time to work now, and you used to have much less. But the Elizabethan actors who started the whole thing off had virtually no time. From what we know of their conditions they more or less just learned their lines and put the play on. How they did it, God knows.

Peggy Ashcroft: *We've been learning a bit of that here, haven't we?*

Donald Sinden: *And when we do have time, and too much time, we dig too much and try to be too clever and to do too much.*

Peggy, let me ask you one naive but important question. What to you is the most important thing to go for in playing Shakespeare?

Peggy Ashcroft: *I think it's too simple to say: the truth. What do we mean by truth? Truth of reality. Truth of poetry, which is a little bit of super-reality. And truth of character. It's the fusion of poetry, truth and character that is required in Shakespeare.*

Reality, poetry and character: three balls that we have to juggle with all the time. If we throw one up too far, that is to say if we concentrate on one only, then we'll drop the other two. That is why acting is often so difficult.

Peggy Ashcroft: *I think we'd all agree that it's like the chicken and the egg. You can appreciate a line, but it's no good thinking you know how to say it until you've found the character. Only when we have found the character are we able to say the line as it should be said. Not by everybody, or anybody, but by us, because we've made that particular character. So it has to fit with that, and then it comes out naturally.*

That's why I haven't talked about poetry until this final session. We have to start by finding the character. Though in the end the poetry may well be the most important thing, it's not the thing the actor can start with. No . . . I don't think that's quite true. Peggy has just spoken of finding truth and character and poetry. The real truth is, I think, that the three should never be split. Any actor who does split them will run into problems. So never split them.

What else have the passages we've heard this session proved but this? In Shakespeare the character and the poetry go together. More than that, they are one. Yet of course it's easier said than done. It's hard to keep those three balls in the air. All work on Shakespeare's like that. We never do him justice because we keep pushing something at the expense of something else. What seems good and splendid at one moment is only so for that moment. We go too far one way or the other. Too heightened, too naturalistic. Too hot, too cold. Too quick, too slow. The list is endless. But as we've covered so much ground I suppose I should try—though I hate generalizations—to sum up our exploration. What, if any, are the key points or what are the golden rules?

We've talked of possibilities, not rules,/of questions, balances, not absolutes./So are there any rules? Yes. Try to find/what goes on in the text and ask yourself/if you can *use* it. You must not reject it/until you've smelled it out and asked the questions./Never forget the verse is there to help you./It can be heightened, and yet very often/it's close to our own humdrum human speech./Which of you noticed while I have been talking/that what I've just said was in bad blank verse?

But let's not finish with my words. Let's go on a little longer with just listening to Shakespeare. First of all, the obvious farewell from Shakespeare is Prospero's much-quoted speech after the masque in *The Tempest.* This has often been quoted out of context and debased as an anthology speech; taken by itself it can easily become sentimental. But I think it's relevant here because it is about actors and it does catch something of the elusiveness we've been talking about of any theatrical performance. Shakespeare himself was an actor and he must have known better than we do that playing him could never entirely do him justice. They say it is his farewell to the theater.

> PROSPERO (*Alan Howard*): You do look, my son, in a moved sort,
> As if you were dismayed. Be cheerful, sir.
> Our revels now are ended. These our actors,
> As I foretold you, were all spirits, and
> Are melted into air, into thin air;
> And, like the baseless fabric of this vision,

The cloud-capped towers, the gorgeous palaces,
The solemn temples, the great globe itself,
Yea, all which it inherit, shall dissolve,
And, like this insubstantial pageant faded,
Leave not a rack behind. We are such stuff
As dreams are made on; and our little life
Is rounded with a sleep.   *The Tempest: IV.1.*

We hardly ever know what Shakespeare himself thinks about it all. But let's listen one final time to the text we've quoted the most often in these sessions: Hamlet's advice to the Players.

HAMLET (*Donald Sinden*): Speak the speech, I pray you, as I pronounced it to you, trippingly on the tongue. But if you mouth it as many of our players do, I had as lief the town crier spoke my lines ...
Lisa Harrow: Nor do not saw the air too much with your hand, thus ...
Peggy Ashcroft: For anything so o'erdone is from the purpose of playing, whose end, both at the first and now, was and is to hold, as 'twere, the mirror up to nature, to show virtue her own feature, scorn her own image, and the very age and body of the time his form and pressure.
                                   Hamlet: III.2.

Now let me end by speaking a personal choice. It's not an obvious one and it may surprise you. But it is a bit of text that always moves me and I love it. It too is about Time and its poetry also is very simple. It's the little dialogue from *Troilus and Cressida* between Ulysses and Hector. They are both looking at the walls and towers of Troy. In my own private mythology I always think of them as the same cloud-capped towers that Prospero spoke of.

ULYSSES: I wonder now how yonder city stands
When we have here her base and pillar by us.
HECTOR: I know your favour, Lord Ulysses, well.
Ah, sir, there's many a Greek and Trojan dead,
Since first I saw yourself and Diomed
In Ilion, on your Greekish embassy.

ULYSSES: Sir, I foretold you then what would ensue.
My prophecy is but half his journey yet;
For yonder walls, that pertly front your town,
Yon towers, whose wanton tops do buss the clouds,
Must kiss their own feet.
HECTOR: I must not believe you.
There they stand yet; and modestly I think
The fall of every Phrygian stone will cost
A drop of Grecian blood. The end crowns all,
And that old common arbitrator, Time,
Will one day end it.
ULYSSES: So to him we leave it.   *Troilus and Cressida: IV.5.*